VICTORIA AND ALBERT

Also by Richard Hough

The Fleet that had to Die (1958)
Admirals in Collision (1959)
The Potemkin Mutiny (1960)
Dreadnought: a History of the Modern Battleship (1960)
First Sea Lord: a life of Admiral Lord Fisher (1961)
The Hunting of Force Z (1963)
The Pursuit of Admiral von Spee (1969)
The Blind Horn's Hate (1971)
Captain Bligh & Mr Christian (1972)
Louis & Victoria: the first Mountbattens (1974)
Mountbatten, Hero of our Time (1980)
The Great War at Sea: 1914–1918 (1983)
The Ace of Clubs: a History of the Garrick (1986)
The Battle of Britain: the Jubilee History (with Denis Richards) (1989)
Winston & Clementine: the Triumphs & Tragedies of the Churchills (1990)
Bless our Ship: Mountbatten and the Kelly (1991)
Other Days Around Me: a Memoir (1992)
Edward & Alexandra (1992)
Captain James Cook (1994)

VICTORIA AND ALBERT

RICHARD HOUGH

St. Martin's Press
New York

Front endpapers: Prince Albert, the Prince Consort by John Lucas
Victoria by Franz Xavier Winterhalter
Back endpapers: Albert in 1855
Victoria in 1866

Library of Congress Cataloging-in-Publication Data

Hough, Richard Alexander.
    Victoria and Albert / by Richard Hough.
        p.   cm.
    ISBN 0-312-14822-4
    1. Victoria, Queen of Great Britain, 1819–1901.   2. Albert, Prince Consort of Victoria, Queen of Great Britain, 1819–1861.   3. Queens—Great Britain—Biography.   4. Princes—Great Britain—Biography.
I. Title.
DA554.H68   1996
941.081'092—dc20
[B]   96-25614
                                                                                      CIP

First published in Great Britain by Richard Cohen Books

First U.S. Edition: November 1996

10   9   8   7   6   5   4   3   2   1

For Jenny Tricker

Contents

Acknowledgements   viii
List of Illustrations   ix
Chronology   xi
Genealogical Tree   xiv

1   The Baron's Plans   1

2   The Frustrated Salute   15

3   'I feel so *safe* when he is with me'   32

4   An End to Loneliness   53

5   'Oh Madam, it is a Princess'   67

6   The Difficult Prince   87

7   The Great Exhibition   107

8   'More dead than alive from overwork'   122

9   War and Mutiny   135

10   What to do with Bertie   153

11   The Conflicts of Mature Marriage   172

12   Tragedy in the Blue Room   178

13   'You will not desert me?'   195

Appendix   211
Condensed Bibliography   213
Index   215

Acknowledgements

I must again list first my debt to Christopher Hibbert, whose knowledge of Victoriana is extensive and reliable. The same may be said of his library. Mrs Jenny Tricker, who graciously allowed me to dedicate this book to her, has once again been tireless in her checking and correcting.

My own interest in the Victorian royal family extends back to the early 1970s when I embarked on the official history of the Battenberg/Mountbatten family, authorised and encouraged by Lord Mountbatten himself, who arranged numerous introductions to help me in my research. Included among them were two of the last surviving grandchildren of Queen Victoria, Princess Alice, Countess of Athlone with whom I had long conversations at Kensington Palace, and Lady Patricia Ramsay, the daughter of Arthur, Duke of Connaught.

Working in a specialised field results in an ever-increasing accumulation of knowledge, some of it rejected at the time but available and sometimes found to be invaluable later. For example, while working in the Royal Archives at Windsor in the 1970s I discovered material which proved useful in my dual biography *Edward and Alexandra* in 1992.

Finally, the staff of the London Library and the Public Record Office have been as helpful and diligent as they always prove to be.

RICHARD HOUGH
September 1995

List of Illustrations

1 Victoria's father
2 Victoria's mother
3 Albert's father
4 Albert's mother
5 Albert at the age of thirteen
6 Victoria at the age of fourteen
7 Victoria receives the news of her accession
8 Victoria's coronation
9 Victoria on horseback
10 Victoria in her bridal dress
11 The wedding of Victoria and Albert
12 Victoria's sketch of Lord Melbourne
13 Lord Melbourne
14 Albert as a medieval knight
15 Victoria's sketch of Albert
16 Portrait of the royal family by Winterhalter
17 Photograph of the royal children at Windsor
18 Photograph of the whole family at Osborne
19 'Bringing the stags home to Balmoral'
20 View of Balmoral
21 Victoria and Albert in early middle age
22 The blue room at Windsor Castle
23 The Queen, Princess Alice and Princess Louise
24 Victoria planting a memorial oak to Albert
25 The Royal Mausoleum

Illustration Credits

The author and publishers are grateful to the following for permission to reproduce illustrations:

Chronology

1819, 24 May	Princess Alexandrina Victoria born at Kensington Palace, London
26 August	Prince Francis Charles Augustus Albert Emanuel born at the Rosenau, Saxe-Coburg-Gotha
1820, 23 January	Death of Duke of Kent, Victoria's father
1824	Albert's mother leaves Coburg, never to see him again
1831, April	Victoria and Albert's uncle, Prince Leopold, becomes King of the Belgians
1835, 12 April	Albert confirmed
30 July	Victoria confirmed
1836, May	Albert visits England and meets Victoria for the first time
1837, 20 June	Accession of Queen Victoria
26 June	Albert writes to congratulate Victoria on becoming Queen
13 July	Victoria moves her court from Kensington Palace to Buckingham Palace
1838, 28 June	Victoria crowned
1839, 10 October	Albert visits England again
15 October	Victoria proposes marriage to Albert who accepts
1840, 10 February	Victoria and Albert's wedding
1 June	Albert delivers his first speech
10 June	Victoria and Albert are the target of a first assassination attempt
26 August	Albert's twenty-first birthday. King Leopold visits to celebrate
21 November	Prince Victoria, 'Vicky', born
1841, 9 November	Prince of Wales, 'Bertie', born

1842,	September	Albert engineers the departure of Baroness Lehzen from the Court and country
	September	Victoria and Albert visit Scotland for the first time
1843,	September	Victoria and Albert visit France
	October	Victoria and Albert visit Belgium
	29 January	Albert's father dies and is succeeded by Albert's brother
	25 April	Princess Alice born
1844,	March	Albert visits Coburg
	June	Czar of Russia and King of Saxony visit England
	6 August	Prince Alfred born
	August	Victoria and Albert, in search of a country residence, visit the Isle of Wight and a property for sale, Osborne House
1845,	23 June	Work starts on a new Osborne House
1846,	25 May	Princess Helena born
	September	Reconstruction of Osborne House completed
1847,	25 March	Albert installed as Chancellor of Cambridge University
1848,	18 March	Princess Louise born
	8 April	The Court retreats rapidly from London to Osborne House in face of threatened Chartist riots
	August	Victoria and Albert purchase Balmoral Castle
	September	Victoria and Albert and four of their children travel to Scotland to examine their new property Albert plans to rebuild it
1849,	1 May	Prince Arthur born
	July	Albert conceives a great international exhibition
	August	Victoria and Albert visit Ireland
	8 October	George Anson, Albert's secretary, dies
1850,	3 January	The royal commission for the Great Exhibition meets for the first time
	26 July	Paxton's vast Crystal Palace in Hyde Park is authorised and building begins
1851,	1 May	Great Exhibition formally opened
1852,	14 September	Duke of Wellington dies Albert much concerned with the nation's defences against invasion
1853,	7 April	Prince Leopold born

1853		Albert plans four museums to be built from the Great Exhibition's profits
	28 September	Victoria lays the foundation stone of the new Balmoral Castle
		Albert attracts venomous criticism in the press in connection with 'the Eastern problem'
1854,	30 January	Albert defended by the Prime Minister, silencing his critics
	1 March	Death of Sir John Conroy
	28 March	Britain declares war on Russia – the Crimean War
	20 September	Russia defeated by Anglo-French forces at the battle of Alma
1855,	18 August	Victoria and Albert visit Paris at the invitation of Emperor Napoleon III
	7 September	The new Balmoral completed and Victoria and Albert go to stay, coincidentally with the fall of Sebastopol
1856,	April	Peace with Russia declared
	29 September	Vicky becomes engaged to Prince Frederick 'Fritz' William of Prussia
1856		Victoria institutes the Victoria Cross (VC), the conception of Albert
1857,	14 April	Princess Beatrice, Victoria's last child, born
		War in China, and mutiny in India
1860,	July–November	Bertie tours Canada and briefly visits USA
	23 September	Victoria and Albert visit Coburg and Vicky and Fritz
	30 September	Albert injured in carriage accident
1861,	16 March	Duchess of Kent, Victoria's mother, dies
	March	Bertie despatched to the Curragh Camp, Dublin, to train as a guards officer
	November	Albert learns that Bertie has been seduced by an actress in Ireland
	22 November	Albert, weak and miserable, knows he is seriously ill
	25 November	Albert visits Cambridge to talk to Bertie
	30 November	Albert resolves crisis with the Union in the American Civil War in spite of his terminal typhoid fever
	1–9 December	Albert weakens
	14 December	Albert dies
1901,	22 January	Victoria dies

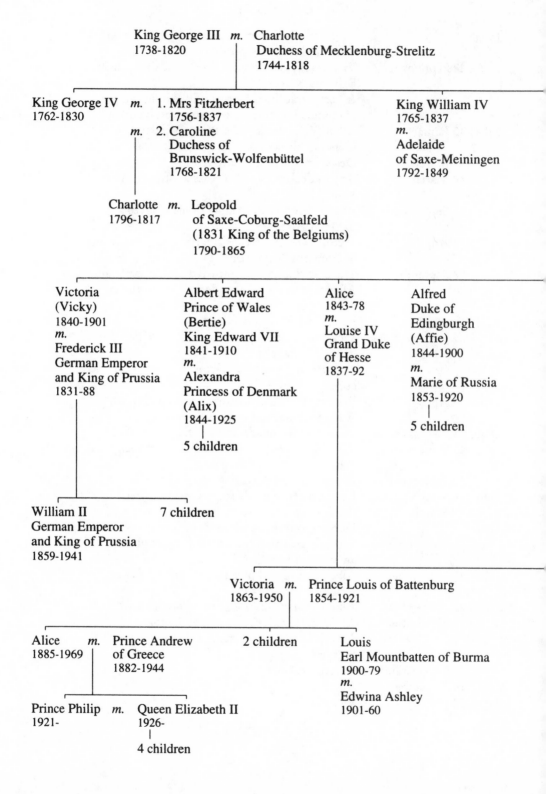

King George III m. Charlotte
1738-1820   Duchess of Mecklenburg-Strelitz
                    1744-1818

King George IV m. 1. Mrs Fitzherbert   King William IV
1762-1830   1756-1837   1765-1837
                m. 2. Caroline   m.
                       Duchess of   Adelaide
                       Brunswick-Wolfenbüttel   of Saxe-Meiningen
                       1768-1821   1792-1849

          Charlotte m. Leopold
          1796-1817   of Saxe-Coburg-Saalfeld
                         (1831 King of the Belgiums)
                         1790-1865

Victoria   Albert Edward   Alice   Alfred
(Vicky)   Prince of Wales   1843-78   Duke of
1840-1901   (Bertie)   m.   Edingburgh
m.   King Edward VII   Louise IV   (Affie)
Frederick III   1841-1910   Grand Duke   1844-1900
German Emperor   m.   of Hesse   m.
and King of Prussia   Alexandra   1837-92   Marie of Russia
1831-88   Princess of Denmark   1853-1920
                      (Alix)
                      1844-1925   5 children

                      5 children

William II   7 children
German Emperor
and King of Prussia
1859-1941

                    Victoria m. Prince Louis of Battenburg
                    1863-1950   1854-1921

Alice   m. Prince Andrew   2 children   Louis
1885-1969   of Greece   Earl Mountbatten of Burma
                1882-1944   1900-79
                                                    m.
                                                    Edwina Ashley
Prince Philip m. Queen Elizabeth II   1901-60
1921-   1926-

                4 children

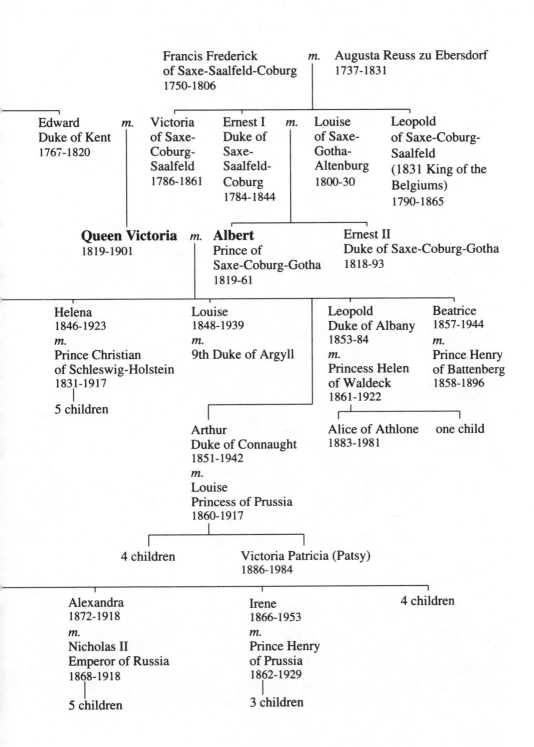

Francis Frederick
of Saxe-Saalfeld-Coburg
1750-1806

m.

Augusta Reuss zu Ebersdorf
1737-1831

Edward
Duke of Kent
1767-1820

m.

Victoria
of Saxe-
Coburg-
Saalfeld
1786-1861

Ernest I
Duke of
Saxe-
Saalfeld-
Coburg
1784-1844

m.

Louise
of Saxe-
Gotha-
Altenburg
1800-30

Leopold
of Saxe-Coburg-
Saalfeld
(1831 King of the
Belgiums)
1790-1865

Queen Victoria
1819-1901

m.

Albert
Prince of
Saxe-Coburg-Gotha
1819-61

Ernest II
Duke of Saxe-Coburg-Gotha
1818-93

Helena
1846-1923
m.
Prince Christian
of Schleswig-Holstein
1831-1917
|
5 children

Louise
1848-1939
m.
9th Duke of Argyll

Leopold
Duke of Albany
1853-84
m.
Princess Helen
of Waldeck
1861-1922

Beatrice
1857-1944
m.
Prince Henry
of Battenberg
1858-1896

Arthur
Duke of Connaught
1851-1942
m.
Louise
Princess of Prussia
1860-1917

Alice of Athlone
1883-1981

one child

4 children

Victoria Patricia (Patsy)
1886-1984

4 children

Alexandra
1872-1918
m.
Nicholas II
Emperor of Russia
1868-1918
|
5 children

Irene
1866-1953
m.
Prince Henry
of Prussia
1862-1929
|
3 children

GENEALOGICAL TREE

Victoria and Albert as newly-weds riding in Windsor Great Park in 1840

CHAPTER ONE

The Baron's Plans

Queen Victoria's birth was the outcome of high risk-taking. She was born into a welter of family debt, virtually homeless, and was the object of mixed joy and anxiety. There was no proper monarch in the land, only an unstable Prince Regent who was standing in for his father, George III. The king was still alive, but had become mad, and blind. The future succession of the Hanoverians was in grave doubt.

Until the last days of March 1819, the Duke of Kent, the Prince Regent's younger brother, had been living with his pregnant wife at the palace of Amorbach in the German dukedom of Gotha. Far from medical aid, Amorbach was an unsuitable place for giving birth. Moreover, any child of the marriage was a likely candidate for the English throne, and should therefore be born in England. Joseph Hume, the influential radical, had written to the duke, 'The greatest and most important duty your country looks for from you is for the [German] Duchess to give birth on English soil.' Anything else 'will be thought by the nation to arise from the wish of the Duchess to remain in her own country'.

The first impediment to travelling to England was the cost. The Duke of Kent was borne down by debt, and the expense of removing his entire entourage from Gotha to Calais, for the crossing to Dover, was far beyond his means, and he calculated that the cost of the duchess's *accouchement* alone would be over £1,100. However, as a result of letters of appeal to friends and relations in high places and to those interested in ensuring that the royal line should pass to the Kents, by

1

the middle of March 1819 the improvident duke had been guaranteed £15,000, more than enough to secure a successful journey overland. At Calais, thanks to the Prince Regent, the royal yacht, *Royal Sovereign*, would carry them to Dover.

There was now no time to waste. The roads were rough, and a miscarriage en route would be a disaster. The man in charge of the arrangements for the 400-mile journey was Captain John Conroy. An extraordinary man, claiming descent through a distinguished line stretching back to the King of Ireland in AD 400, Conroy was tall and good-looking, with immense vanity, charm, and ambition. He was also a genuinely able administrator, who by devious channels was granted the appointment of equerry to the Duke of Kent. At times like this, he was worth every penny of his £60 a month salary.

The Duchess of Kent's mother, the Dowager Duchess of Coburg, saw off the cavalcade on 28 March. Grieved to be losing her beloved daughter, this estimable woman was also alarmed that the young duchess was undertaking such a taxing journey while eight months pregnant. However, she had full confidence in her son-in-law who, among other precautions, had insisted that they should take with them a woman obstetrician.

Seen off with much fluttering of handkerchiefs by all the staff of Amorbach, a veritable living museum of contemporary carriages set out in the early spring sunshine. In the vanguard the duke drove a lightweight, well-sprung cane phaeton, with the duchess beside him, well wrapped against the cool air. The duchess's landau followed with the suite and several English maids of Princess Feodora, the eleven-year-old child of the duchess's former marriage to Prince Emich Charles of Leiningen. Next came the duke's barouche with the obstetrician, Madame Siebold, and the duchess's lady-in-waiting. Behind the barouche was a large covered post-chaise, empty but reserved for the duchess in the event of rain.

Taking up the rear were two gigs, a cabriolet and finally a curricle for the duke's doctor, an ex-Royal Navy officer.

As for the luggage, this ranged from the family plate to the duchess's own bed and linen.

Conroy aimed to travel twenty-five miles a day, although the distance was determined by the availability of accommodation at the various hostelries en route. There were also days of complete rest for the benefit of the duchess, who remained in good health and spirits, leading the duke to report in a letter to a friend, 'I am happy to say that on the whole the Duchess is even *less* fatigued of an evening on her journey than she used to be when resting quietly at home.'

Everything seemed to conspire in favour of the Duchess of Kent and her unborn child: the weather was calm and mainly sunny, there were no breakdowns, no sickness nor accident of any kind among the retinue. 'Providence absolutely prospered our undertaking,' the jubilant duke reported.

On 5 April they caught sight of the towering spires of Cologne cathedral and entered the city that evening for the night's rest. Thirteen days later, they reached Calais where, moored in the harbour, was the *Royal Sovereign*, ready to take them to England.

Conroy was much praised for his organisation and strict adherence to the timetable, but even this Irishman could not control the weather, and day followed day with fierce headwinds which prohibited departure. The duke fretted and contemplated the dreadful irony of his wife giving birth twenty-three miles from English soil. The duchess, however, remained serenely unconcerned and confident of a successful outcome.

At last, on 24 April, the wind abated, and though the sea remained boisterous, the yacht was able to depart. They crossed in three hours, the duchess sick all the way.

'All has ended well,' wrote the duke in relief to the Dowager Duchess of Coburg.

Four days later, the party reached London and Kensington Palace, where the Regent had offered accommodation for the Kents and their retinue. The duke was familiar with the palace:

he had lived in rooms there as a young man, until obliged to leave for the Continent, accompanied by his mistress and pursued by his creditors. Since then, the condition of the building had greatly deteriorated.

Kensington Palace had had a chequered existence. It is situated at the west end of Hyde Park, the great open space given to the people of London in the early years of the seventeenth century. The house is of Jacobean origin, and was purchased from its first owner by King William III, whose hatred of his official residence equalled that of his wife, Mary. Christopher Wren, who was shortly to rebuild St Paul's after the previous cathedral had been burnt down in the Great Fire of London, was commissioned to reconstruct what was then called Nottingham House. He and his clerk, Nicholas Hawksmoor, were constantly hurried by Queen Mary with the result that some of the work was skimped. The Queen herself narrowly escaped injury when part of the structure collapsed, killing a number of people.

The palace became more or less habitable by Christmas 1689. The Queen especially loved the rural isolation, for Kensington was then a mere village to the west of the capital, and the King enjoyed working in the garden. Unfortunately the fabric of the palace was badly neglected, and matters were not helped when the building was damaged by fire in 1691.

The Hanoverian 'Georges' – I, II, and III – either preferred the new 'Buckingham House', later Palace, or lived intermittently at 'KP', as it has always been known by the royal family. Only the King's brother, the Duke of Sussex, the mesmerist, collector, and co-founder of the Garrick Club, lived there for any length of time. No one with the required wealth and authority took the necessary steps to maintain the building satisfactorily.

The Kents' apartment, on the ground floor and mainly overlooking present-day Kensington Gardens and Hyde Park, was generous in size, but according to the Regent's architect, unfit for human habitation. Orders were therefore issued for a comprehensive refurbishment, to be completed by 18 April, Conroy's predicted date for the ducal party's arrival in Calais.

Kensington Palace's congenital ill-fortune held. There were complications over the cost and other delays, with the result that much remained to be done when the ducal party arrived. Apart from lack of decoration and furnishings, no repairs had been carried out to the windows, which were rotten and let in the rain. John Conroy would have done better, as, no doubt, he made clear. The first priority was to have ready a nursery for the unborn child. A north-facing room was selected and furnished with a crib of mahogany and hangings of white glazed cambric.

The duke and duchess's bedroom with its two four-poster beds, had wonderful views over the round pond of Kensington Gardens, and more distantly the great lake surrounded by trees and sweeps of grassland grazed by sheep. It might, indeed, have been the depths of rural England. There was much to be done during these first days, and John Conroy was busy from dawn to dusk.

The duchess's lying-in room was not ready until 22 May, barely in time for the birth. On the evening of the next day, and rather later than expected, the duchess went into labour. The duke, in accordance with traditional practice, despatched a message to his comptroller, General Wetherall, who in turn urgently commanded the presence at Kensington Palace of the Regent's ministers, the Privy Councillors.

These gentlemen, who included the Duke of Wellington, Manners-Sutton, the Archbishop of Canterbury, the Bishop of London, and the Duke of Sussex – who merely walked in from his own apartment in the palace – all assembled quietly in the adjoining room at around midnight, and prepared to endure the tedium of awaiting the birth.

Meanwhile, after a labour of six and a half hours, assisted by her obstetrician, and in the presence of the anxious duke, the Duchess of Kent gave birth to 'a pretty little Princess, as plump as a partridge'.

*   *   *

Among those who gave thanks to God for the safe delivery was the baby's German grandmother, the Dowager Duchess of Coburg. 'I cannot find words to express my delight ... to God be praise and thanks eternally that everything went on smoothly ... The English like Queens.' But there were others less pleased, particularly the Prince Regent who loathed his younger brother the Duke of Kent, and detested the idea of his offspring possibly succeeding to the throne at some future date.

Precisely one month later, on 24 June 1819, with the princess already showing signs of unusual strength and sturdiness, she was carried to her christening in the Cupola Room at Kensington Palace. The event lived up to the palace's reputation for mishaps. The Prince Regent, perhaps for mischievous reasons, agreed to stand as godfather. The baby's names had been chosen with care: Alexandrina Georgiana Charlotte Augusta Victoria. Alexandrina was out of respect for the Emperor of Russia, Alexander I, who had consented to be godfather *in absentia*; Charlotte was a traditional Hanoverian name, as was Augusta; while Victoria was for both her mother and her Coburg grandmother, who was also to be godmother. The Prince Regent knew of these proposed names but waited until the evening before the ceremony before writing 'that the name of Georgiana could not be used – as He did not chuse to place his name before the Emperor of Russia's – and He could not allow it to follow'.

A gold font had been placed in the centre of the Cupola Room. At the most sacred moment in the service, the archbishop, with the plump infant in his arms, turned enquiringly to the Prince Regent, waiting for the names to be pronounced. There was a long pause and at last the prince uttered with evident reluctance the name of Alexandrina. And that, apparently, was all. The Duke of Kent then interceded and pronounced the name Elizabeth. This produced a shake of the Regent's head, as did Charlotte, the name of his daughter who died in childbirth. Augusta also received an emphatic negative.

By now the mother was sobbing, and the duke turned on his

brother. 'Then what name would you suggest?' he demanded. 'Give her the mother's name, but it cannot precede that of the Emperor.'

And so the future Queen Empress was baptised by royal order Alexandrina Victoria; and throughout her infancy and early childhood was called simply Drina, later choosing Victoria.

My earliest recollections [wrote Victoria some fifty years later] are connected with Kensington Palace, where I can remember crawling on a yellow carpet spread out for that purpose – and being told that if I cried and was naughty my 'Uncle Sussex' [the

Victoria's drawing of herself after she had contracted typhoid at Ramsgate in October 1835

royal duke who lived in Kensington Palace] would hear me and punish me, for which reason I always screamed when I saw him! I had a great horror of *Bishops* on account of their wigs and *aprons* but recollect this being partially got over in the case of the then Bishop of Salisbury . . . by his kneeling down and letting me play with his badge of Chancellor of the Order of the Garter. With another Bishop, however, the persuasion of showing him my 'pretty shoes' was of no use. Claremont [the home of beloved Uncle Leopold] remains as the brightest epoch of my otherwise rather melancholy childhood . . . I used to ride a donkey given me by my Uncle, the Duke of York, who was very kind to me. I remember him well – tall, rather large, very kind but extremely shy. He always gave me beautiful presents . . .

To Ramsgate we used to go frequently in the summer, and I remember living at Townley House (near the town), and going there by steamer. Mamma was very unwell. Dear Uncle Leopold went with us.

To Tunbridge Wells we also went, living at a house called Mt. Pleasant, now an hotel. Many pleasant days were spent here, and the return to Kensington in October or November was generally a day of tears . . .

The independent state of Coburg, where the Kents had begun their journey, was so small it risked being lost among the multitude of dukedoms and principalities that made up greater Germany. Yet it produced a flow of candidates for the highest offices in Europe. The dukedom of Saxe-Coburg gained additional lustre through the family of Duke Francis, who died in 1806, leaving three sons and four daughters. The youngest child, Prince Leopold, eventually became the first King of the Belgians, when that nation was created in 1831. He had earlier married Princess Charlotte, daughter of the Prince Regent and heiress to the English throne. (She died giving birth to a still-born child eighteen months later.) His sisters married respectively a French *emigré* called Mensdorf; a brother of the Empress Marie of Russia; the Grand Duke Constantine of Russia; and, as her second husband, the Duke of Kent, father of Queen Victoria.

Ernest, who inherited the dukedom from Francis, married

Louise, the daughter of the heiress of the Duke of Saxe-Gotha. They had two sons, Prince Ernest and Prince Albert.

These brothers, born in 1818 and 1819, were so dissimilar in character and appearance that there were mischievous rumours that the younger was illegitimate. Prince Albert was born on 26 August 1819, just three months after his cousin Princess Victoria. The birth took place at one of the ducal country estates, the Rosenau, a turreted and castellated mock castle shooting-lodge overlooking a lake and surrounded by heavily wooded hills. Almost from the day of his birth Albert's beauty was remarked upon. 'Lovely as a little angel,' his mother recorded in his infancy. His eyes, like his mother's, were deep blue and his curly hair was at first fair.

Albert's brother Ernest 'was as unattractive as Prince Albert was attractive. His complexion,' ran the harsh description by Marie, Queen of Roumania, 'was sallow with liver spots, his eyes were bloodshot, and his lower teeth, like those of a bull-dog, protruded far above his upper ones'. But the same Queen had to concede that he was 'a mighty hunter of wine, women and song'. Even from their infancy, it was plainly evident that the elder son took after his father, in character and appearance, while Albert strongly resembled his mother in most respects, certainly in his features, and in his steadiness of character. 'The Prince was,' according to the biographer Roger Fulford, 'by nature affectionate, intelligent and confiding', all qualities lacking in his brother.

Baron Stockmar, who was to have such a strong influence over Prince Albert, found it puzzling that he turned out to have so fine a character 'with such a father and such a brother, both equally unprincipled'. When Albert was still only four, his mother suddenly disappeared from his life for ever. It was a tragic and shocking event, but it was typical of the boy, and later of the man, that he never uttered a bitter comment on this occurrence, and always thought of his mother with great tenderness.

The cause of her departure was the almost ceaseless womanising of Duke Ernest, who increasingly neglected his wife. After a long period of such treatment, the Duchess Louise left home in the company of an officer in the Coburg army, who took her to live in Paris. Here this sad, beautiful woman died from a lingering and painful disease. She was only thirty-one.

The two boys derived consolation from each other. In spite of the gulf that separated them in many respects, they felt great mutual affection, which was fortunate as they were so much in each other's company, especially during their early boyhood. From time to time members of their widespread German family came to stay at the Rosenau or in the palace in Coburg, often bringing their children. But for the most part the boys were dependent on each other, whether studying, making music, playing games together – or fighting.

Their father was too occupied in gambling and roistering in Paris and elsewhere to give much time to his sons. But there were two figures in the duchy who were loved by the boys and had a strong early influence on them. The first was Christoph Florschütz, the tutor who took over their education when Albert was four, and his brother five. Florschütz from the beginning did not attempt to conceal his special regard for Albert, sometimes carrying the little boy up and down stairs. 'Every grace,' he once wrote of Albert, 'had been showered by nature on this charming boy. Every eye rested on him with delight, and his looks won the hearts of all.' He also admired Albert's academic work, but, surprisingly perhaps, there is no evidence that Ernest took offence at this favouritism.

The other influential and important figure, almost a surrogate mother, was the dowager duchess, a most amiable, affectionate and intelligent woman. Once when they returned home after a short absence, she wrote in her diary, 'Yesterday morning, my dear little boys came back from Gotha, and I was overjoyed. Ernest is very much grown . . . Albert is very much smaller than his brother, and lovely as a little angel with his fair curls.' Later, perhaps feeling her age, she wrote, 'They are very good boys on the whole, very obedient and easy to manage. Albert used to rebel a little sometimes, but a grave face brings the little fellow to submit.' Another entry reads, 'The boys are very wild, and Ernest flies about like a swallow.'

In the early, rather skimpy records of Albert's young boyhood, there are several references to poor health which in retrospect can be seen as ominous. Theodore Martin in his authorised five-volume biography writes, 'The sweetness of his nature showed itself conspicuously during the attacks of illness to which he was subject up to the age of ten. His heart seemed then to open to the whole world. He would form the most noble projects for execution after his recovery – and, though not apparently satisfied with himself, he displayed a temper and disposition, in thought and deed, perfectly angelic.'

At the age of eleven, Albert is recorded as having written, no doubt without a trace of self-consciousness, 'I intend to train myself to be a good and useful man.' Herr Florschütz was doing his utmost to help the boy along this path. Noting that he possessed 'a rather too strong will of his own', he also found that 'he surpassed his brother in thoughtful earnestness, in calm reflection and self-command, and evincing at the same time, more prudence in action'.

In another more prosaic observation, the tutor noted Albert's tendency to fall asleep as soon as he was tired, and he became tired all too readily. One reason for this was his frail constitution, another the need to get up early. It appeared to be as impossible for Albert to stay in bed after an invariably early awakening as it was for him to remain awake in the evening. If he could not go to bed for any reason, he 'would suddenly disappear', as Florschütz recounted, 'and was generally found sleeping quietly in the recess of the window . . .' This tendency was to remain with him for all his life, frequently with embarrassing consequences.

If Florschütz was Albert's loving and close guide and mentor, Baron Stockmar was his assiduous and – for the present – distant observer. It was, for instance, Stockmar who found and recommended Florschütz as tutor. Christian Frederick

Stockmar was born in Coburg in 1787, and, his father dying young, was brought up by his shrewd and admirable mother. He qualified as a doctor, and served in the last years of the Napoleonic wars. He married and had children, but he was besotted by power, and had the skill and wit to ease himself towards the centre of a highly influential circle. In 1815 he entered the service of Prince Leopold of Saxe-Coburg-Saalfeld who had married Charlotte, daughter of the Prince Regent and heiress presumptive to the English throne. Stockmar became not only personal doctor to Prince Leopold and his wife, but also general factotum and confidential secretary.

He made himself essential to them and, as Princess Charlotte lay dying, it was to Stockmar that she uttered her last memorable words – 'Stocky, they have made me drunk.'

When it had appeared that Leopold might become the Prince Consort, with Charlotte as Queen, he had been granted a lifetime annuity of no less than £50,000 a year. As his niece Victoria grew up in England, he took an increasing interest in her welfare and upbringing and made generous grants to her penurious mother.

This avuncular figure took an equal interest in the welfare of his motherless nephew, Albert of Coburg, although when Leopold became King of the Belgians in 1831, neither he nor Stockmar had designs on Victoria as a wife for Albert. It was not until the second half of 1835 when niece and nephew were sixteen and it had become evident that the Duchess of Kent's daughter would succeed King William IV as monarch, that these two scheming men contrived a plan to bring about a match in which Albert would become Prince Consort to Victoria's Queen – a position which Leopold had been denied by the death of his first wife.

Why should King Leopold have chosen the younger rather than the older of his two nephews? The answer was that both he and Stockmar judged Albert to be the superior for the role assigned to him. This was based on Leopold's own observation and on a report sent back from Coburg to Brussels by Stockmar, who had found Albert 'a handsome youth'.

The report continued,

... with pleasant and striking features; and who, if nothing interferes with his progress, will probably in a few years be a well-built man with a pleasant, simple, and yet distinguishing bearing. Externally, therefore, he has everything attractive to women, and possesses every quality they find pleasing at all times, and in all countries. It may also be considered as a fortunate circumstance that he had already a certain English look about him. He is said to be prudent, cautious, and already very well informed. All this, however, is not enough. He must not only have great capacity but true ambition, and a great strength of will. To pursue so difficult a political career a whole life through requires more than energy and inclination – it demands also that earnest frame of mind which is ready of its own accord to sacrifice mere pleasure to real usefulness.

During his late teens Albert was taken on a tour of Italy to broaden his mind and introduce a cultural element to his education. This was a joint Stockmar–Leopold enterprise. The visit to Berlin was certainly not. It was the idea of the boys' father, perhaps to show them a slice of what he termed 'the real world'. Without informing any of the family, Duke Ernest whisked the boys away immediately after their joint confirmation. The two experiences could not have been more contrasting. Berlin in the 1830s was regarded as the most decadent city in Europe and the father knew the places and people who helped to sustain this reputation.

King Leopold was outraged when he heard of the visit and worried how it might affect Albert. He need not have been concerned: Albert hated the place from the moment of his arrival, and refused to join his brother and father on their dissipated rounds of clubs and places of entertainment. He spent most of his time in the Hotel Angleterre, reading and ignoring the jeers no doubt uttered by the other two. Albert the Good indeed!

The Berlin experience did at least harden the resolve of Leopold and Stockmar to press ahead with their plans for Albert. If they could not save both boys from their father, they could do their best for the younger boy. Princess Victoria's seventeenth birthday, which would bring her only one year from the qualifying age to succeed without an intervening regent, was on 24 May. And there were plenty of contenders for the hand of the world's most powerful and rich future monarch. Moreover, the health of William IV was very poor: he was asthmatic, his liver, from years of heavy drinking, was in a terrible state, and he was confined to a wheelchair.

His condition had not improved King William's temper and had increased his antagonism to any plan for his successor to marry into the Coburg family. Determined that Princess Victoria should marry one of the sons of the Prince of Orange, he was not in the least concerned that, on meeting them, she had vowed to have nothing to do with either of them. 'The boys are both very plain,' she wrote to her Uncle Leopold, much to his relief, 'and have a mixture of Kalmuck and Dutch in their faces, moreover they look heavy, dull, and frightened and are not at all prepossessing. So much for the *Oranges*, dear Uncle.'

King William was beside himself with frustration and fury when he heard that the Coburg princes were on their way to stay at Kensington Palace, and tried to persuade the Foreign Secretary, Lord Palmerston, to forbid their landing on English soil. Palmerston refused to comply.

On hearing through courtiers' gossip that the Orange princes were also coming to London for the birthday celebrations, Leopold instructed Grand Duke Ernest to set out at once. The duke had remarried but had not brought his wife with him, no doubt fearful that her presence might restrict his womanising in London, and later in Paris.

In early May sunshine, the party of three with their staffs slipped down the Rhine on the ferry for Rotterdam, thence by pacquet to Dover. Albert spent most of the journey studying an English grammar book, breaking off to contemplate with some anxiety his imminent meeting with the English princess and wondering what she would make of him.

CHAPTER TWO

The Frustrated Salute

Victoria's childhood was scarred by royal rows. The Hanovers fed on acrimony. Of George III's children, the eldest, Prince George, 'Prinny', acting as Prince Regent, was a thoroughly unpleasant character, unable to produce an heir but furious at the idea of any of his brothers, especially Edward, Duke of Kent, doing so. Cumberland was as improvident and disreputable as most of his brothers. Sussex, with his fascination for mesmerism and clocks, was eccentric almost to the point of dottiness. By far the best of the bunch was Victoria's father, although his capacity for keeping some sort of order with his finances was no better than his brothers'. But at least he did not engage in family vendettas nor relish court infighting.

The christening row was typical of the quarrelsome nature of Victoria's childhood. She may not have been conscious of the dreadful atmosphere on this occasion but, as she grew, so did her realisation of the rancorous nature of those immediately about her. The worst of these was John Conroy, the best his bitter enemy Baroness Lehzen.

There was no limit to the ambitions of the Irishman who had organised the complicated journey from Gotha to Kensington Palace. The fine weather which had accompanied them for most of the way, and the unfailing reliability of the vehicles, were typical of the luck of the Irishman, although appropriate credit must also be given to his organisational skills. With the successful delivery of his master's child, Conroy recognised that, more than ever, he must maintain his position with this family. He had overheard time and again the father instructing visitors to 'Look at her well for she will be Queen of England.' Conroy accepted, as did his master, that this was not a certainty. At the time of her birth Princess Victoria was fifth in line to the throne – after her uncles the Prince Regent, Frederick Duke of York, William Henry Duke of Clarence, and her father, Edward Duke of Kent. However, unless other legitimate children, notably Clarence's, intervened, which seemed unlikely, she would succeed.

Conroy's ultimate ambition was to become private secretary to this girl when and if she became Queen.

Victoria was only seven months old when Louise Lehzen was appointed governess to Princess Feodora, now aged twelve. Lehzen was thirty-five years old, the daughter of a Lutheran clergyman of Hanover. By all accounts she was not beautiful, and she had the distasteful habit of chewing caraway seeds when off duty, but she was dedicated to her job and almost fanatically loyal to all the Kent family. She had the ear of the duchess who became deeply fond of her, as, in due course, did both the duchess's daughters.

While Britain went to war in Afghanistan, and in London the National Gallery was opened and Charles Dickens began publishing his serial *Nicholas Nickleby*, the Kents settled into Kensington Palace. Unfortunately, neither the Prince Consort nor Parliament allowed them a penny, deeming it the responsibility of the duchess's brother Leopold, with his generous allowance of £50,000 a year, to look after her. He did, but only to the tune of £3,000 p.a. The duke himself enjoyed a settlement of £6,000 p.a., and that was all. There were servants, a lady-in-waiting, Conroy, Lehzen and others to pay; the upkeep of the household, carriages, appropriate dresses for a royal duchess, and, most demanding of all, keeping creditors at bay.

The duchess insisted on feeding Victoria herself, an eccentric practice for one of her class, and so no wet nurses were required which proved both a convenience and an economy. A nursemaid was engaged, a Mrs Brock, who was almost a caricature of the typical nurse of the time – bulky, homely, affectionate, much starched; her charge called her 'dear Boppy' when she could speak.

Not many more months of 1819 had passed before the duke and duchess were obliged to fall back on the charity of Leopold. In England Leopold stayed at his country residence at Claremont, west of London. The Kents were now granted free accommodation at Claremont as Leopold's guests. Later that autumn the family moved farther west to the seaside at Sidmouth in Devon for Christmas. The duke judged that the air would be beneficial to mother and daughter, especially at a time when Victoria was being weaned. On the journey, the duke caught a chill, but such was his faith in sea air that he paced up and down the promenade at Sidmouth, doing his cold no good at all. Within a few days he was laid up in bed with pneumonia.

In answer to the duchess's calls for help as her husband's condition worsened, Stockmar and Prince Leopold hastened to Sidmouth. In the last hours of the life of Edward Duke of Kent, Stockmar persuaded him to make a will. The sole beneficiary was his widow who inherited all his mountainous debts. John Conroy succeeded in getting his name on the list of executors.

Victoria was just seven months old when her father died on 23 January 1820. Six days later the insane George III, Edward's old father, died, to the relief of those responsible for him. Both men were buried together in the family vault at Windsor: Princess Victoria was one step closer to the throne, a fact of which she, unlike John Conroy, remained totally unaware.

Added to the widow's grief was her fear for the future. For the present, she did not even have the money to bring herself and her party back to London. Brother Leopold at length came to her rescue and Conroy organised the journey. The duchess realised that she was now more than ever dependent on these two men, and also on the wisdom of Stockmar.

Victoria's early upbringing was extremely austere and the subject of much deliberation by her mother, Stockmar, John

Conroy and, when the first simple lessons were introduced to her daily timetable, by Lehzen. 'I was brought up very simply,' the Queen later wrote, 'never had a room to myself till I was nearly grown up – always slept in my mother's room till I came to the throne.' This, however, was as much for security as austerity reasons.

Her day started with breakfast of bread, milk and fruit on a table placed between her bed and her mother's. This was at 8 a.m., after which her mother retired to her private sitting-room, Mrs Brock would dress her charge and, according to the weather, take her for a walk or a ride in the little pony cart.

The duchess would not long be absent from her daughter's daily routine. When Victoria was ready for lessons, she began at first on a very simple basis, mostly drawing, which she loved, but, she said, 'I baffled every attempt to teach me my letters up to five years old' – a considerable exaggeration. Before luncheon was served, again with her mother, she played at games or with her dolls. There was never any mention of a rest period afterwards, although as a child of four or five she must have had a 'lie down'. Lessons and playing followed until dinner for her mother, and supper of bread and milk at her side for Victoria. She was encouraged to get down when she had finished, but returned to the table for dessert. Then bed at 9 p.m.

Conroy found a professional teacher for Victoria when she was still very young, the Reverend George Davys. He remained at Kensington until Victoria was twelve, when he left to become Dean of Chester.

The young princess saw very few children, and in spite of the age difference her one dearest friend remained her step-sister Feodora, who slept on the other side of the duchess's bed. These two played harmoniously together for hours. When for whatever reason they were separated, they exchanged frequent and loving letters. Princess Feodora grew into a beautiful young woman, tall and graceful, with the exquisite manners her mother had taught her.

Early portraits of Victoria show fair, curly hair, parted in the middle, a resolutely poised head, bright blue eyes, already somewhat protruding, a negligible chin in the Hanoverian style, dimpled cheeks, tiny pudgy hands and unusually small feet. Even when she was only six or seven years old there was an air of authority about her as if she were in training for her destiny, although no hint had yet been offered that she might well one day be crowned Queen of England. A certain astuteness was also evident. Quite able to hold her dignity in the presence of the appalling George IV, she suffered without a flinch being dandled on his gouty knees, and even being kissed by the rouged and powdered 'Uncle King'.

Once when out walking in Windsor Park with her mother, they found themselves overtaken by the grand royal phaeton. It drew to a halt just ahead of them, and the King called out, 'Pop her in!' Powerful arms plucked her up and into the carriage where she was seated between the King and Aunt Mary of Gloucester. They clattered away at high speed. 'I was greatly pleased,' she recounted later, but her mother was terrified, not of an accident but rather of a kidnap.

That same evening Uncle King put on a special entertainment for his little niece. At one point she was asked by the King to choose the next piece for the orchestra. She responded at once with unerring tact, 'God save the King'. At the end of the evening the little girl was asked what she had enjoyed most that day. Equally judiciously and quickly she replied, 'The drive with you.'

'He took notice of me,' Victoria later reminisced modestly. George IV's love of children was about his only endearing characteristic. 'He always was fond of children,' Prime Minister Lord Melbourne later reminded the Queen. 'He bought an enormous amount of playthings to give away as presents. His accounts are replete with bills for dolls and lead soldiers, boxes of ninepins, miniature farmyards, play houses, mechanical animals, rocking horses, games and toys of every description.'

As she grew older – say nine or ten – she became more

conscious of her status in society, although probably not yet fully aware of her closeness to the throne. For example, she had already noted and no doubt drawn conclusions from the way gentlemen meeting them took off their hats to her before turning to Feodora.

She was once overheard saying to a rare visitor of her own age about to play with her toys, 'You must not touch those, they are mine; and I may call you Jane but you must not call me Victoria.' No wonder she was sometimes lonely, especially when her half-sister went off to Germany to marry.

There remained, however, John Conroy's daughter Victoire of her own age. But Victoria was already becoming canny about the comptroller of her mother's household.

It is not possible to lay down who was the most responsible for what came to be known as the Kensington system, which ruled Princess Victoria's life from the age of six almost until she acceded to the throne. Conroy himself gave all credit to the duchess. 'From 1825 Your Royal Highness,' he wrote later, 'conceived and acted on a System, that was to make the Princess "The Nation's Hope", "The People's Queen" – it would take volumes to narrate your difficulties, your anxiety, your efforts to accomplish this mighty design.'

It is most likely that the system grew out of discussions with prominent Whigs of the time, notably the first Earl of Durham, who owned vast sources of coal in that area, and became known as King Coal, or King Jog because he managed to jog along on £40,000 a year. Others who formed a sort of council were Lord Dunfermline, Lord Duncannon, and most important of all Baron Stockmar, who divided his Machiavellian talent between the Duchess of Kent and her daughter and Prince Leopold.

Conroy once declared that the Kensington system had been created 'to give the Princess Victoria an upbringing which would enable her in the future to be equal to her high position'. This was typically vague and high sounding. In effect it was to ensure that she was properly taught the languages she would most need, mathematics and economics (which she loved and was good at), art and music, and history and politics, which were not favourite subjects.

Above all, the system was devised to keep Victoria as far as possible isolated from the decadent English Hanoverian court, and the almost equally dissipated and extravagant Coburg court, of which the parents of Prince Ernest and Prince Albert were prime examples. Like some locked-away fairy-tale princess, Victoria was never allowed to be alone with another person, above all not alone with anyone from outside the Kensington court. Lehzen was her most frequent 'guard', with instructions always to hold her hand going up or down stairs, until she was almost adult. And it was Lehzen who sat in her bedroom, often reading aloud until Victoria fell asleep and leaving only when the duchess came to bed.

Although not made unhappy by this security and isolation, Victoria certainly became self-sufficient and resourceful. She read and painted, but above all grew more and more dependent on her collection of dolls. Her punctiliously kept list numbers 132 of them, each named and given a character. As Cecil Woodham-Smith has told us, 'The Princess found an outlet for her imagination and affection in dressing and playing with her dolls and they continued to be a favourite amusement until she was nearly fourteen.'

The stakes were too high for risk-taking. The constant fear of the duchess and Conroy was that Victoria would be whisked away, perhaps by one of her ageing, eccentric and unscrupulous uncles with their unauthorised marriages and illegitimate children. But there was no question that the Duke of Clarence would succeed to the throne as William IV on the death of his brother George IV.

This occurred on 26 June 1830. The new King was sixty-five years of age, looked a good deal older, was asthmatic and although cheerful enough and informal in his manner, did not appear likely to last the seven years before his niece Victoria came of age. After a struggle, for she was not a popular woman, Parliament appointed the Duchess of Kent as regent should the need arise. Also as a bonus of good news, the House granted Victoria an extra £10,000 a year 'for the Princess's education'.

Victoria was by now fully aware that, barring some miracle, such as King William and Queen Adelaide conceiving a child, she was heiress presumptive. She had never been told formally, but the special treatment and privilege she enjoyed, the unusual respect accorded her in public places, seemed to confirm that she would one day be Queen. The proof, however, was still lacking.

Then on 11 March 1830, shortly before the death of George IV, Lehzen was conducting a history lesson, using Howlett's *Tales of the Kings and Queens of England*. Victoria recognised that an extra loose page had been inserted and she studied it carefully. It revealed a genealogical table which showed numerous possible heirs to the throne. All had died and the dates of death had been included. At the end came Uncle George, Uncle William, and finally her own name.

'I never saw that before,' she exclaimed.

'No, Princess,' Lehzen replied. 'It was not thought necessary that you should.'

Lehzen described in later years how Victoria exclaimed, 'I am nearer to the throne than I thought,' and burst into tears, explaining when she had recovered that many young people might be thrilled at the splendour of the prospect, but that she was aware of the weight of responsibilities with which she would be burdened. Then, again according to Lehzen, she raised the tiny forefinger of her right hand and spoke the now-famous words, 'I will be good.'

A little later she told Lehzen that now she understood why she had learned Latin so carefully: 'You told me Latin is the foundation of English grammar.' Putting her hand in Lehzen's, she repeated the words, 'I will be good.'

Many years later Albert recounted how 'The Queen perfectly recollects this circumstance and says the discovery that morning made her very unhappy.'

*   *   *

22

Elizabeth Longford defined Sir John Conroy, the Duchess of Kent's comptroller, and with the death of George IV more powerful than ever, as 'a man of extravagant ambitions, an intriguer, a vulgarian and a scamp'. Partly to demonstrate the closeness of his own connection with the future Queen and also to strengthen Victoria's position among the people, he devised a series of tours across the nation, staying at the houses of rich and powerful aristocrats, like Blenheim (the Marlboroughs) and Madresfield, the home of the Beauchamps. Between these journeys, Conroy arranged visits to great cities like Birmingham where she was shown some of the largest factories of the time, which were at the heart of the industrial revolution and the nation's wealth. Bristol, Bath, Gloucester were all included in the south-western leg of their tour and they stayed for several nights at Badminton with the Beauforts.

The party was a large one, including Victoria's mother and grandmother Gotha, Conroy and members of his family, ladies-in-waiting and a dozen or so servants and coachmen. In the cities and towns the people turned out in thousands to see and cheer their enchanting little future Queen. The King, however, was not best pleased. The duchess had not bothered to obtain his authority for this tour or those that followed. Conroy himself had explained to King William that the purpose was to graft upon the princess's education 'a more extended knowledge of the internal concerns of the country, which she could not fail to imbibe from visiting the great seats of manufacture and commerce': a laudable motive, but less vexatious to the monarch, if he had been fore-warned. Both Conroy and the duchess had been fearful of a prohibition.

It was during these tours that Victoria's name first became associated with urban features in England. She named a park at Bath 'Royal Victoria' and a street in Malvern became 'Victoria Drive'. Over the next seventy years and more Victoria's name would be found on railway stations, roads and hundreds of buildings from great offices to pubs.

One event of the early 1830s that was of particular concern to Victoria was the departure of Prince Leopold to become King of the Belgians. His wisdom and kindness and earlier financial contributions to the duchess and her children had been of crucial importance. The family had become accustomed to his regular visits to Kensington Palace and would greatly miss him.

It is hard to judge at this distance of time whether Leopold could have fended off the first great crisis of Victoria's childhood to occur after she learned she was next in line to the throne. The event seemed to confirm all her fears for the responsibilities of this great office.

The problem arose over her relationship with John Conroy and her mother, originating in what, at the time, was called 'the Cumberland plot'. George Duke of Cumberland, later King of Hanover, was said to have become aware of Conroy's too-close relationship with his employer, the Duchess of Kent. Conroy was a fine-looking man, and the twice-married Duchess of Kent was not without her allure. This alleged improper relationship was considered by Cumberland to be the justification for the King to intervene and remove Victoria from Kensington in order to complete her upbringing at the royal court. Rumour also had it that the plot was scotched by the Duke of Wellington. On the other hand, it was also known that the duke, when asked if the duchess was her comptroller's mistress, had replied that he assumed so.

How much of all this came to Victoria's ears we shall never know. Certainly in later years, as a mature woman, she pooh-poohed the existence of this plot – 'A total untruth,' she wrote. The other undeniable historical fact remains that at or about this time, Victoria showed the first signs of distrust for Conroy, which rapidly grew into a deep hatred. She also disputed his claim that her father on his deathbed held Conroy by the hand and entreated him to do all he could for his widow and never, never desert her.

It is pure speculation to consider whether Victoria witnessed over-intimacy between her mother and Conroy, and was appalled by the sight. However, the relationship with her mother was never to be the same again.

It was not only from Princess Victoria that Conroy and the duchess were isolating themselves. There was also the row over the royal salute, and the row over Victoria's confirmation.

During the royal progresses the Isle of Wight had been more than once on the itinerary. Conroy ensured, quite improperly, that because their ship had the heir to the crown on board, the royal standard should be flown. This led to the Royal Navy correctly greeting their ship with a royal salute of twenty-one guns. King William, 'our sailor King', was outraged and gave instructions through his ministers that the practice must cease. Conroy replied mischievously that, as Her Royal Highness's *confidential adviser* 'he could not recommend her to give way on this point'. The King responded with an Order in Council which decreed that the royal standard should only be saluted when the sovereign or his consort was on board. And that was the end of the matter.

The next controversial event to affect Victoria directly and much distress her was the occasion of her confirmation. King William was concerned about the arrangements and discussed them with Victoria's lady-in-waiting, the Duchess of Northumberland. The Duchess of Kent was furious at being bypassed and replaced the duchess with Lady Flora Hastings, the duchess's own lady-in-waiting and firmly in the Conroy camp. Louise Lehzen was then threatened with dismissal from Kensington Palace, which would have been a terrible blow to Victoria. The duchess also defied the King by proceeding with her own arrangements for the confirmation.

King William's counter-blow was a letter in his own hand to the Bishop of London forbidding him to allow Princess Victoria to be confirmed in any of the Chapels Royal. As any other venue was out of the question, the Duchess of Kent yielded, but with the worst possible grace.

Victoria was confirmed in the Chapel Royal, St James's Palace, at midday on 30 July 1835 by the Archbishop of Canterbury, assisted by Victoria's one-time tutor Dr Davys.

Conroy attempted to enter the chapel but the King ordered him out, to his fury and chagrin.

The ridiculous warfare continued with the preparation of an extended tour which the duchess and Conroy knew would infuriate the King. And so it did. Lord Melbourne intervened this time in order to discourage the King from banning the tour, which would only add to the tension. Instead there was an acrimonious exchange of correspondence, and another letter from the King direct to Victoria, expressing the hope that the princess would not be 'travelling this year'. However, he indicated his affectionate concern for his niece in these words: 'It is your real good and permanent happiness I have really at heart and I therefore write these my sentiments as being the best advice I can give.'

After this, in a bid to bring some peace into the royal court, Victoria tried to persuade her mother to cancel the tour, pleading fatigue as one of the reasons why she did not wish to go. The duchess responded with a devious last-minute letter, clearly composed by John Conroy, the burden of which was that if it became widely known that the heir to the throne lacked the energy to undertake journeys 'you would fall in the estimation of the people of this country'.

Victoria surrendered once again and endured the rigours of the tour. When it was all over her mother and Conroy took her to the seaside to recover. It was too late. The exhausted adolescent succumbed to what was thought to be typhoid fever. For five weeks the princess was exceedingly ill, and at one point it was feared she might not recover. When she was at her weakest Conroy and her mother attempted to obtain her signature to a letter promising Conroy the post of private secretary when she became Queen.

'They (Mamma and John Conroy) attempted (for I was still very ill),' she told Lord Melbourne, 'to make me promise beforehand, which I resisted in spite of my illness and their harshness, my beloved Lehzen supporting me alone.'

The girl's obstinacy (as Conroy saw it) and refusal to co-operate in his plans for self-advancement, drove Conroy to ever-more outrageous behaviour. William IV knew what was going on. 'I have great distrust of the persons by whom [the duchess] is surrounded,' the King told Lord Melbourne, while expressing the hope that he would live long enough for the nation to avoid another regency.

The nadir in relations between the King and the Kensington court was reached at a dinner at Windsor when the King replied to the loyal toast in these terms:

> I trust in God that my life may be spared for nine months longer, after which period, in the event of my death no regency would take place. I should then have the satisfaction of leaving the royal authority to the personal exercise of that young lady [pointing at Victoria], the heiress presumptive to the crown, and not in the hands of a person now near me, who is surrounded by evil advisers and who is herself incompetent to act with propriety in the station in which she would be placed. I have no hesitation in saying [the King continued implacably] that I have been insulted – grossly and continually insulted – by that person, but I am determined to endure no longer a course of behaviour so disrespectful to me ... I would have her know that I am King, and I am determined to make my authority respected ...

A tidal wave of embarrassment struck the diners, including the Queen. No one had ever heard anything like this. Victoria burst into tears; her mother called for her carriage.

When it appeared likely that Princess Victoria would become Queen of England, the richest and most powerful nation in the world, her marriage prospects became a favourite topic of conversation in some circles and it is hardly surprising that appropriate or likely suitors were discussed in drawing-rooms and coffee houses, and in foreign (especially French) magazines and newspapers. *The Times*, however, stamped on this speculation from the first, pointing out that the princess was not yet ten years old. The rumours never quite died. By 1836, when Victoria was fifteen and King William IV over seventy, the matter had to be taken more seriously. The inevitable division surfaced between the royal court and Kensington.

The King still favoured strongly the introduction of another injection of Dutch blood.

Leopold's own plan to counter the King's preference for the sons of the Prince of Orange and, he hoped, to please his sister and his niece, was to persuade the duchess to invite to Kensington Palace two of his nephews, Princes Ernest and Albert of Saxe-Coburg and Gotha, together with the grand-duke, their father. Before her seventeenth birthday, therefore, Victoria had paraded before her no fewer than four princes, together with the threat of another from the court of Berlin. He was Prince Adelbert of Prussia, but his candidature was withdrawn when the duchess wrote a needlessly dismissive letter to the prince's father.

The two Coburg princes were not to know, at the time, how close they had come to being sent home on orders from King William, before they could land at Dover from Rotterdam. It took Lord Melbourne to prevail upon the King not to eject these guests of his niece. However, Melbourne was informed by the King's private secretary: 'The King has ordered me to repeat to your Lordship that nothing will induce Him to consent to the marriage of the Princess Victoria to a Prince of Coburg.'

At the same time the King knew better than anyone, except perhaps his wife and physician, how old and tired he was. William IV had difficulty in breathing and during the months before he died lost the use of his legs and was confined to a wheel-chair. Victoria was fond of her uncle and sorry for his condition. She was well aware that she might be called to the throne at any time, and was prepared in her heart and mind for that momentous event.

All this was quite sufficient to occupy her thoughts. At the same time she accepted the inevitability of eventual marriage and by no means feared it – rather, she welcomed the promise of romance and security that marriage would offer.

For the present Uncle Leopold, in the role of a surrogate father, met these needs in some degree. She wrote of him in her Journal at this time, 'I love him so very very much. He is

Il mio secondo padre or rather *solo padre*! for he is indeed like my real father, as I have none!'

This 'real father' was, predictably, outraged at King William's plot to 'bring over the Oranges' from the Netherlands to present them to Victoria, and even more furious at William's attempt to prevent Leopold's protégés from landing in England. A few days before the arrival of all the candidates, he wrote to Victoria:

> I am really *astonished* at the conduct of your old Uncle the King; this invitation to the Prince of Orange and his sons, this forcing him upon others, is very extraordinary ... Not later than yesterday I got a half official communication from England, insinuating that it would be *highly* desirable that a visit of *your* relatives *should not take place this year – qu'en dites-vous?* The relations of the Queen and the King, therefore, to the God-knows-what degree are to come in shoals and rule the land, when *your relations* are to be forbidden the country, and that when, as you know, the whole of your relations have ever been dutiful and kind to the King. Really and truly I never heard or saw anything like it, and I hope it will a *little rouse your spirit* ...

Leopold also wrote to his friend and ally, Baroness Lehzen, pointing out that 'The Princess's 17th birthday marks an important stage in her life: only one more year and the possibility of a Regency vanishes like an evil cloud. This is the perfect time for us, who are loyal to take thought for the future of the dear, dear child. An immediate alliance is out of the question; she must reach her 18th birthday, perhaps even more ...'

The epochal visit to London of Prince Albert was a conditional success for him, a quite unconditional success for Princess Victoria.

> At a $^1/_4$ to 2 we went down into the Hall, to receive my Uncle Ernest, Duke of Saxe-Coburg Gotha, and my cousins, Ernest and Albert, his sons [wrote Victoria in her Journal for 18 May 1836] ... Ernest is as tall as Ferdinand and Augustus [the Dutch princes]; he has dark hair, and fine dark eyes and eyebrows, but the nose and mouth are not good ... Albert, who is just as tall

as Ernest, but stouter, is extremely handsome; his hair is about the same colour as mine; his eyes are large and blue, and he has a beautiful nose, and a very sweet mouth with fine teeth; but the charm of his countenance is his expression, which is most delightful; *c'est à la fois* full of goodness and sweetness, and very clever and intelligent.

Prince Albert was much more restrained in his letters home. The visit was soured by the terrible crossing he and his party endured, which gave him, he told his stepmother, 'such a disgust for the sea that I do not like even to think of it'.

At home he had always led a quiet life, walking in the woods, reading a lot, and playing music with his brother. Now he was thrown into the hurly-burly of late dinners, drawing-rooms, receptions, levées, balls and concerts, and the opera and theatre. As an early riser and early retirer, Albert found it required a superhuman effort to remain awake, and he did nod off once or twice.

'The climate of this country, the different way of living, and the late hours, do not agree with me,' he wrote home. 'You can well imagine that I had many hard battles to fight against sleepiness during these late entertainments.'

Many people, and especially Victoria herself, had been dreading the inevitable meeting between the Coburg boys and the King. It occurred at a royal ball. William IV was weak and unwell, Albert feeling seedy and tired and none the better for facing yet another late night. To everyone's delight and astonishment, the old King took an immediate fancy to Albert, which was reciprocated. Victoria cherished the memory of that evening when the only meeting between her uncle and her future husband took place so successfully.

Unlike Albert, Victoria loved all the celebrations and entertainments. She enjoyed nothing more than dancing the night through and retiring to bed at dawn, the normal time for Albert's rising. She would comment that 'poor Albert' looked pale and delicate, whereas the next day she felt all the better for her night-long dancing.

Albert's comments on his cousin were extremely muted,

and the best he could say of her was that she was 'very amiable'. He improved on this on later reflection: 'Princess Victoria and myself, both at the age of 17, were much pleased with each other, but not a word in allusion to the future passed either between us, or with the Duchess of Kent.'

Over the following months occasional letters were exchanged between the cousins, but Victoria in particular was deeply preoccupied with preparations, if only in her mind, for succeeding to the throne. Besides, the Princess was also deeply engaged in the conflict at Kensington Palace between herself, loyally supported by Lehzen on the one hand, and her mother and Conroy on the other. The contest grew more intense with every week that passed before Victoria's eighteenth birthday; from that day the duchess would lose the opportunity of acting as Regent on the King's death, with John Conroy controlling the household.

The King's strength was fading fast, but, kept informed by Melbourne of the situation ('God I don't like this man,' he commented of Conroy), he was determined to outlive his niece's eighteenth birthday. At a last meeting between the present and future monarchs, William IV told Victoria that it was his intention to apply to Parliament for an annuity of £10,000 a year for her, and recommended her to form her own establishment and appoint her own Privy Purse in preparation for the throne.

As Wellington said of the battle of Waterloo twenty-two years earlier, it was a near-run thing. Princess Victoria reached her majority and the age at which she could ascend the throne on 24 May 1837; King William IV died on 20 June.

CHAPTER THREE

'I feel so *safe* when he is with me'

The young Queen of Lord Melbourne

The day before William IV died, Victoria wrote to King Leopold about her imminent accession, 'I look forward to the event which it seems is likely to occur soon, with calmness and quietness. I am not alarmed at it, and yet I do not suppose myself quite equal to all.'

Within hours, at 2.12 a.m. on 20 June 1837, the King died at Windsor Castle. Two of those at the death bed, Dr Howley, the Archbishop of Canterbury, and Lord Conyngham, the Lord Chamberlain, immediately ordered a carriage. Galloping the full twenty-two miles to Kensington Palace, with one change of horses, they arrived as dawn was breaking at 5 a.m., to find the gates locked and the porter fast asleep. They rang and knocked for some minutes before they could raise him, and the coachman drove them to the Clock Court and halted at the great door. Again there was a delay before they could gain entry. Even then they were told that it was too early to awaken Princess Victoria. But Lord Conyngham insisted with these words, 'We are come on business of State to the Queen and even her sleep must give way to that.'

So at last the waiting and uncertainty were over. Her journal records her excitement and determination as she awoke to the events of that dawn and what followed:

I was awoke at 6 o'clock by Mamma, who told me that the Archbishop of Canterbury and Lord Conyngham were here, and wished to see me. I got out of bed* and went into my sitting

* This was the last night she slept with her mother.

room (only in my dressing gown) and *alone*, and saw them. Lord Conyngham then acquainted me that my poor Uncle, the King, was no more . . . and consequently that I am *Queen*.

Queen Victoria correctly and swiftly extended her little right hand to the Lord Chancellor, who kissed it. She then withdrew and in the privacy of her bedroom fell into her mother's arms, weeping on her shoulder. She wept not for the fearfulness of her responsibilities at the age of eighteen, but for her old uncle whom she had been unable to see before his death. Elizabeth Barrett Browning was mistaken when she wrote:

> The Maiden wept;
> She wept to wear a crown!

Victoria's own words show her real feelings:

> Since it has pleased providence to place me in this station, I shall do my utmost to fulfil my duty towards my country; I am very young and perhaps in many, though not in all things, inexperienced, but I am sure that very few have more real goodwill and more real desire to do what is fit and right than I have.

If it revealed nothing else, that first morning as Queen was proof that she would never again be without occupation, nor much alone. Even at breakfast Baron Stockmar joined her to pay his respects and offer any needed advice. None was asked for. Time and again the Queen had rehearsed in her mind her first duties. But she was glad to have 'good, faithful Stockmar' beside her. She then dressed, wearing black bombazine, the long dress stiffening out at her feet. She completed her toilet, and wrote letters to King Leopold, her friend and half-sister Feodora and to the bereaved Queen Adelaide at Windsor. She also received several letters, including one from her Prime Minister, Lord Melbourne, who would 'do himself the honour of waiting upon Your Majesty a little before nine this morning'.

Melbourne arrived promptly and in full dress. There was deep bowing and kissing of the Queen's hand before he read the Declaration he had composed for the Queen to read later that morning to the first Privy Council meeting of her reign. 'He is a very straightforward, honest, clever and good man,' she commented. It was the beginning of the most important relationship of the early years of her reign.

She approved of the Declaration, and at the appointed hour descended the stairs – alone and with no hand to hold – to the red salon below.

It was only eleven o'clock in the morning, but over 200 Privy Councillors, displaying curiosity as much as duty, had hurried to Kensington Palace. A brief, whispered debate occurred on the question of who should escort the new Queen. Instead, when the doors were opened she entered quite alone, a diminutive but utterly self-composed figure:

> She looked very well [wrote Charles Greville, the Clerk of the Council], and though so small in stature, and without much pretension to beauty, the gracefulness of her manner, and the good expression of her countenance give her on the whole a very agreeable appearance, and with her youth inspire an excessive interest in all who approach her . . .

As much as her appearance and dignity, the Queen's voice left its mark on all present, even the half deaf (and there were a number of them), such was its fine tune, pitch and clarity. 'Naturally beautiful', 'clear and untroubled', were other expressions used to describe it.

The elderly figures of the two royal dukes, her uncles Sussex and Cumberland, stepped forward to greet her, bowing and then leading their niece to the throne. Their obeisance served to bow out her three Hanoverian predecessors, aptly described as 'an imbecile, a profligate and a buffoon'. This young woman, little more than a girl, symbolised a refreshing new era in which the monarchy would put in the past imbecility, profligacy and buffoonery – and all other Hanoverian characteristics.

She read out the Declaration without a slip, giving generous credit to her late uncle:

I place my firm reliance upon the wisdom of Parliament and upon the loyalty and affection of my people. I esteem it also a peculiar advantage that I succeed to a sovereign whose constant regard for the rights and liberties of his subjects and whose desire to promote the amelioration of the laws and institutions of the country have rendered his name the object of general attachment and veneration . . .

Having completed this declaration, the swearing-in commenced, a titanic task which she completed swiftly but without seeming haste, and without change of expression even for those she already knew, like Melbourne, Wellington and Sir Robert Peel. Many remarked afterwards on the coolness and softness of her hand.

John Wilson Croker, the Tory politician and author of *Stories for Children from English History*, summed up the observations of many present: 'Her eye was bright and calm, neither bold nor downcast, but firm and soft. There was a blush on her cheek which made her look both handsome and more interesting; and certainly she *did* look as interesting and handsome as any young lady I ever saw.'

As the great doors closed behind the Queen, a murmur of wonder and approbation ran through the crowd of Privy Councillors, soft and discreet, without a dissenting note. There were copious tears, too. It had been an heroic, historic performance, leaving not a man unmoved nor unconscious of future greatness.

From Germany, among many hundreds of letters, there was an especially welcome one from Prince Albert:

Bonn, 26th June 1837

My Dearest Cousin,

I must write you a few lines to present you my sincerest felicitations on that great change which has taken place in your life.

Now you are Queen of the mightiest land of Europe, in your hand lies the happiness of millions. May Heaven assist you and strengthen you with its strength in that high but difficult task.

I hope that your reign may be long, happy, and glorious, and that your efforts may be rewarded by the thankfulness and love of your subjects.

May I pray you to think likewise sometimes of your cousins in Bonn, and to continue to them that kindness you favoured them with till now. Be assured that our minds are always with you.

I will not be indiscreet and abuse your time. Believe me always, your Majesty's most obedient and faithful servant,

Albert

No monarch had come to the English throne with more excitement and zest for the task. Everything about being Queen, even the seemingly tedious routine tasks, like signing innumerable papers, appealed to her. She adored the exercise of power, unrestrained by consideration for anyone else if she so wished. The warmth of that first summer's sunshine was made all the more welcome by the flattery and ingratiation which surrounded her. Her status provided all the power and freedom anyone could aspire to.

Snippets from her hastily composed letters to her uncle, King Leopold, give some idea of how happy and fulfilled she felt during that summer of 1837. 'I have been so busy, I can say but two words more, which are that I prorogued Parliament yesterday in person, was very well received, and am not at all tired today, but quite frisky.' On another occasion she wrote, 'I have very pleasant large dinners every day. I invite my Premier once a week to dinner as I think it right to show publicly that I esteem him and have confidence in him . . .'

Victoria relished laying down instructions and ensuring that they were properly carried out. She enjoyed efficiency and being unyielding to pleas and excuses. Only a few weeks after her accession she decided to move her court to Buckingham Palace. Built on the site of Buckingham House for the first Duke of Buckingham, it had been bought as a private house by George IV, reduced to a husk, totally redesigned by John Nash, and renamed King's House, Pimlico. At vast expense, it grew and grew in size but was not completed in time for the King to move in. William IV never lived in this white elephant, but Victoria had long since nursed plans to leave Kensington Palace with all its melancholy associations, and have Buckingham Palace, now renamed, as her London home. It was, however, in a terrible state of disrepair.

She determined to move in in the middle of July; and was swiftly told that this was impossible, Ma'am. She then wrote a letter in her own hand saying that she was moving in on 13 July – and that was that. An army of builders invaded the Mall, housed in tents for their brief stay. If a railway could be built to link London and Bristol in five years, a month should suffice for finishing off a single building in London.

On 11 July, Queen Victoria wrote to Uncle Leopold, 'I *really* and *truly* go into Buckingham Palace the day after tomorrow.' And so she did.

In these early days of her reign William Lamb, second Viscount Melbourne, effectively replaced King Leopold as surrogate father to Victoria. For four years, he was the most important figure in her life. They rode together, dined together – he always on her left – discussed the affairs and the personalities of the day. She turned to Melbourne for advice on the multitudinous problems she had to face, especially in the early months of her reign; Melbourne was as willing an adviser as Queen Victoria was a disciple.

There was additionally a real affection between this eighteen-year-old monarch of the world's greatest power and the fifty-eight-year-old Whig Prime Minister. Melbourne's life had been tinged with tragedy. At the age of twenty-six he had married Lady Caroline Ponsonby, a wild but enchanting young woman, who led him a pretty chase. She had a prolonged affair with Lord Byron until he tired of her tantrums, whereupon she attempted to stab him at a ball. She conceived one child with Melbourne, a mentally defective boy who died at twenty-nine. Queen Victoria learned of her Prime Minister's tragic story in detail and was deeply moved. 'The Duchess of Sutherland spoke to me last night about Lady Caroline Lamb, Lord Melbourne's wife,' she wrote in her Journal entry for 1 January 1838. 'The strangest person that ever lived, really half crazy, and quite so when she died; she was not good looking, but very clever, and could be very amusing. She teased that excellent Lord Melbourne in every way, dreadfully, and quite embittered his life . . . He was the kindest of husbands to her, and bore it most admirably . . .'

Melbourne was approaching old age when the Queen first depended upon him so strongly, but he remained a magnificent figure of a man. Her passion for him was deep. 'I feel so *safe* when he is with me,' she once wrote. 'I am very sorry to lose him even for one night.'

As for Melbourne, Victoria had come into his life at a time of great loneliness and depression at the loss of his son. 'She was more to me than anyone ever was, or ever will be,' he once said. Despite belonging to the party associated with reform and concern for the underprivileged, Lord Melbourne was a heavy reactionary, opposing change in all things as a political instinct. The Queen soon came to admire these views and the uncompromising quality of his conversation. Undoubtedly some of his beliefs rubbed off on her.

In these early months of her reign, Victoria spent about six hours of every day with her Prime Minister, 'an hour in the morning, two on horseback, one at dinner, and two in the evening,' according to her journal. She would have enjoyed at least two more if the opportunity were there. His company was a constant delight, even after she married. She loved the way he 'never scrupled to declare boldly and frankly his real opinions, strange as they sometimes sounded, and unpalatable as they often were'. Above all other qualities, the Queen admired candour and probity.

The move from Kensington Palace to the newly refurbished Buckingham Palace by no means doused the fire of acrimony within Victoria's court. Her mother moved with her though she was offered only austere accommodation far from Victoria's quarters. Nor was it possible to dispose entirely of Conroy, who remained as pressing as ever for the post of private secretary to the Queen. The man was shameless in his demands; finally, Victoria ignored him entirely. She could not, without enormous disturbance, discharge him as her mother's comptroller.

The post of private secretary to the sovereign was a recent innovation, stemming back to the time when George III became blind. No one doubted that George IV and William IV were perfectly able to check any aspirations to power of their private secretaries. But an eighteen-year-old girl? That was different. She might become the victim of the power and prejudices of this post to the point where it became a threat to the constitution itself.

The problem was solved, like so many others, by Lord Melbourne, who offered to step in and act as private secretary as well as first minister to the Queen.

Conroy aside, the joy and happiness of that summer of 1837 was unconstrained. With the happiness of being Queen, Victoria's health improved, almost as if the drains and climate of Kensington had been replaced by the healthy character of Pimlico and the River Thames. 'Everybody says that I am quite another person since I came to the throne. I look and am so very well,' she wrote to her half-sister. 'I have such a pleasant life; just the sort of life I like . . . It is not the splendour of the thing or the being Queen that makes me so happy, it is the pleasant life I lead which causes my peace and happiness.'

Another factor, which perhaps she was too modest to mention, was her evident popularity with her people. The crown had not enjoyed much esteem since before George III went mad. Not only did this beguiling young woman attract the natural sympathy of the people by contrast with her mainly appalling predecessors, but here, suddenly, was a queen of dignity and grace who conducted herself with both modesty and authority.

Scarcely a month after her accession, Victoria had to conduct the dissolution of Parliament. The House was packed, the parliamentary robe dreadfully heavy. Thanks in part to the presence of Melbourne 'bearing the sword of state walking just before me' and standing 'quite close to me on the left-hand side of the throne', she survived the arduous ceremony and was greatly praised for her conduct.

On the afternoon of the Lord Mayor of London's Guildhall dinner, Victoria made her first public progress to the city. 'I met with the most gratifying, affectionate, hearty and brilliant reception from the greatest concourse of people I ever witnessed,' she wrote wonderingly, 'the streets being immensely crowded as were also the windows, houses, churches and balconies everywhere.'

Soon after moving to Buckingham Palace, Victoria determined to take up temporary residence at Windsor. The castle had recently suffered many alterations, mostly for the worse, though they were nothing like as extensive as those made to the palace. It also needed cleaning and refurbishment, all of which was carried out with thoroughness and speed.

A great crowd had collected in the streets of the town to welcome their new sovereign – 'a remarkably friendly and civil throng'. The shadow of Uncle William and his dying days still haunted the stone interior of this great castle. 'There is a sadness about the whole which I must say I feel,' Victoria wrote on the day of her arrival but all that was soon driven out by her high spirits and the presence of friends and relations. Military bands played frequently, Lord Melbourne came to stay, and so did the King and Queen of the Belgians, Uncle Leopold and Aunt Louise. 'It is an inexpressible happiness and joy to me,' Victoria wrote 'to have these dearest beloved relations with me and in my house.'

She liked to have plenty of children around, too, and could be found playing ball-games with them down the 550-foot-long Great Corridor, her spaniel Dash joining in enthusiastically. She also enjoyed battledore and shuttlecock with her ladies, and out of doors (it was a long hot summer) there was the endless joy of riding. The Queen had a very good seat, was as bold as any of the men accompanying her, and looked beautiful in the saddle, dressed in a black velvet riding habit, top hat and veil.

Victoria also looked extremely attractive in the evening,

wearing a favourite crimson velvet dress from Paris. She told of a game of chess with Queen Louise. Victoria, inevitably, was the Red Queen, but both contestants were confused by the authoritative but contradictory advice about where to move their queens on the board. 'I got quite beat,' the English Queen lamented, '& Aunt Louise triumphed over my Council of Ministers' – which included Lords Melbourne, Palmerston and Conyngham.

Queen Victoria might suffer defeat at chess, but there was no disputing her ultimate triumph of that summer, the military review in the Great Park. For this she wore a habit of dark blue with red collar and cuffs – 'the Windsor uniform' – and rode one of her favourite and aptly-named horses, Leopold. Those who were present would remember for all their lives, the style with which their young sovereign rode up to the colours to be saluted by her regiments. She returned the salutes 'by putting my hand to my cap like the officers do, and was much admired for my manner of doing so', she wrote of this day. She then cantered up and down the lines as if she were a colonel who had been doing this all his service life. By the time she returned to London the Queen had fallen in love with Windsor, and for all her long reign would be pleased at the prospect of returning there from London.

Brighton was less of a success. She had never visited the Marine Pavilion on which her uncle, first as Prince of Wales in 1787 and then as King, had spent so much money and time. She had never seen anything like it before, though she must have seen drawings. 'The pavilion is a strange, odd Chinese-looking thing,' she complained. 'Most rooms low.' She also complained that from her rooms she could view only 'a little morsel of the *sea* . . .' She decided that she would rarely revisit Brighton – anyway, for the time being. The Queen's mind was now much concerned with her coronation.

'The crowning of the Sovereign,' runs one definition, 'is a most ancient ceremony, rich in religious significance, historic association and pageantry.'

For days before the coronation, now fixed for Thursday, 28

June 1838, the roads into London were packed with passenger vehicles of all kinds. Other visitors came into the metropolis by rail, notably to Euston station and the wooden station at Paddington, opened a month earlier. There was not a room to be had in hotel or lodging house, and many begged for a bed in private houses, or simply slept out on the grass of St James's or Green Park, which were the nearest open spaces to Buckingham Palace. The Queen remarked on the number of tents she could count from her windows. For the well-connected and affluent, rooms overlooking the route of the procession could be rented; or for a lesser price seats in the temporary stands which had been constructed from scaffolding and planks. Fortunately, the weather was benign; buskers and tradesmen with hand-carts did great business.

The government had been determined that this should be a spectacular and memorable occasion that would help to restore the reputation of the monarchy after its rapid recent decline. The length of the route had been extended through Westminster, flags and bunting were everywhere to be seen, military bands played continuously to while away the hours before the start of the procession at 10 a.m.

It was a grey morning but warm and with a hint in the air of later sunshine, which proved to be the case.

> I was awoke at four o'clock by the guns in the Park [wrote the Queen in her Journal of this great day] and could not get much sleep afterwards on account of the noise of the people, bands, etc. etc. Got up at seven, feeling strong and well. The Park presented a curious spectacle, crowds of people ... soldiers, bands, etc. At half-past nine I went into the next room dressed exactly in my House of Lords costume ...
>
> At 10 I got into the State Coach with the Duchess of Sutherland and Lord Albemarle and we began our Progress ... It was a fine day, and the crowds of people exceeded what I have ever seen ... Millions of my loyal subjects were assembled *in every spot* to witness the Procession. Their good humour and excessive loyalty was beyond everything and I really cannot say *how* proud I feel to be the Queen of *such* a nation ...

Up Constitution Hill proceeded the state coach drawn by eight cream-coloured horses, following twelve royal carriages of the Queen's household, mounted bands, the Queen's bargemaster, a squadron of the Household Brigade, foreign ambassadors, and many more bodies such as the Yeoman Prickers and Foresters. They were accompanied by the sound of shouting, cheering crowds and the discharge of cannon so that some covered their ears. Up Piccadilly, right down St James's Street, along Pall Mall to Trafalgar Square, not yet adorned by Nelson's Column, and down Whitehall, the procession was greeted by cheering spectators at every window, some balanced precariously on roof tops.

> I reached the Abbey amid deafening cheers at a little after half-past eleven; I first went into a robing-room quite close to the entrance where I found my eight train-bearers – all dressed alike in white satin and silver tissue with wreaths of silver corn-ears in front, and a small one of pink roses round the plait behind, and pink roses in the trimming of the dresses . . .

As in the streets outside, accommodation inside the Abbey had been greatly increased by galleries specially erected for one thousand additional spectators. Each gallery was covered with crimson cloth fringed with gold, and beneath the galleries stood lines of Foot Guards.

The Chair of Homage faced the altar, itself covered with heavy gold plate, while in the chancel was St Edward's chair, to which the Queen proceeded, and sat down. Next came the ceremony of the recognition, the boys of Westminster School first who cried out in unison, 'Vivat Victoria Regina'; next, the Archbishop of Canterbury who recognised her as the 'undoubted Queen of this Realm'.

As the Queen turned to face the four points of the compass, everyone assembled in the Abbey, from Members of Parliament to the royal dukes, cried out, 'God Save Queen Victoria'. Next the oath – 'Will you solemnly promise and swear to govern the people of the United Kingdom of Great Britain and Ireland,' demanded the Archbishop of Canterbury, 'and the dominions thereto belonging according to the statutes in Parliament agreed on, and the respective laws and customs of the same?'

Without hesitation the Queen replied, 'I solemnly promise so to do.'

'Will you, to your power, cause law and justice, in mercy, to be executed in all your judgements?'

'I will.'

Then there was the oath referring to the maintenance of the laws of God, the preservation inviolably of the settlement of the United Church of England and Ireland, and the preservation 'unto the bishops and clergy of England and Ireland, and to the churches there committed to their charge, all such rights and privileges as by law do or shall appertain to them or any of them?'

'All this I promise so to do,' rang out that clear silvery voice.

After the solemn anointing, the Queen had the dalmatic robe held round her by the Lord Great Chamberlain. The culmination was now approaching:

> ... the Crown being placed on my head – which was, I must own, a most beautiful impressive moment; *all* the Peers and Peeresses put on their coronets at the same instant.
>
> My excellent Lord Melbourne, who stood very close to me throughout the whole ceremony, was *completely* overcome at this moment and very much affected; he gave me *such* a kind, and I may say *fatherly* look. The shouts, which were very great, the drums, the trumpets, the firing of the guns, all at the same instant, rendered the spectacle most imposing.

The ceremonies continued, seemingly without end – the enthronisation, the homages by the dukes, the bishops and the peers, all first touching the crown and then kissing the Queen's hand. There were occasional human touches: one eighty-two-year-old peer fell on the steps and rolled right down on to the stone floor, without apparent damage. When he tried again, Victoria got up and walked to meet him. Then it was Melbourne's turn and when he knelt to kiss the Queen's hand, 'I grasped his with all my heart, at which he looked up with his eyes filled with tears.'

The Queen also exchanged glances and smiles with her 'dearly beloved angelic Lehzen', who witnessed the proceedings from a box immediately above the royal box.

A human touch of a less welcome nature was the confused performance of the aged Archbishop of Canterbury, who presented the heavy orb to the Queen far too early, and then attempted to give it to her again during the brief pause in St Edward's Chapel where the altar was covered with refreshments, sandwiches and bottles of wine. He disappeared in total confusion, returning later with the ring, which he thrust roughly on the Queen's wrong finger. 'I had the greatest difficulty to take it off again, which I at last did with great pain.'

It was nearly over. At half past four the Queen reentered her carriage, wearing the crown and carrying the heavy sceptre and orb. Later she recounted:

> We proceeded the same way as we came – the crowds if possible having increased. The enthusiasm, affection, and loyalty were really touching, and I shall ever remember this day, as the *Proudest* of my life! I came home at a little after six, really *not* feeling tired.

For four days after the coronation the celebrations continued. A fair was set up in Hyde Park, the theatres were free and there was a prodigious consumption of ale and gin.

The second half of 1838 marked the culmination of Queen Victoria's popularity in the early part of her reign. But royal popularity, she was to learn, was a volatile factor, and one incident alone in 1839 was to bring with it grave problems. The trouble was presaged in January by the sudden death of the Queen's good friend Princess Marie of Orleans, sister of the Queen of the Belgians, and 'a sweet, amiable creature'. Next, Lord Melbourne's government found itself in difficulties and Victoria had to face the unacceptable possibility of losing Melbourne, whose friendship and fatherly guidance had supported her so stoutly since her accession.

Finally there was the Lady Flora Hastings affair. Lady Flora was the eldest child of the first Marquess of Hastings, thirty-two years of age and unmarried. As a lady-in-waiting to the Duchess of Kent, she allied herself with the ubiquitous John Conroy and thus became a subject of Queen Victoria's gravest suspicion, 'an amazing spy,' she told Melbourne, 'who would repeat everything she heard.'

After suffering from a prolonged 'bilious illness', Lady Flora consulted the Queen's own physician, Dr James Clark. He diagnosed 'derangement of the bowels', and noted 'a considerable enlargement of the lower part of her abdomen'.

Others had noted this phenomenon and drawn different conclusions. The Queen, for one, wrote in her diary that she had no doubt 'that she is – to use the plain words – with child'. And who could be responsible for this condition? Why, none other than John Conroy, her mother's paramour – as she truly believed him to be. For several weeks rumours echoed about the corridors of Buckingham Palace. Greville recorded that 'Lady Flora Hastings . . . has been accused of being with child. It was first whispered about, and at last swelled into a report, and finally into a charge.'

Sir James Clark's disgraceful role in this affair brought discredit on his profession. When Lady Flora refused to have an intimate examination, he bullied her and advised her to make an immediate confession. 'Are you secretly married?' he demanded, because no one could look at her and doubt that she was with child.

The pressure to have an examination to clear up the matter or leave the court altogether became so strong that Lady Flora at last reluctantly gave way. The two doctors who eventually conducted the examination both agreed that, while there was certainly an enlargement of the stomach, she was definitely not with child.

The Queen was both relieved and deeply upset by this turn

of events. She sent a message to Lady Flora begging for a meeting so that she could apologise personally. This took place on 23 February. '. . . on my embracing her, taking her by the hand, and expressing great concern at what had happened – and my wish that all should be forgotten, she expressed herself exceedingly grateful to me, and said, that for Mama's sake she would suppress every wounded feeling, and would forget it etc.'

Far from forgetting it, however, Lady Flora informed her uncle by marriage, Hamilton Fitzgerald, and her brother. Her honour, she complained, had been 'most basely assailed'. Lord Hastings regarded the false accusations as a plot against, and insult to, the whole family, and acted accordingly.

In spite of all the efforts of Melbourne and others, including the Duke of Wellington, nothing could now quench the flames of scandal, and conceal from the public the great rift at court between the Queen on the one hand and her mother, with Conroy, Lady Flora and the rest of the duchess's court on the other. Lehzen figured prominently, along with Lady Tavistock, as the guilty parties who had originated the false rumour of pregnancy.

It was now open warfare. Greville wrote of 'the scandalous story': 'The Court is plunged in shame and mortification at the exposure . . . the palace is full of bickerings and heart-burnings,' he continued, 'while the whole proceeding is looked upon by society at large as to the last degree disgusting and disgraceful.'

The Hastings family published in the *Morning Post* Lady Flora's letter to the Queen, and the correspondence with Melbourne. The Queen was beside herself with rage, and claimed that she 'would have wished to have hanged the editor and the whole Hastings family for their infamy'. There was worse to come. It now emerged that not only was Lady Flora not pregnant but she was dying from cancer. The Queen refused to believe that this was so, weakening her position yet more seriously. Even Melbourne failed to satisfy her of the truth of the illness. It took James Clark, who had failed to diagnose cancer earlier, to convince Victoria that the poor woman's days were numbered.

On 26 June Victoria visited the woman in her bed.

> I went in alone; I found Lady Flora stretched on a couch looking as thin as anybody who is still alive; literally a skeleton, but the body *very* much swollen like a person who is with child; a searching look in her eyes, a look rather like a person who is dying ... she was friendly, said she was very comfortable, and how very grateful for all I had done for her ...

The Queen was clearly very much more shocked by the experience than she recorded. She hastened from the room as soon as she decently could. When she rejoined Lord Melbourne, he remarked, 'You remained a very short time.'

This implied rebuke from her old friend, of all people, signalled the opening of a campaign against the Queen and her fellow conspirator Baroness Lehzen. After the death of Lady Flora on 5 July, the attacks came from several quarters simultaneously and overwhelmed Victoria by their viciousness and implacability.

What the Queen did not at first understand fully was that there was strong political motivation behind the attacks, for she was widely recognised as being a strong Whig and an ally of Melbourne. The Hastings family was more bent on revenge than ever after Lady Flora's death. The *Morning Post*, continuing to act as a mouthpiece for the Tory-Hastings faction, gave up two pages on 14 September 1839 to a letter from the Marquis, accompanied by Lady Flora's statement, correspondence between the Marquis and Melbourne, a letter from Lady Flora to Hamilton Fitzgerald, and other related correspondence. The Marquis's letter included this passage:

> I have been told on high authority that if I bring this subject before the House of Lords it will be immediately silenced as an attack upon the Throne. Insurmountable technical difficulties prevent my exposing in a court of justice the vile conduct of those who have slandered my sister; but one course therefore

remains open to me and that is to publish the accompanying correspondence.

At the same time, anonymous pamphlets were sold on the streets of London and in the coffee houses. There were few direct attacks on the Queen, she was seen more as a victim of the 'uncleansed court'. Sir James Clark, who had failed to diagnose Lady Flora's condition, was one of the chief targets. One pamphlet in verse wrote of the court as a place

> Where arts and luxury are most refined
> And all is fair and polished – but the mind.
> Strange destiny that Britain's mighty isle
> Should hang dependent on a schoolgirl's smile.
> The court physician, with his cringing back
> And coward sneer, the leader of the pack . . .

Another leader of the pack was Lehzen, whose influence over the Queen was considered by the opposition as baleful. A pamphlet with the title, *Warning Letter to Baroness Lehzen*, described her as 'a certain foreign lady [who] pulled the wires of a diabolical conspiracy of which Lady Flora was to be the first victim'.

It is impossible to know how aware the Queen was of these pamphlet attacks and of the heavy criticism in the Tory provincial newspapers. Many were certainly concealed from her. What could not be hidden was the reaction in the streets and public places in London. She was hissed while riding in Rotten Row, men failed to raise their hats to her, and she never knew what abuse to expect when a crowd collected. After the adulation she had previously enjoyed, the effect was extremely jolting.

Queen Victoria had not behaved with the discretion and wisdom which she later acquired. She should not have allowed her hatred of John Conroy to lead her to give evidence to the public of her unkindness to her mother, who, like Lehzen, might be of foreign birth, but scarcely deserved to be almost sealed out of her daughter's life. Certainly Victoria's elevation to the throne had added a touch of disdain and even arrogance, to her manner, but she had only just passed her twentieth birthday and can surely be forgiven for this early misjudgement.

As though the Lady Flora affair were not enough, the long-feared fall of the government took place, and with it the loss of Lord Melbourne. The fall was brought about by the narrowest of votes in the Commons.

In passing this grim news to the Queen on 7 May, the Prime Minister wrote: 'Lord Melbourne is certain that your Majesty will not deem him too presuming if he expresses his fear that this decision will be both painful and embarrassing to your Majesty, but your Majesty will meet this crisis with that firmness which belongs to your character, and with that rectitude and sincerity which will carry your Majesty through all difficulties.'

In this moving letter Melbourne emphasises his own pain at quitting the service of 'a Mistress who has treated him with such unvarying kindness and unlimited confidence'. Melbourne also advised the Queen to call on the Duke of Wellington as Tory Prime Minister, but to remember that the old general was very deaf. In the event, the duke declined and suggested that the Queen should call on Sir Robert Peel.

With the utmost reluctance, Victoria did so, and they had an hour together. Peel put forward a number of proposals, but it was the Queen who raised the contentious issue of her 'ladies', and in particular those of her household whose husbands were among Peel's strongest opponents in Parliament. Peel gave no clear answer. Melbourne, still quite improperly giving advice, recommended caution.

It was too late. The idea had suddenly occurred to the Queen that if she refused to dispense with any of her ladies, it might be impossible for Peel to form a government, these ladies for the most part being married to Whig opponents of a Tory Peel government.

This indeed proved to be the case. On 9 May the Queen was warning her beloved Melbourne of 'what *may* happen in a very few hours. Sir Robert Peel has behaved very ill, and has insisted on my giving up my Ladies, to which I replied that I never could consent, and I never saw a man so frightened . . .'

The Queen refused to yield, and while there were several more exchanges of views, by holding to her monarchical rights, the Queen won. To his astonishment, Melbourne found himself Prime Minister again. The Queen was delighted by her triumph.* So was Uncle Leopold. Melbourne was not so sure. He had reconciled himself to the loss of office and prepared himself for a rest from the responsibilities of power.

An invaluable witness to events at court at this time was Lady Lyttelton. In 1838, after the early death of her husband, Sarah Spencer, Lady Lyttelton, was appointed lady-in-waiting to the Queen. Four years later, she became governess to the royal children, a task for which she was well equipped, being an extremely sensible woman who had brought up five children of her own. She remained in this post for nine years and had a strong influence on all the Queen's older children. Her letters, many to her own children, give a vivid picture of her observations and her day-to-day life. Here she describes the prorogation of Parliament, which wound up the critical period of late summer 1839:

> London, August 28, 1839
> . . . The prorogation was very fine. Beyond my expectations, though the House of Lords is a shabby poky little place enough, compared to the old burnt down one. The day was glorious, till after all was over, when we had a deluge. The finest moment I thought was while the Queen, dressed in crimson velvet and ermine, advanced through the entrances and passages, at a slow pace, *alone*, preceded and followed by all the Court and Ministers. Lord Melbourne (who begins to look picturesquely old) with the Sword of State. The Blues and Beefeaters and all the splendour of her entourage lining her path, and loads of full-dressed people looking down from every place where they could stick themselves. All this in the light of a dazzling sunshine, and

---

* Sixty years later, during a conversation with her private secretary, the Queen said, 'I was very young then, and perhaps I should act differently if it was all to be done again.'

to the sound of a great number of most royal trumpets, *in unison*, quite close to us, and a fine bass accompaniment of cannon outside. The trumpets were, I thought, quite sublime. Then her speech was most beautifully read. Her voice is, when so raised and *sostenuto*, quite that of a child, a gushing sort of richness, with the most sensible, cultivated, and *gentlemanlike* accent and emphasis. She raised her head, and uttered, 'Gentlemen of the House of Commons!' with a little air of grandeur that was very pretty. She was frightened, but no one could have guessed it; *we* knew it by the crimson colour of her face and neck, and a little trembling. The effect of the whole is to my taste spoilt by the shoals of ladies and the very few peers who have room. It looks like a mere pageant, and would be much finer if she (child as she looks) were speaking evidently to a crowd of grey-haired senators and sturdy statesmen.

My duties turned out unexpectedly important and arduous, and frightened me very much. After the Duchess of Sutherland had changed Her Majesty's robe, with the help of the dressers, *I* had (in the library as it is called, a great room adjoining the body of the house), in presence of the whole Court, and surrounded by all the great officers of State, to unpin and remove from Her Majesty's head her diamond diadem, and taking the great Crown of England (weighing 12 pounds) from some grandee (whom I did not see very distinctly) to place it and *pin it on* with two diamond pins through the velvet and her hair at the back of her head! Feel for me! All this I did however pretty well. But when I had to do it all over again in reverse, on Her Majesty's return, she was in a hurry, and the *last* pin I *could* not find the proper place for in the diadem, and first ran it against her royal head (upon which she looked up with a comical arch look of entreaty), and then could not put it in at all anywhere. So she went without it. Luckily it was by no means a necessary circumstance. It has furnished a most invaluable story against me to Her Majesty ... On returning to the palace, of course I made an immediate confession to Mme. de Lehzen. She answered, 'Oh, do not mind! Do not *care a pin for de pin!* All deed so well, it does not matter at all!'

CHAPTER FOUR

An End to Loneliness

As early as June 1839, before the death of Flora Hastings and the ladies of the bedchamber crisis, Queen Victoria was showing signs of restlessness, impatience and dissatisfaction. Isolated, at her own wish, from her mother, she had only Lehzen and Melbourne with whom she could discuss her feelings, and though entirely dependent on the sixty-year-old Prime Minister for guidance on political matters and affairs of state, she became increasingly impatient with his indications of age and general slowing down. She began to upbraid him for going to sleep over dinner and during church services, missing things in conversation. At the same time she was too sensitive not to feel shame at her impatience with the old man to whom she owed so much.

The fact was that she was badly missing the company of people of her own age. She was a passionate young woman who wanted not just young people about her, but especially young men. In short, she was ripe for marriage, while at the same time deceiving herself that this was not the case, that she did not wish to be rushed, either in time or choice.

Since she had first met Prince Albert of Saxe-Coburg more than two years earlier, Victoria had been aware that an assumption had developed among some of her relatives – not least Uncle Leopold – that this cousin might well prove to be the first choice.

Victoria did not care for assumptions. When she learned that her Saxe-Coburg cousins were due to make a second visit to England, she protected herself by a letter to Uncle Leopold asking 'if *Albert* is aware of the wish of his *Father* and *you* relative to me?' She continued that 'if I should take Albert, [in marriage] I can make *no final promise* this year, for, at the *very earliest* any such event could not take place *till two or three years hence.*'

Anxious to make her feelings completely clear to her uncle, and at the same time to cover every contingency, Victoria added with typical common sense, 'One can never answer beforehand for *feelings*, and I may not have the *feeling* for him which is requisite to ensure happiness. I *may* like him as a friend, and as a *cousin* . . . but not *more*; and should this be the case (which is not likely), I am *very* anxious that it should be understood that I am *not* guilty of *any* breach of promise for *I never gave any.*'

Victoria could scarcely have made her position clearer. 'I have now spoken open to you,' she concluded her letter, which went at once by courier to Belgium.

Two more reluctant guests to the English court than Prince Ernest and his younger brother Prince Albert could scarcely be imagined. Ernest had no interest in the Queen and knew that he was acting as no more than a companion to his brother. As for Albert, he was quite as resentful as the Queen that assumptions be made simply because his Uncle Leopold and his own father held ambitions for him to marry into the English royal family.

What Albert had learned about Victoria since his last visit to London was mainly discouraging. She was, it seemed, a young woman with a short temper, subject to tantrums, proud and over-assertive. On their way to Rotterdam and their boat to England, the two princes stayed with King Leopold at Laeken. Albert especially was always glad to see his uncle, whose opinions were so wise and whose kindness was so evident. For his part Leopold could not fail to discern Albert's depression at the prospect of facing his cousin again now that she was Queen. Leopold therefore wrote an urgent letter to Victoria warning her of Albert's downcast mood and suggesting she would have no trouble shaking him out of it.

The Queen had already drawn the conclusion that her guests were scarcely burning with eagerness for the visit. Her letter to Leopold, dated 1 October 1839, reveals: '... the *retard* of these young people puts me rather out, but of course cannot be helped. I had a letter from Albert yesterday saying that they could not set off, he thought, before the 6th. I think they don't exhibit much *empressement* to come here, which rather shocks me ...'

The auguries failed to improve during the final days before the meeting. The brothers did their best to keep up their spirits by playing music on the instruments Leopold made available to them. The autumn weather remained dreadful, and the sea looked unwelcoming when at last they reached Rotterdam. Once on board, they immediately went below and were so seasick that they scarcely recognised the sudden stability of their vessel when the captain manoeuvred her through the entrance to Dover harbour.

Albert and Ernest dragged themselves ashore in the pouring rain. Their valets searched unsuccessfully for their baggage but assumed that it would be put into the carriage automatically. The princes prepared themselves for the sixty-three-mile drive to London and twenty-three more to Windsor.

Neither of them looked or felt at his best when, some five hours later, their fly ran up the steep, cobbled slope, past St George's Chapel to the main entrance to Windsor Castle. Albert's spirits remained low. As he wrote later, he had come to Windsor 'with the quiet but firm resolution' to declare that he was weary of the delay over an engagement with the English Queen, and that he would 'withdraw entirely from the affair'.

Albert first caught sight of Queen Victoria again, after the interval of three years, from the bottom of the stairs leading to her private quarters. She was leaning over the banister rail, dressed for dinner, smiling and waving a welcome.

The Queen wrote of this moment to Uncle Leopold: 'The dear cousins arrived at half-past seven on Thursday, after a very bad and almost dangerous passage, but looking both very well ... Ernest is grown quite handsome; Albert's *beauty* is *most striking*, and he is so amiable and unaffected – in short very *fascinating* ...' Many people attested to Prince Albert's handsomeness at this time, before he grew heavy and lost his hair. Walter Bagehot, the distinguished economist and journalist, described him as 'very, very handsome'.

The next day, when the young men's luggage had arrived, the three cousins with Albert's great greyhound, Eos, rode together in Windsor Great Park, Ernest acting the part of chaperon. Victoria was already conscious of an entirely fresh and novel sensation. Admiration for beauty in young men was nothing new to her, and time and again in her late adolescence she had experienced the pangs of hero-worship. But what she was feeling now was the onrush of mature love for this 'extremely handsome' young man. She wrote in her Journal, 'My heart is quite going.'

That evening, there was dancing and the two young men played Mozart and Haydn. Victoria, who loved music, was captivated. They all made a great fuss of gentle Eos, who at dinner circulated the table offering her paw and receiving tit-bits on a fork as a reward.

Three days passed, as if in a dream. Victoria had to spend most of the morning working on papers presented to her by Melbourne, who, with Albert's valet and Lehzen, were alive to the situation and amazed at the speed with which the mutual love had grown. They now awaited the inevitable outcome.

Ernest fell ill with jaundice and was confined to his bed. Victoria scarcely noticed, but enjoyed the freedom of having no chaperon. She and Albert rode together for hours on end, sometimes coming so close that they could hold hands. One evening they were caught in Windsor Great Park late in the day and with black clouds accelerating the onset of darkness. For a while they became lost, and relished the experience, while the storm broke and Victoria had to guide them home with the help of familiar landmarks momentarily exposed by the flashes of lightning. That evening they danced later than ever and the Queen awoke with a headache, but her heart was high and she did not care.

At her first meeting of the day with Lord Melbourne, Victoria confided in the old man who had guided her so closely and kindly since she had become Queen. She confessed that she felt agitated, but that now that she had seen her cousin again, she had quite changed her mind about waiting two or three years before marrying.

'Very naturally,' was Melbourne's only verbal comment. Then, after a few minutes, he advised that, having made up her mind, she would be well advised not to delay the marriage. They settled down to work out a timetable and discuss the details. February should be the month, the Prime Minister urged, after Parliament had met and authorised the prince's allowance. He should have the customary honours, be appointed a field marshal, addressed as Royal Highness, but not be given a peerage as that would involve him in politics. For the present, the engagement would be confidential. Many more details were discussed during the next hour. When the emotionally charged meeting ended, with Melbourne and the Queen close to tears, she took his hand and thanked him for being so helpful and *'fatherly'*.

There could be no question of Prince Albert proposing to the Queen of England: it had to be the other way round, an arrangement which had led to laughter between the Queen and her minister. When, on the morning of 15 October, Albert received a message that his presence was required in the Queen's most private retreat, the Blue Closet, he knew that his time had come, that, for better or for worse, his fate was sealed. Too much had happened for there to be any doubt that a deep and passionate love had grown up between them during the last few days.

In the most significant and deeply felt entry in her lifelong Journal, Queen Victoria wrote of that meeting:

> I said to him that I thought he must be aware *why* I wished him to come here, and that it would make me *too happy* if he would consent to what I wished (to marry me); we embraced each other

over and over again, and he was *so* kind, *so* affectionate; Oh! to *feel* I was, and am, loved by such an angel as Albert was *too great delight to describe*. He is *perfection*; perfection in every way – in beauty – in everything! I told him I was quite unworthy of him and kissed his dear hand – he said he would be very happy 'das Leben mit dir zu zubringen' and was so kind and seemed so happy, that I really felt it was the happiest brightest moment in my life, which made up for all I had suffered and endured. Oh! *how* I adore and love him, I cannot say!! *how* I will strive to make him feel as little as possible the great sacrifice he has made . . .

Albert's comment on this meeting was briefer and more succinct: 'The openness of manner in which she told this quite enchanted me, and I was quite carried away by it.'

The proposal and engagement had occurred at noon. There was therefore plenty of time after luncheon for Albert to write with more passion to his fiancée. 'How is it,' he asked, 'that I have deserved so much love, so much affection?' And it concluded, 'In body and soul ever your slave, your loyal Albert.'
Victoria also wrote to her 'dearest Uncle' Leopold:

> Windsor Castle, 15th October 1839
> This letter will, I am sure, give you pleasure, for you have always shown and taken so warm an interest in all that concerns me. My mind is quite made up – and I told Albert this morning of it; the warm affection he showed me on learning this gave me *great* pleasure. He seems *perfection*, and I think that I have the prospect of very great happiness before me. I *love* him *more* than I can say, and I shall do everything in my power to render the sacrifice he has made (for a *sacrifice* in my opinion it is) as small as I can . . .

On the following day Albert divulged the news of the engagement to Stockmar, King Leopold's confidential factotum and also Albert's close guide and adviser:

> I am writing to you today on one of the happiest days of my life to send you the most joyful possible news. Yesterday in a private

Queen Victoria's proposal to Prince Albert, 15 October 1839

audience V. declared her love for me, and offered me her hand, which I seized in both mine and pressed tenderly to my lips. She is so good and kind to me that I can scarcely believe such affection should be mine. I know you take part in all my happiness, and so I can pour out my heart to you.

During four more wonderful autumn weeks the young couple were together as often as the Queen's duties allowed – in the Blue Closet, out riding or walking, and in the evening dancing and singing. They embraced and kissed whenever opportunity occurred, the secrecy of their love an added savour. To the few who knew of their engagement, they both wrote extravagantly of their love.

Late on 13 November Queen Victoria had her last dance with Albert 'as an *unmarried girl*'. Early the next morning, it was the last kiss, his cheek 'fresh & pink like a rose' as she described it. Then came the tears of parting, the consolation being the passionate love letters that raced by courier between Coburg and England, and the brevity of their separation.

Nine days after Prince Albert's return home, the Queen had to face the ordeal of addressing the Privy Council to announce her engagement, effectively to the nation as well. No fewer than eighty-two Privy Councillors arrived at Buckingham Palace that morning to hear the declaration. The Duchess of Gloucester, who knew nothing of the engagement, asked the Queen if she were nervous. 'Yes,' came the reply, 'but I did a much more nervous thing a little while ago.'

'What was that?'

'I proposed to Prince Albert.'

The Queen's hands were visibly shaking so that those present wondered that she could read her paper. As always, she was up to the occasion, and the Council listened with polite attention but without excitement or comment.

This lack of enthusiasm was reflected throughout the land. People still remembered the shaming Lady Flora Hastings affair and the glow which Victoria had enjoyed early in her reign had faded. They did not disapprove of the principle of marriage, but they could find no enthusiasm for a *German* prince, who might be Catholic in religion. (It was pointed out in this connection that Lord Melbourne in his declaration had made no reference to the prince's religion. Wasn't that significant?) Then surely the Queen of the richest and most powerful nation on earth warranted a husband of higher status than the younger son of a minor and impoverished German duke? The Queen was not in the least amused by such reflections on her *beloved* Albert, expressed in this popular ditty of the time:

> He comes the bridegroom of Victoria's choice,
> the nominee of Lehzen's vulgar voice;
> He comes to take 'for better or for worse'
> England's fat Queen and England's fatter purse.

The Queen was not always in a good temper at this time, as though the stress of the engagement taxed her patience. Even Melbourne was the victim of her irritation:

The Queen has received both Lord Melbourne's notes; she was a good deal vexed at his not coming, as she had begged him herself to do so, and as he wrote to say he would, and also as she thinks it right and of importance that Lord Melbourne should be here at large dinners; the Queen *insists* upon his coming to dinner tomorrow, and also begs him to do so on Wednesday, her two last nights in town, and as she will probably not see him at all for two days when she goes on Friday; the Queen would wish to see Lord Melbourne *after* the Prorogation tomorrow at any hour *before* five he likes best.

The Queen has been a good deal annoyed this evening at [Lord] Normanby's telling her that John Russell was coming to town next Monday in order to *change* with *him*. Lord Melbourne *never* told the Queen that this was definitely settled; on the contrary, he said it would 'remain in our hands', to use Lord Melbourne's own words, and only be settled during the Vacation; considering all that the Queen has said on the subject to Lord Melbourne, and considering the great confidence the Queen has in Lord Melbourne, she thinks and feels he ought to have told her that this was *settled*, and not let the Queen be the last person to hear what is settled and done in her own name; Lord Melbourne will excuse the Queen's being a little eager about this, but it has happened once before that she learnt from other people what had been decided on.

Meanwhile, the elaborate preparations went ahead for the wedding, the first between a reigning Queen and her Consort since Mary Tudor married Philip II of Spain in 1554.

As soon as he had crossed the Channel, Prince Albert had headed straight for Wiesbaden for a discreet discussion with Baron Stockmar and King Leopold, both of whom were now privy to the engagement.

Albert's English was not bad but they all agreed that it could be much improved and that it was important to conceal as far as possible his German origins, however proud he was of them. A teacher was found for him, and at the age of twenty he went back to school – at least in this one subject. A stiffer task was the study of a copy of Blackstone's *Commentaries on the Laws of England* which the Queen had given to him before he left for home.

The subject of home was much on his mind during the following weeks. It sometimes seemed unimaginable to this young man that he was cutting all his old ties, leaving the people and places of his childhood. If only he had not been so happy, so attached to his older brother, his father and grandmother, to the staff of the ducal household, it would be easier. At least there would be his greyhound Eos who had already accompanied him on a visit to England.

In one of his letters to Victoria at this time, be broached the tense subject of having his household chosen for him in his absence rather than bringing with him people he knew and could trust:

Think of my position, dear Victoria, I am leaving my home with all its old associations, all my bosom friends and going to a country in which everything is new and strange to me . . . Except yourself I have no one to confide in. And is it not even to be conceded to me that the two or three persons, who are to have the charge of my private affairs, shall be persons who already command my confidence?

But Victoria, while revealing to others the sympathy she felt for the sacrifice Albert was making in marrying her, was clearly not going to encourage any lurking feelings of self-pity in her fiancé. Her reply to this appeal was brief, almost tart: 'Once more I tell you that you can perfectly rely on me.'

Victoria's favouring of the Whig cause remained as powerful as her hatred for the Tory Party. She still regarded the Tories as a cabal of the super-rich, the great landowners, who treated their labourers like slaves, opposed all progressive influence, and by tradition disliked and distrusted the court. And she disliked the Tory leader, Sir Robert Peel, almost as much as she loved her faithful Melbourne.

Albert had recognised this prejudice in the Queen early in his visit and later, when he was engaged and had committed the remainder of his life to his adopted country, he expressed his concern. No doubt he was sharply reprimanded by Victoria, whose trust in Melbourne and his administration was total. Late in January 1840, Albert learned of a debate in Parliament which seemed not only to bear out his view of the importance of the monarch adopting a neutral stance, but also, unfortunately, directly affected him. The matter of Albert's grant came up for debate on 29 January. The standard figure was thought to be £50,000: that is what Queen Anne's Consort had been voted, and neither Victoria nor Albert had reckoned on anything less.

To the consternation of Melbourne and all the Whig hierarchy, a Radical member put forward a motion that Albert's annuity should be no more than £21,000. This could be interpreted as the people's answer to 'England's fatter purse'. The motion was defeated but a Tory, Colonel Sibthorp, now proposed £30,000. This was supported by every Tory and Radical in the House, leading to a vote in favour of 262 to 158.

Unlike the Queen, Albert reconciled himself to this

reduction of his expected annuity, but he was angered and hurt by the parallel debate concerning his precedence. For a while it looked as if he might be deprived of his position immediately following the Queen. Eventually the question was resolved but only after the Queen had almost exploded with wrath. 'The Tories . . . do everything that they can,' she wrote to Albert, 'to be personally rude to me . . . The Whigs are the only safe and loyal people.'

Despite their access to sound advice, especially from King Leopold, Baron Stockmar and Prime Minister Melbourne, these two young people could sometimes be seen, during the early years of Victoria's reign, as babes in the wood, lost for lack of experience and knowledge. Blinded by love, Queen Victoria had no understanding of the country's suspicion of Albert's nationality, low rank and penury. Most people had never heard of Saxe-Coburg-Gotha, and only recognised that it sounded decidedly alien. What the Queen did possess, in full measure, was a consciousness of her rank, and there was no lack of imperiousness when she felt it right to exercise it.

For both Albert and Victoria, those early weeks of 1840 passed like the view from a train window on the recently completed London to Birmingham railway.*

There were distressing as well as loving letters between the prince and the Queen. Albert could not entirely ignore a widely distributed lampoon:

> She's all my Lehzen painted her,
> She's lovely, she is rich,
> But they tell me when I marry her
> That she will wear the *britsch*.

For her part, the Queen continued to cause Albert anxiety by her unremitting support for the Whig cause.

---

* Two years later when the Paddington to Windsor line was opened, Victoria and Albert travelled by railway for the first time. She was enchanted; he warned, 'Not so fast next time, Conductor.'

His departure from Gotha was for Albert a sombre if impressive occasion. After long and tearful farewells to the staff and numerous friends, Albert mounted his father's somewhat ramshackle travelling carriage. Victoria had sent out three more carriages to help with the passengers, and two britzkas and two fourgons for the luggage, all rather more respectable in appearance than the prince's mode of transport.

Albert had been deeply depressed by the last letter he had received from Victoria in reply to his express wish for a honeymoon at Windsor Castle. Victoria had reminded him 'that I am the Sovereign, and that business can stop and wait for nothing. Parliament is sitting,' she continued, 'and something occurs almost every day, for which I may be required.' In the event, she relented and they had one week there.

When the ducal caravan arrived at Brussels for a night, King Leopold reflected in a letter to Victoria, that Albert seemed 'rather exasperated about various things, and pretty full of grievances ... He is not inclined to be sulky, but I think he may be rendered a little melancholy if he thinks himself unfairly or unjustly treated.'

This scarcely seemed the most promising augury for a marriage that was only a few days distant.

To compound Albert's unhappiness, the crossing from Calais to Dover was, if possible, even worse than the one of the previous October, taking in all five hours and leaving almost the entire Coburg party prostrate. However, despite the gale and pouring rain, there was a splendid reception by the local citizenry. Albert pulled himself together and composed a letter to his fiancée: 'Now I am in the same country with you. What a delightful thought for me! It will be hard for me to have to wait till tomorrow evening. Still, our long parting has flown so quickly, and tomorrow's Dawn will soon be here ... There were thousands of people on the quay, and they saluted us with loud and uninterrupted cheers.'

Only two and a half months had passed since Albert had

last seen London but in that time it had been transformed almost beyond recognition. The nearer he approached Buckingham Palace from London Bridge, the more elaborately decorated were the buildings, with union flags and even some Saxe-Coburg-Gotha flags, secured to the windows. Nothing had been prearranged but when the long cavalcade was recognised, crowds gathered and cheered the ducal carriage and its passengers. For Albert, this unexpected recognition and greeting would now follow him everywhere for the rest of his life, a chastening thought for a young man who had certainly been loved and admired in his home dukedom but had never before experienced a reception on this scale. His arrival had, it seemed, reversed national prejudice against him.

The cavalcade with its weary passengers made its way up the Mall soon after four o'clock in the afternoon of 8 February. The Queen was at the main entrance to greet them. 'My dearest precious Albert looking beautiful and so well ... put me at ease about everything,' Victoria wrote of this moment, when all the sharp or discomfiting exchanges of the past weeks were put behind them. They embraced and exchanged presents.

The following day was filled with formalities and ceremonies, the most important being the brief rehearsal of the wedding itself and Albert's oath of naturalisation conducted by the Lord Chancellor. Albert wrote a loving letter to his grandmother, who was the nearest person in his life to a surrogate mother, and who – he knew – had been almost distraught with grief at his departure.

The tenth of February dawned wet, cold and windy. Victoria awoke early and wrote from her room a last letter to Albert as her fiancé:

> Dearest, how are you today, and have you slept well? I have rested very well, and feel very comfortable today. What weather! I believe, however, the rain will cease. Send one word when you, my most dearly beloved bridegroom, will be ready.
> Thy ever-faithful Victoria R.

CHAPTER FIVE

'Oh Madam, it is a Princess'

Although, as with the coronation, there was no full rehearsal of the royal wedding, the bride and groom did spend an hour on the previous evening practising with the ring and reading over the marriage service. The following morning, after a good night's sleep, the Queen arose at 8.45 a.m., wrote her letter to Albert, and breakfasted three-quarters of an hour later.

Prince Albert's procession was the first to leave the palace on the brief journey to the Chapel Royal in St James's. The pouring rain and high wind in no way discouraged the crowds who cheered the future Prince Consort all the way. The previous day he had been made a field marshal by the Queen and appointed to the Order of the Garter, the highest honour, and he now wore its collar over his shoulders. The band struck up 'See the conquering Hero comes', which seemed to some excessive considering the brevity of his service, youth and lack of action.

Lord Melbourne, too, was wearing a new coat of great splendour and 'built like a 74-gun ship', though his only armament was the sword of state, which he carried with great dignity.

As soon as Albert was standing correctly before the altar, looking pale but tall and splendidly handsome, the Lord Chamberlain left to fetch the Queen. Victoria travelled in the royal coach with her mother and her mistress of the robes. She wore a dress of rich white satin, trimmed with orange-flower blossoms and with a broad flounce of lace. Her wreath was of the same flowers, her veil, arranged to expose her face, according to tradition. The lace was from Beer, near Honiton in Devon, and had provided work for 200 people; the satin was made at Spitalfields in east London. All the designs were destroyed as a precaution against copying. As jewellery she wore only her Turkish diamond necklace and earrings, and a sapphire brooch, a present from Albert.

Victoria came up the aisle with cheerful dignity to the tune of the national anthem, her train held by her twelve brides-maids, dressed simply in tulle and carrying white roses. One of them, Lady Stanhope, complained later that the bridesmaids were either too numerous or the train too short. 'We were all huddled together, and scrambled rather than walked along, kicking each other's heels and treading on each other's gowns.' There was only one other *faux pas* during the ceremony and that was created by one of the royal dukes, Cambridge, who chattered loudly to no one in particular, but in jovial terms. Then, as a gesture of ducal gallantry, he helped the bridesmaids down the steps one by one 'with many audible civilities'.

The service was performed by the Archbishop of Canterbury, the Archbishop of York and the Bishop of London. It proceeded with notable smoothness, Victoria par-ticularly enjoying being addressed simply by her name. Then, 'Albert, wilt thou . . .' and she turned and looked up at him, her face expressing total love as he spoke the words, 'I will.' Her uncle, the Duke of Sussex, gave away the bride.

There was great applause in the chapel when the ceremony was concluded. Victoria kissed her aunt, the Dowager Queen Adelaide, but only shook hands with her mother, an omission widely remarked upon. *The Times* reporter thought he saw traces of tears on Victoria's cheek, and wrote that she 'appeared somewhat disconsolate and distressed'.

Others noticed the signs of crying but it was only from emotion, not grief. Lady Lyttelton reported:

Being a compound part of the procession, I, of course, saw very little of its effect, and especially was prevented by the portly forms and finery of the Duchess of Bedford and Lady Normanby, who walked before me, from seeing the Queen and her trainbearers at all; and they were said to have formed much the most striking part of the show, in their pure and simple white dresses. They looked like village girls, among all the gorgeous colours and jewels that surrounded them. The Queen's look and manner were very pleasing; her eyes much swoln with tears, but great happiness in her face; and her look of confidence and comfort at the Prince as they walked away as man and wife was very pretty to see. I understand she is in extremely high spirits since. Such a new thing for her to *dare* to be *unguarded* in conversation with anybody; and with her frank and fearless nature, the restraints she has hitherto been under from one reason or another must have been most painful . . .

As a reward for their strenuous and uncomfortable service, the Queen presented to each bridesmaid a brooch she had designed. It featured a gold eagle, the beak a diamond, the eyes rubies, the claws resting on pearls. One hundred wedding cakes had been baked by London's finest confectioners, to be distributed not to the poor but as gifts to foreign ambassadors (who also received gold snuff boxes with portraits of the happy pair set in the lids).

Only two Tories had been invited to the wedding, none to the wedding breakfast, not even the Duke of Wellington. The couple were expected at Windsor Castle in the evening but after changing and before leaving, Victoria had ten minutes with Lord Melbourne alone. The Prime Minister was full of praise for the way the ceremony had been conducted. '"Nothing could have gone off better." Before leaving him, I pressed his hand once more, and he said, "God bless you, Ma'am," most kindly.'

The sun at last broke through as they left, 'I and Albert alone, which was SO delightful' on the arduous three-hour drive. For the first part they had a cheering escort of riders on horseback or in gigs. It was pitch dark at Windsor but there were plenty of lanterns on the streets held by the cheering crowd. Like excited school-children, Victoria and Albert explored the suite that had been prepared for them. Victoria changed again, and returned to the sitting-room to find Albert playing the piano, wearing his Windsor coat.

They embraced, as man and wife, and then dinner was served in the sitting-room, but Victoria could not eat anything. She had suddenly been seized by a sick headache and had to retire to a sofa in the Blue Room, worn out by the experiences of the day, and the anxious days before.

> But ill or not, I NEVER NEVER spent such an evening!!! My DEAREST DEAREST DEAR Albert sat on a footstool by my side, & his excessive love & affection gave me feelings of heavenly love & happiness, I never could have *hoped* to have felt before! – really how can I ever be thankful enough to have such a *Husband*!

There were two aspects of the royal marriage which perhaps neither of them had fully anticipated. While on the one hand they shared a deep passion, the depth of which certainly surprised Albert, Victoria found herself unwilling or unable to share with her husband the responsibilities of power. She was eager to share everything else with Albert – their joy in music and pictures, their riding, their dancing and games of all sorts, but not the power of the monarchy.

Before her marriage Victoria customarily spent long hours of each morning with Lord Melbourne. There was always much to discuss, much to arrange. Not for one moment did the Queen contemplate sharing this work with her husband. Sometimes, almost as if it was a child's treat, Albert was allowed to hold the blotting paper and blot Victoria's signature as she worked her way through a pile of documents and letters. That was all.

Albert had great difficulty in concealing his dismay. To an old friend he wrote, 'In my home life I am very happy and contented; but the difficulty in filling my place with the proper dignity is, that I am only the husband, and not the master of the house.' It was a strange contrast with that day, just a few weeks ago, when Victoria had insisted that 'love, honour and *obey*' should be included in full in her marriage vows.

Victoria continued to see her ministers alone, and never

revealed the contents of the document boxes that passed through her hands in great numbers every day. The Queen had members of her household, Lehzen and Melbourne, in whom to confide. Albert did have a secretary but no one to whom he could talk intimately. And in spite of his love for his wife, there were moments of dreadful loneliness.

This political isolation was the more dismaying because it crippled, anyway for the time being, his ambition to bring about first an understanding, later an alliance, between Britain and Germany. When he left Germany Albert declared before his family that he would remain 'a loyal German, Coburger, and Gothaner'. Although destined to live in Britain, and to accept British nationality, he determined to remain a German in spirit and the destiny of Germany was always close to his heart.

Albert's ambition, however far distant it might seem in 1840, was to create a Germanic *bloc* made up of Germany, Britain, Belgium and Denmark at the northern end, and Switzerland in the south. This was to be formed in self-protection against the 'military despotism and red republicanism' of Russia and France. He was confident that German unification was inevitable, and that it would be Prussia that would bring this about.

Although Albert's English was much improved, domestically he spoke German, as did Victoria and, later, their children. Every child was bi-lingual, and was also fluent in French. Albert continued to dress in the German style, which led to occasional ribaldry on the hunting field, though it had to be accepted that he was a bold rider.

This further 'Germanisation' of the English court, already well established by the Hanovers, was to have consequences unimagined in the 1840s.

Another factor in the relations between Victoria and Albert, though less serious in its consequences, was their timetable disparity. Victoria's robust constitution and love of evening life after a hard day's work led her to dance late into the night whenever the opportunity occurred. Albert loved to dance, too, and Victoria admired his skill, but his stamina in no way matched hers. Long before she was ready for bed, he sat out a dance, and fell at once into a deep sleep. It was the same at concerts, the opera and theatre, and even at the dinner-table.

> The Queen took a more lively interest [in the concert] than the greater part of her guests did [remarked one observer]. Prince Albert slept. She looked at him, half smiling, half vexed. She pushed him with her elbow. He woke up, and nodded approval of the piece of the moment. Then he went to sleep again still nodding approval . . .

Prince Albert preferred to be in bed as soon after ten o'clock as was seemly and practical. The Queen enjoyed dancing until there was light in the summer sky.

It is not surprising that Victoria and Albert's first year of marriage brought with it a number of uncomfortable surprises and disappointments as well as pleasures. They were both so young (celebrating their twenty-first birthdays in May and August respectively); they had no training for married life, one without a father, the other without a mother; they had known one another well for only a few weeks before their marriage; their heredity might be similar but their upbringing could scarcely have been more contrasting.

Neither Victoria nor Albert knew what to expect of married life beyond the realisation that they must lose their freedom and expect new responsibilities. To Albert's distress and puzzlement, these responsibilities continued to elude him.

Their love and passion survived these early months intact. Lady Lyttelton witnessed many occasions which revealed the strength of the marriage. On a drive in Windsor Park, for example, she recorded:

> I went in the Queen's carriage yesterday, for the first time, with Lady Palmerston. I enjoyed it from watching her [the Queen] and the Prince, who rode a fine horse alongside, and was so delightful! Leading the drive through every beautiful turn, which he knows as he does every tree, and cantering up to point out 'a fine swarm of bees just settling on that bough', and then some talk about the queen-bee and their ways; our Queen listening

like a good child, and answering 'How curious!' and asking little questions. And then we got to the larger paddock, where his Arabians and their foals and his fine hunters were galloping about; and he brought them up to shew her, and she was so worthy! knowing them all by name, and seeming to long to get a gallop herself. And then pointing out the magnificent scarlet geraniums, seen through the glass of the Conservatory, and then rather begging the Queen to alight and go in to see them better. She could not, being engaged at the Castle by a particular hour, but refused very gracefully and kindly; and I envied for her the simple tastes and pleasures, and happy, active temper and habits of her husband.

Albert's interest in horses and bloodstock came as a surprise to Victoria, but she took care to encourage it. In early June 1840 she arranged to stay at Claremont for part of Epsom week. Albert reported to his father:

We came back yesterday (3 June) from Claremont, where we have again passed two days. We went there this time in order to be able to go from the neighbourhood to the celebrated Epsom races, which were certainly very interesting. The numbers of people there were estimated at from one to two hundred thousand. We were received with the greatest enthusiasm and cordiality. I rode about a little in the crowd, but was almost crushed by the people.

But sharp words were sometimes exchanged and it was not only in their sexual activities that passions ran deep. One of the causes of acrimony, and one which might have been anticipated, was Baroness Lehzen, who was bitter about the inevitable loss of influence over her mistress. That influence remained powerful enough to disturb Albert and create counter-jealousy.

Melbourne, Stockmar and George Anson, Albert's private secretary, combined forces to eliminate or at least diminish these early disputes and misunderstandings. The Queen's reluctance to involve Albert in any political matters, which he so resented, was explained to Anson by Melbourne: 'My impression is that the chief obstacle in Her Majesty's mind is the fear of difference of opinion and she thinks that domestic harmony is more likely to follow from avoiding subjects likely to create difference.'

It was true that Albert had a clearer view than Victoria of the crown's correct role in domestic politics. His attitude was one of neutrality rather than the blatant anti-Tory prejudice of the Queen. Victoria was well aware of this difference of opinion between them and avoided discussion for fear of enflaming it.

Nature found a partial cure for this unhappy situation. The anticipation of pregnancy and childbirth were two consequences of married life which Victoria had hated to contemplate – 'the ONLY thing I *dread*'. She had believed that she could somehow escape pregnancy for, say, six months after her marriage. Scarcely six weeks passed, however, before she knew, by her sickness and instinct, that she was pregnant. 'I cannot in any way see the good side of this sad business,' she wrote to Uncle Leopold. To her grandmother-in-law, the Dowager Duchess of Saxe-Coburg-Gotha, she wrote, '. . . my prayers have not been answered and I am really most unhappy. I cannot understand how any one can wish for such a thing, especially at the beginning of a marriage.'

Queen Victoria never became reconciled to the miseries of pregnancy, though she suffered them so frequently. One year after the birth of her last child in 1857, she wrote to her pregnant eldest daughter of 'the sufferings and miseries and plagues – which you must struggle against – and enjoyments etc. to give up – constant precautions to take, you will feel the yoke of a married woman . . . I think our sex a most unenviable one . . .'

The one consequence of pregnancy – 'the shadow side of marriage' as she defined it – which she resented more than any other was that it put her on the level of any other woman. But she was not 'any other woman': she was Queen of England, the most powerful woman in the land, if not the world. She resented how pregnancy increasingly restricted her activities, especially on horseback and the dance floor. In a fit of irritation she wrote indignantly to Uncle Leopold of the foetus in her womb, '*the thing* is odious and if all one's plagues are rewarded only by a nasty girl, I shall drown it, I think. I *will* know nothing else but a boy. I never will have a girl!'*

However, even before the birth of their first child, Albert's position in the household began to improve. The death of Princess Charlotte while giving birth to a child who would have been heir apparent to the throne, emphasised the importance of having a Prince Regent standing by in the event of a similar catastrophe. With typical common sense, Victoria accepted this need. There was talk and rumour of the setting up of a regency council, or of a joint regency with the Duke of Sussex and Albert. Sensibly, Albert remained silent during the intriguing and negotiation between the two principal political parties. Stockmar got his way, as usual, and on 17 July 1840 Albert was able to write to his brother (with somewhat unseemly excitement), 'In case of Victoria's death and her successor being under eighteen years of age, I am to be Regent – *alone* . . . You will understand the importance of this matter and that it gives my position in the country a fresh significance.'

An incident which improved still further the Queen's popularity and brought new credit to Albert, but which might have put the royal succession into renewed chaos, occurred in the early days of the Queen's pregnancy. On 10 June 1840 in the late afternoon, according to custom, Victoria and Albert left the palace in a low open phaeton for a drive in the park. They were some way up Constitution Hill when there was a loud crack. Albert spread his arms over Victoria and exclaimed, 'My God, don't be alarmed!' She was not, until she noticed 'a little man on the footpath with his arms folded over his breast, a pistol in each hand.' Victoria ducked. There were shouts from the crowd of 'Kill him! Kill him!' One man†

---

* Over seventeen years, Queen Victoria gave birth to five girls.

† He was John Millais, father of John Everett Millais, then aged eleven and to become a famous painter. He was also present, having just raised his cap to the Queen.

seized the would-be assassin who turned out to be a mentally inadequate youth of eighteen, named Edward Oxford. He spent the remainder of his life in a lunatic asylum.

The Queen insisted on continuing their drive. On returning to the palace, the royal phaeton was surrounded by hundreds of cheering citizens. Her popularity was raised to the level of the early days of her reign, and Albert's coolness under attack was widely praised.

During that first summer of their marriage, Albert's standing with the British people showed signs of further improvement. For all his married life it was fashionable among the 'smart set' to lampoon him. With his guttural accent, quaint German-cut clothes, and serious mien, he was an easy target. But among people who mattered, Albert's qualities were soon recognised. His interest in the sciences led to his election to the Royal Society. Then, on his twenty-first birthday in August he was made a Privy Councillor. Albert also began to make a mark as an administrator and organiser. Buckingham Palace was seething with corruption, grossly over-manned, inefficient and extravagant. Old court practices had been perpetuated through several reigns. It was also insecure, as was proved when a twelve-year-old boy was discovered to have lived undetected in the palace for a year. Another older boy was found at the same time. He had penetrated the security guards several times without any difficulty, and continued to do so, in spite of barbarous punishment on the treadmill. (He was eventually sent away to sea.)

Albert made himself unpopular within the palace by his economies and the sacking of indolent and unnecessary staff. He also thoroughly upset Lehzen who resented his 'interference' and was soon set on a collision course with him which could have only one outcome.

Albert continued to learn about the law of the land and studied practices and activities which at first utterly confused him. The Duchy of Cornwall, for example, was a complete enigma. There was no duke, but the title to this extensive land had, since the days of the Black Prince, been vested in the sovereign's eldest son, namely the Prince of Wales, when there was one. After studying the finances, Albert soon discovered that one-third of the duchy's income of £36,000 a year went on administration. Here, then, was another Augean stable ripe for cleaning.

Many other features of British, and court, life continued to puzzle Albert. Why did the men remain behind to drink, smoke and talk, at the end of dinner, while the hostess and the ladies sat alone in the withdrawing room? Not only did this extend the evening (sufficient alone to damn it in Albert's eyes), but it seemed ill-mannered, and, final condemnation, Victoria hated it. On hearing of Albert's plan to scrap the practice, Melbourne recommended caution, considering that such an attempt to 'Germanise' life at court would make Albert more enemies than friends. A compromise was reached: a time limit of five minutes, which did not satisfy either the ladies or the gentlemen. It was also a rule made for breaking, and so it was.

As Queen Victoria's pregnancy advanced, so did Albert's involvement in her political life. She began sharing her despatch boxes with him and discussing problems on an equal basis. The one thing they never talked about was the reason for this change. It is possible that the shadow of poor Princess Charlotte and her death in childbirth was darker than Victoria was prepared to concede; perhaps subconsciously she was preparing her husband for the duties that might fall upon him in the event of her own death and the survival of her child. But Victoria remained well. 'I take long walks,' she boasted to Feodora, 'some in the highest wind, every day, and am so active, though of a *great* size I must unhappily admit.'

However, as the pregnancy advanced at Windsor she was recommended to leave the castle for Buckingham Palace, where medical facilities were more readily available. A week later, and three weeks earlier than expected, she felt the first pains early on Saturday morning, 21 November 1840. The labour continued through the morning, and the Queen later wrote, 'the last pains that are generally thought the worst I thought nothing of, they began at half past twelve and lasted till ten minutes to two [in the afternoon] when the young lady appeared.' Albert was at Victoria's side during the twelve-hour labour, and the Duchess of Kent was there, too. No one else besides Dr Locock and the midwife, Mrs Lilly, remained in the room; the Privy Councillors, including Lords Palmerston and Melbourne, stayed in the adjoining room, with the door open as witnesses. They heard Dr Locock's voice clearly as he said, almost as an apology, 'Oh Madam, it is a princess.'

'Never mind,' said the Queen briskly, 'the next will be a prince.'

As soon as the little princess had been washed and wrapped in flannel, she was carried into the room and laid briefly for examination on a table.

Later, Victoria wrote of the princess as 'a perfect little child ... but alas a girl and not a boy, as we both so hoped and wished for. We were, I am afraid, sadly disappointed.' Of course they both became fond of 'our little lady' or 'Pussy' or 'Pussette' as she came to be called.

As a signal that a new era had begun in his marriage, almost immediately after the birth Albert had to hurry to a Privy Council meeting, the first he had ever attended. He wrote to his brother, 'Albert, father of a daughter, you will laugh at me.' But in spite of the self-mocking tone, they both knew that Albert's status had been transformed. Albert was now father of the heiress to the throne, at least until a son was born when he would become father to the heir, a much higher position than Consort to the Queen. Letters of congratulation for both Victoria and Albert arrived from all the courts of Europe. From Laeken, Louise, King Leopold's second wife, wrote:

> I hope as you are, thank God, so well, I may venture a few lines to express *a part* of my feelings, and to wish you joy on the happy birthday of your dear little girl. I need not tell you the *deep deep* share I took in this most happy event.

Baron Stockmar was full of congratulations, too, but his letters to Albert were also full of fussy instructions. 'You ought not yourself to be too much about the Queen just now, for your being near or talking with her may be too exciting.' On this occasion Albert ignored Stockmar's orders, knowing that Victoria was greedy for his comforting presence at any time, whether reading or talking. 'His care was like that of a mother, nor could there be a kinder, wiser or more judicious muse,' the Queen observed. He was also kind to the Duchess of Kent – he always was – and dined with her every evening, refusing all other invitations.

Victoria recovered so rapidly and fully from her confinement that they decided to go to Windsor for Christmas. Queen Charlotte had been the first to introduce Christmas as a special celebratory festival, before Victoria's birth. But it was still a comparatively muted affair which had not spread widely among the people. Albert determined that the celebration should be on the German scale, with fir trees, decorations and the sending of cards to friends and relations. As part of the revels, the prince joined the skaters on the lake at Frogmore,* outdoing them all with his grace, dexterity and speed. The exchange of gifts on 25 December was effectively a postponement of the feast of St Nicholas – or Santa Claus – on the sixth of the month.

The Queen, with the little Princess Royal beside her, relished every aspect of the day, as did the members of her court. In later years it became a national religious celebration, with strong commercial undertones, and Albert did nothing to dispel the widespread belief that he had introduced the festival into his adopted country rather than developing and enlarging its importance.

Unlike her mother, Victoria did not attempt to feed her child. She remained in bed for the usual two weeks. Then she was up and walking the corridors with increasing pace and

---

* Frogmore was the Duchess of Kent's home, in the grounds of Windsor Castle.

vigour, keen to become fit and strong again. She saw her baby twice a day, which was quite often enough – at least until the child was about six months old and had lost her similarity to a wrinkled frog. At the same time Victoria boasted of her daughter's handsome looks – 'just like *dear* Albert', she wrote in her letters.

Pregnancy she always regarded as an act of God from which there was no escape. She enjoyed with gusto the act of union which brought it about, but not the consequences. No sooner had Pussy been christened then she discovered that she was pregnant again. She was not at all amused. Her mother lamented, 'I wish she could have waited a little longer.'

'The christening will be at Buckingham Palace on the 10th February, our dear marriage day,' Victoria wrote to her Uncle Leopold.

Before that happy event, a shadow was cast over the last days of that eventful year. There were usually a number of dogs gambolling around Victoria wherever she went, but Dash was her favourite spaniel, her companion for ten years or almost half her life. Now he was dead. He was buried under a marble effigy, with a long carved tribute, including '. . . His attachment was without selfishness/ His playfulness without malice/ His fidelity without deceit . . .'

The Princess Royal behaved well at her christening – she was a placid child – and so did everyone else. The Duke of Wellington, in spite of a seizure in the House a few days before, was able to represent Albert's father as sponsor. King Leopold was another sponsor, an uncle the Queen was always glad to see. But to Victoria's regret, Lord Melbourne was too stricken with gout to attend the ceremony.

Lady Lyttelton got her first glimpse of the princess at her christening.

> She is a fine, fat, firm, fair, royal-looking baby, sitting bolt upright, and too *absurdly* like the Queen. She wore a very plain white pelisse of muslin, and a droll little quaker-shaped straw bonnet; no bows or bustle about her, and she surveyed us all most composedly for a minute. She was shewn at her carriage-

window to all the standers-by, and it was amusing to us who followed to see the universal grin left upon all faces after their look at her. She will soon have seen every pair of teeth in the kingdom. They say she laughs, crows, and kicks very heartily, and the Prince tosses her often.

The princess was christened Victoria Adelaide Mary Louise. As an infant she continued to be called Pussy, or simply The Child, but as she grew older she was called Vicky, a name which remained with her for the rest of her life.

In spite of his gout and other manifestations of old age, Melbourne remained Prime Minister. But for how long? On 9 May 1841, in answer to the Queen's question, if he would mind leaving office, he replied, 'Why, nobody *likes* going out but I'm not well – I am a good deal tired, and it will be a great rest for me.'

As the year advanced it became ever clearer that he would soon be going, like it or not. During the first half of the year, the revenue continued to fall, trade was stultified, and there was real suffering and hunger in the nation's industrial towns. Chartist riots* occurred. In the early months of 1841 Melbourne lost four successive by-elections, and in May the Tories won a fiscal motion by just one vote.

Albert, no longer isolated from the political scene, and possessing confidence in Sir Robert Peel as future premier, understood that this time there must be no ladies of the bedchamber crisis, which might even cause the end of the monarchy. With infinite tact this time, Peel persuaded the Queen to give up three of her Whig ladies. Whether he would have succeeded without the behind-the-scenes support of Albert is doubtful.

The Queen's second pregnancy was less satisfactory than

---

* Chartism was a political reform movement demanding the fulfilment of the People's Charter of 1838 and universal male suffrage. With the rejection of petitions to Parliament, riots frequently broke out, one at Newport, Monmouth, resulting in twenty-four Chartist deaths.

81

the first. She was fretful and nervous, nor did she look so well as before, something noted by members of the household. How much this was caused by her physical condition and how much by political and domestic worries it is impossible to establish. The transformation of the political scene certainly tested her nerves and patience. Albert had blunted to a great extent the hostility she had always felt for the Tories. But the final loss of Melbourne and the day-by-day contact with Tory ministers were hard to contemplate.

As for the Tory leader, 'The Duke [of Wellington] is the best friend we have.' And it was the duke she wished to send for. Melbourne effectively ruled that out. It had to be Sir Robert Peel, he advised her. Albert agreed, and so, less directly, did his private secretary, upon whom the prince increasingly depended for advice.

On 29 June 1841, the Queen dissolved Parliament, and a general election immediately followed. The Tories were returned with a substantial majority and Peel set about forming his administration. Palmerston was replaced by the Earl of Aberdeen as Foreign Secretary; Lord Lyndhurst became Lord Chancellor, and the old Duke of Wellington was appointed Cabinet minister without office. Gladstone considered Peel the greatest man he had ever known. After the warm and sentimental Melbourne, the Queen found him cold and shy, though she came to admire him. His public frigidity was probably due to his industrial 'Lancashire cotton' background and upbringing, which he felt keenly among the landowning grandee Tories whom he led.

One of Peel's early communications to the Queen typically ran, 'It is essential to my position with the Queen that her Majesty should understand that I have the feelings of a gentleman and, where my duty does not interfere, I cannot act against her wishes.' But it was not for a further four months, on 3 September 1841, that she finally said goodbye to Lord Melbourne. The farewell occurred at Claremont, where Victoria and Albert had sought a few days' rest. Melbourne had already said emotionally to the Queen, 'For four years I have seen you daily and liked it better every day.'

Melbourne had also spoken in the warmest terms of Prince Albert. To confirm his opinion and keep it on the record, he wrote to the Queen:

> Lord Melbourne cannot satisfy himself without again stating to your Majesty in writing what he had the honour of stating to your Majesty respecting H.R.H. the Prince. Lord Melbourne has formed the highest opinion of H.R.H.'s judgement, temper and discretion, and he cannot but feel a great consolation and security in the reflection that he leaves Your Majesty in a situation in which Your Majesty has the inestimable advantage of such advice and assistance. Lord Melbourne feels certain that Your Majesty cannot do better than have recourse to it, whenever it is needed, and rely upon it with confidence.

Melbourne's estimate of the quality of Albert's judgement was to be sorely tested over the next domestic crisis. The incompatability of Baroness Lehzen and Prince Albert could have been foreseen by anyone even casually acquainted with their characters, or with the relationship between Lehzen and the Queen, who had every reason to feel gratitude and loyalty to the baroness. Lehzen had stood solidly by Victoria during her days at Kensington Palace: a friend indeed. To Lehzen, Queen Victoria was her whole life. When Albert had written to an old friend, 'I am only the husband, and not the master of the house,' he was referring not to the Queen but to Lehzen who had taken over arrangements in the royal household on the Queen's accession. Lehzen supervised the staff at every level. All the Queen's private expenditure was controlled by Lehzen. The baroness was also in charge of all non-state expenditure, accounts of which were produced quarterly and then submitted to the Keeper of the Privy Purse, who was authorised to pay the bills only if they carried Lehzen's signature.

Prince Albert recognised almost from the beginning of his marriage that Lehzen was determined to drive a wedge between the Queen and himself. She was constantly complaining to Victoria about his views and actions and, above all, his hostility to her. Albert had evidence that Lehzen encouraged the Queen to hold on to her prerogatives and reign alone, without allowing him to participate. Even more dangerous in Albert's judgement, was Lehzen's anti-Tory views and the way she enflamed this dangerous prejudice in the Queen.

Intermittently, this smouldering underground fire burst through the surface of life at court. Captain Childers was a case in point. This officer could not, it seemed, be restrained from making loud protestations of love for the Queen. Quite properly, Lehzen reported the matter to the Lord Chamberlain, Lord Uxbridge. When George Anson, the prince's private secretary, heard about it, he thought she should additionally have informed Prince Albert. Lehzen replied, according to Anson, that the 'Prince's conduct to her had rendered it impossible for her to consult with him. He had slighted her in the most marked manner . . . He had once told her to leave the Palace, but she replied that he had not the power to turn her out of the Queen's house . . . She tried to impress upon me [continued Anson] that the Queen would brook no interference with the exercise of her powers of which she was *most jealous*.'

This occurred only four months after the marriage, and relations deteriorated further, so that by January 1842 Albert was writing to Stockmar that Lehzen was 'a crazy, stupid intriguer, obsessed with the lust for power, who recognises herself as a demi-God, and anyone who refuses to recognise her as such is a criminal.' Albert concluded his long diatribe by emphasising that 'the welfare of my children and Victoria's existence as sovereign are too sacred for me not to die fighting rather than yield them as prey to Lehzen.'

Albert was clearly obsessed by this woman and her behaviour at court. That Lehzen was a real threat to the marriage of Queen Victoria and Prince Albert is proved by letters from them to Stockmar, father-confessor to both. A tremendous argument over Lehzen on 16 January 1842 spilt over, like so many marital rows, into other subjects of dispute, in this case the medical treatment of Pussy, which Albert thought faulty. Victoria had said something which Albert was provoked to describe as 'really malicious'. 'This was enough [wrote Albert] to make Victoria accuse me of wanting to send the mother out of the nursery, I could murder the child if I wanted to etc. etc. I went quietly downstairs and only said "I must have patience."'

In a separate note to Victoria, enclosed with the letter to Stockmar, Albert was seen to have lost control of his words: 'Dr Clark has mismanaged the child and poisoned her with calomel and you have starved her. I shall have nothing more to do with it; take the child away and do as you like and if she dies you will have it on your conscience.'

These outbursts from both parties were modified by expressions of deepest affection, like '... Dearest Angel Albert, God only knows how I love him.'

It was to take months to accomplish, but it was clear to all at the ringside that Baroness Lehzen would have to go. Even the Queen had to recognise that she was the one serious threat to her marriage and the solidarity of the family. 'It was not without great difficulty that the Prince succeeded in getting rid of her,' wrote Stockmar. 'She was foolish enough to contest his influence, and not to conform herself to the change in her position ... If she had done so, and conciliated the P[rince], she might have remained in the Palace to the end of her life.'

In the end the departure of Lehzen was engineered with surprisingly little difficulty or passion. In the last week of July 1842, Albert summoned her and told her that she was being retired and would receive a generous pension. This time, as proof of his mounting authority, Lehzen did not dispute Albert's demand. The Queen knew nothing of this, and as with the departure of the bedchamber ladies, was presented with a *fait accompli*. The baroness wished to retire in two months' time, for the sake of her health, Victoria was told. The Queen was greatly upset. The woman had, after all, been an almost constant companion since Victoria was five. No more loyal servant could be imagined. Lehzen had advised her on clothes and money, had been a Lady of the Bed-chamber, private secretary, confidante, political adviser and much else.

The Queen still did not accept that Lehzen had tried to damage her relations with her beloved Albert, nor that she had enflamed her prejudices against the Tories. But the Queen's common sense told her that, as she put it, Lehzen's departure was 'for our and her best'.

With the severance of the umbilical cord, a calmness fell about the baroness as if she were suddenly starved of the fire and passion of Victoria which had nourished her for so many years. The Queen's doctor, Sir James Clark, visited her for the last time in her quarters and found her covered in the dust of packing. She left Buckingham Palace three days later on 30 September 1842, without saying goodbye for fear of making a scene.

Living on her savings and her £800-a-year pension, she moved in with her sister in Bückeburg, just west of Hanover. She lived a selfless life helping financially with her nieces and nephews, surrounded by mementoes of her royal service and corresponding regularly with the Queen. They also met several times before the baroness died in 1870 at the age of eighty-six.

The Queen would have dearly liked to pension off her Prime Minister as Albert had pensioned off Lehzen. As the days and weeks passed, she could not get over her antipathy for Peel. Sitting next to her at dinner on 2 October, Anson noted, 'Her Majesty alluded to Sir Robert Peel's awkward manner, which she felt she could not get over. I asked if Her Majesty had yet made any effort, which I was good-humouredly assured Her Majesty "thought she really had done".

'"Sir Robert's ignorance of character was most striking and unaccountable," she continued. Feeling this, made it difficult for Her Majesty to place reliance upon his judgement in recommendations.'

CHAPTER SIX

The Difficult Prince

A year before the final departure of Baroness Lehzen, in the late summer of 1841, Victoria was feeling unsettled and unwell. There were other reasons for depression and anxiety than her second pregnancy. Lord Melbourne had gone, and although she kept up a steady correspondence with her old friend and mentor until shortly before his death in 1848, his guiding political and emotional support was greatly missed. At the same time, while accepting the need and desirability for Albert to take over increasing responsibilities, Victoria also resented it.

To compound all this Pussy, who had seemed bursting with good health and cheer earlier in the year, was now proving fretful and generally run down. 'Till the end of August she was such a magnificent, strong fat child, that it is a great grief to see her so thin, pale and changed,' Victoria wrote. A new diet was decreed, which included '*only* asses' milk'.

On 11 October Victoria thought she might have a miscarriage. It was a false alarm but reflected her nervous anxiety. There were two more false alarms, on 26 and 28 October. 'I unfortunately was feeling very wretched'; but as consolation, 'Albert was so dear and kind, and anxious that this trying time of waiting would soon be over'.

Victoria kept recalling her last peaceful pregnancy and wondered when she would deliver this great baby she was carrying. Then, at last, early on the morning of 9 November she felt certain enough that her time had come to call for Mrs Lilly, who summoned Drs Charles Locock, James Clark, Robert

87

Ferguson and Richard Blagden to assist with the delivery if required. 'My sufferings were really very severe,' complained the Queen, 'and I don't know what I should have done, but for the great comfort and support my beloved Albert was to me.'

The official bulletin read, 'The Queen was safely delivered of a Prince this morning at 48 minutes past 10 o'clock.'

As before, the baby was taken to be examined by the Privy Councillors who had assembled in the next room. The news spread throughout the land with astonishing speed and amid unbridled celebration. In London the birth coincided happily with the Lord Mayor's Show, almost to the minute, adding a new zest to the procession's progress. The Archbishop of Canterbury prepared a form of prayer and thanksgiving to Almighty God for Her Majesty's safe delivery of a prince, to be said in all churches.

The Queen wanted her son to be called simply Albert but was at length prevailed upon to add the more Anglo-Saxon Edward. He was to be known informally throughout his life as Bertie, although his mother was at first content to refer to him simply as The Boy. There was an ominous note in the Queen's letter to Uncle Leopold of the Belgians: 'You will understand how fervent are my prayers, and I am sure everybody must be, to see him resemble his father in *every, every* respect, both in body and mind . . . Pussy was not at all pleased with her brother,' the Queen added. But she noted approvingly, 'He is a wonderfully strong and large child, with very large dark blue eyes, a finely formed but somewhat large nose, and a pretty little mouth.'

Lord Melbourne, ever ready with advice even at this early stage in Bertie's life, recommended, 'Be not over solicitous about education. It may be able to do much, but it does not do so much as is expected from it. It may mould and direct the character, but it rarely alters it . . .'

As Victoria and Albert's family grew larger – she was pregnant again at the time of Bertie's christening – so did the young couple's wish to travel throughout the kingdom and to find a place which offered them tranquillity and isolation. Although they both loved Windsor, the castle did not provide the privacy they sought. Motherhood, and Albert, had wrought a fundamental change in Victoria's girlish delight in the tumult of London life. Buckingham Palace must remain the centrepiece of their professional lives, but, as she wrote on 19 October 1843, 'Albert & I talked of buying a place of our own, which would be so nice.'

For them as for many other people with the necessary financial means, travel was being extended, almost monthly, by the growth of the nation's railway system. The London to Birmingham line and the London to Bristol line were fully open by 1838. The great cities of the midlands and the north were rapidly being linked. In spite of Prince Albert's instruction to the conductor not to go so fast after their first ride on the 'iron road', they both took enthusiastically to the royal train. On the road, the coachmen had to keep up a fast pace to prevent crowds mobbing the vehicle. The Queen and Prince Albert felt safe behind the windows of their railway carriage, detached from the world outside.

In the summer of 1842, the Queen determined to visit her subjects in Scotland for the first time. She was disappointed to learn that the railway to Edinburgh had not been completed. Prime Minister Peel judged it unwise, because of '[Chartist] rioting in the North', to travel by road. It would have to be by sea. The Queen approved. 'How delightful to be quite alone together on board,' she exclaimed. There had been two further attempts to assassinate the Queen in London that year, and the Edinburgh authorities were in a state of deep anxiety about security. Victoria and Albert were whisked through the thronged streets, offering the citizens scarcely a glimpse of their sovereign. But the people approved of the visit as much as Victoria approved of Scotland. She later told Uncle Leopold about their travels north of Edinburgh:

We left Dalkeith on Monday, and lunched at Dupplin, Lord Kinnoul's, a pretty place with quite a new house, and which poor Lord Kinnoul displayed so well as to fall head over heels down a steep bank, and was proceeding down another, if Albert had not caught him; I did not see it, but Albert and I have nearly died with laughing at the *relation* of it. From Dalkeith we went through Perth (which is *most* beautifully situated on the Tay) to Scone Palace, Lord Mansfield's, where we slept; fine but rather gloomy. Yesterday morning (Tuesday) we left Scone and lunched at Dunkeld, the beginning of the Highlands, in a tent; *all* the Highlanders in their fine dress, being encamped there, and with their old shields and swords, looked very romantic ... The situation of Dunkeld, down in a valley surrounded by wooded hills, is very pretty. From thence we proceeded to this enchanting and princely place [Taymouth] the whole drive here was beautiful. All Lord Breadalbane's Highlanders, with himself at their head, and a battalion of the 92nd Highlanders, were drawn up in front of the House. In the evening the grounds were splendidly illuminated, and bonfires burning on the hills; and a number of Highlanders danced reels by torchlight, to the bagpipes, which was very wild and pretty ...

For Victoria and Albert a seed had been planted north of the border which was to grow as high as the mightiest Scots pine.

The next visit was to Kent, to Walmer Castle, at the invitation of the Duke of Wellington. The journey, by the Dover Road, was the best part for the Queen. She ensured that they stayed for the night en route at the same hostelries used by Albert when he came to marry her.

The return journey was less relaxed, and on arrival at Windsor Lady Lyttelton found herself short of luggage, and staff:

Windsor Castle
December 4, 1842

... Here we are. Our journey was very prosperous, being almost literally one gallop from Walmer to London, and a railroad rush hither. We arrived at twenty minutes after four, and then came such a regular nursery worry. Mrs. Sly taken ill, with so furious a sick headache that she was obliged to go to bed. Aimée, tho' recovered, not yet allowed to see the children, therefore useless up in her room. One nursery maid detained, as were the maids of honour, and almost everybody's servants and luggage on the train from Walmer, owing to some unexplained blunderation, and all our little possessions, night things, playthings, *rusks*, shawls, etc., left behind in London, to follow by next train, *we* having believed they were coming on with us when we stepped out of our warm littery [*sic*] nursery on wheels, to share the honours of the Queen's special train from London hither, where nothing but royal live persons and their indispensable attendants are admitted. So I and Charlotte and the Queen (who took her full share of the trouble, and even got up and ran an errand for me, of course un-asked, most funnily and kindly) had the sole charge of Prince and Princessy, who were taken with tearing spirits, and a rage for crawling, climbing, poking into corners, upsetting everything, and after a little while being tired, cross and squally for hours, till gradually the most necessary absentee people and things dropped in, and I, more untidy and horrid than a beggar, but easy about the children, came up *home* at last, and enjoyed the great luxury of a nice fire and drawn curtains, and Mr. Sprague [her footman], and my regular fine dinner . . .

Brighton, by contract with Walmer Castle, was a disaster, even worse than the first visit. The crowds mobbed and obstructed them. The Queen noted, 'The people are very indiscreet and troublesome here really, which makes this place quite a prison.' After February 1845 she never returned.

The nation had given the Queen a steam yacht, and in the late summer of 1843 she and Albert determined to use it to make the first royal visit to France since Henry VIII and King Francis I of France met in 1520 at the Field of the Cloth of Gold.

On 2 September 1843, her magnificent new paddle steamer dropped anchor at Tréport, to be met by the much smaller but equally impressive French royal barge, crewed by fifty oarsmen, all in white with red sashes and red ribbons round their hats. The sole passenger was the King of France, Louis Philippe, smiling and saluting a welcome. The Queen and the prince proceeded on board, the English royal standard was hoisted alongside the French royal standard – a unique occurrence – and the oarsmen took the joint party ashore.

Here the French Queen and the whole court were assembled, along with a regiment of crack troops and thousands of citizens cheering, 'Vive la Reine d'Angleterre!'

They were then transported to the Château d'Eu, thence to a clearing in the nearby forest for a déjeuner. Later there was swimming in the sea for some of the men, including Albert, and a tour of the château for the Queen. Victoria was delighted with everything she saw and everyone she met, 'in a family circle of persons of my own rank, with whom I could be on terms of equality & familiarity'.

Next they steamed up-Channel for a brief visit to Brussels and the King and Queen of the Belgians – Uncle Leopold and Aunt Louise. Among the crowds on the streets of the capital to watch the English royal family pass by was Charlotte Brontë, who recounted to her sister Emily how she had seen the Queen

> for an instant flashing through the Rue Royale in a carriage and six, surrounded by soldiers. She was laughing and talking very gaily. She looked a little, stout, vivacious lady, very plainly dressed, not much dignity or pretension about her. The Belgians liked her very well on the whole – They said she enlivened the sombre court of King Leopold, which is usually as gloomy as a conventicle.

Both Victoria and Albert were entranced by their brief holiday which, with the trip to Scotland, led them to recognise that there was no need to restrict their lives to Buckingham Palace and Windsor. They sought advice on a place they could call their own, a family home for holidays for themselves and the children. Sir Robert Peel firmly advised the Isle of Wight, accessible yet distant enough to insulate them from the cares of palace life and from the germs of Pimlico and Windsor.

Before they could begin house-hunting, however, domestic affairs at Gotha intervened. The old duke died on 29 January 1844. In spite of the infidelities which had driven out his wife, the dissolute ways, and improvidence, Albert never lost his love and respect for the old man.

Both Victoria and Albert experienced much anguish and grief, yet the prince knew that he must return to his first home to sort out Coburg affairs, which were in a state of disarray, especially the exchequer. His brother Ernest, the new duke, was already showing signs of the same dissolute behaviour and extravagance as his father.

'My darling stands so alone,' Victoria told Stockmar, 'and his grief is so great and touching...' But as poignant for Albert was the return to an earlier chapter in his life at the Rosenau with its secret woodlands, streams and waterfalls, which represented his happy childhood, when life was so much simpler and less demanding.

Albert was away for barely two weeks, yet every day without him was agony for the Queen, almost as if she were mourning son *and* father. So great was her suffering that the King and Queen of the Belgians came over to London to offer their company and comfort.

With the Gotha situation resolved and Albert back home, the royal couple were able to return their attention to a possible home on the Isle of Wight. The Prime Minister was helpful and recommended several properties that might be suitable, but it took many months before Peel discovered that an estate of some 1,000 acres and a pleasant old Georgian house, was for sale. The estate was at the east end of the island, high above the sea but with exclusive access to it.

They went down to see it in April 1845, and both Victoria and Albert were enchanted by the situation and the privacy it offered. Victoria wrote to Melbourne:

> It is impossible to see a prettier place, with wood and valleys, and *points de vue* which would be beautiful anywhere; but all this near the sea (the woods grow into the sea) is quite perfection; we have a charming beach quite to ourselves. The sea was so blue and so calm that the Prince said it was like Naples. And then we can walk about anywhere by ourselves without fear of being followed and mobbed, which Lord Melbourne will easily understand is delightful.

The name of the house was Osborne, and after some limited renovation, they spent a week there in October. Although there were sixteen bedrooms and sitting-rooms on two floors, plus servants' quarters, Albert decided that the accommodation was inadequate. This was confirmed when a Privy Council was held there and everyone complained about the lack of space. He persuaded a reluctant Victoria that they should demolish the old house and clear some of the land for an entirely new building.

Albert fancied himself as an architect and set about designing their holiday home with the utmost relish, forgetting temporarily about politics, the Corn Laws, the troubles in Ireland, and on the other side of the world: in New Zealand with the Maoris, and in western Canada with the Americans. The Queen observed with amused satisfaction Albert's absorbed dedication to their new house. She laid the first cornerstone on 23 June 1845, and the building proceeded rapidly. Albert commissioned Thomas Cubitt, who had built most of Belgravia in London and much else, to prepare the drawings and execute the work. It was all done to Albert's design, which in turn was inspired by the Italian style. Lady Lyttelton was a witness to Victoria and Albert's enthusiasm for the building work and also their concern for the workforce:

> I had a little conversation on the road to church with Prince Albert, and it was pleasant to see how earnestly he tries to do his best about this place, giving work to as many labourers as possible, but not making any haste, so as to make it last, and keep at a steady useful pitch, 'not to over excite the market'. His bailiff (I mean of course the Queen's) has dismissed quantities of men lately, because it is harvest time [June 1846], that they may work for others, telling them all that the moment any man is out of employment he is to come back here, and he will without fail find him work to do. This is doing good very wisely.

In its original form, Osborne House consisted of two ranges around an open courtyard, the whole dominated by two campanili, one at each end, but dissimilar in design and even height, one called the Flag Tower and the other the Clock Tower. Later additions tended to add to the impression that several architects had been at work and at odds with one another. It is only the sheer size of the building that gives any impression of majesty.

The main range, or pavilion wing, faced north-east and out to the sea and the Solent. On the ground floor were the billiards room, drawing-room and dining-room. The interior decoration, supervised by Ludwig Gruner and the prince, was dominated by imitation marble columns, a screen of them separating the drawing-room from the billiards room. There were also innumerable marble statues, including lifesize representations of the royal children.

In this wing of the house was the Horn Room, so-called for the good reason that the furniture was made from, or inlaid with, antler. The ceilings of all these ground-floor rooms were elaborately carved, with complex cornices.

On the first floor were the private apartments of the Queen and Prince Albert – bedrooms, dressing-rooms and sitting- and writing-rooms; above were the nurseries for their children and the bedrooms for the staff.

There were many novel features at Osborne. As in many of his London buildings, stucco was widely used by Cubitt to simulate stone, cast-iron girders replaced wooden beams, and a primitive form of central heating by hot air was installed. Another novelty for a royal house was the water closets.

The gardens in front fell away in terraces towards the sea and were as elaborate and Italianate as the house itself. 'The Prince was ably seconded by Mr Toward, our land steward for twenty-six years,' wrote the Queen. While Albert's official biographer (or hagiographer) declared that, 'His labours were amply repaid by the results. His plantations, rich in an unusual variety of conifers and flowering shrubs, gladdened his eyes by the vigorous luxuriance of their growth, and in them the nightingale "trilled her thick-warbled note the summer long".'

This main domestic range was completed with remarkable

speed and was ready for occupation by the middle of September 1846. The entire family with the staff hastened down to the Isle of Wight, crossing the Solent in their yacht, as they were to do many hundreds of times.

Lady Lyttelton, writing the day after they arrived, described their first night:

> Nobody caught cold or smelt paint, and it was a most amusing event the coming here. Everything in the house is quite new, and the dining room looked very handsome. The windows, lighted by the brilliant lamps in the room, must have been seen far out to sea. After dinner we rose to drink the Queen's and Prince's health as a *house-warming*, and after it the Prince said very naturally and simply, but seriously, 'We have a hymn (he called it a psalm) in Germany for such occasions. It begins' – and then he quoted two lines in German which I could not quote right, meaning a prayer to 'bless our going out and coming in'. It was dry and quaint, being Luther's; but we all perceived that he was feeling it. And truly entering a new house, a new place, it is a solemn thing to do.

At Osborne the children had their own elaborate playground, and a complete Swiss Cottage, midway in size between a doll's house and a normal-size house, imported in pre-fabricated form from Switzerland. Sometimes they invited their parents to tea. They had acres of woodland to explore, and, under supervision, went down to the beach to paddle in the sea.

Victoria developed a taste for the sea, too. A bathing machine was purchased and a launching ramp constructed upon which to run it. She mounted this machine for the first time in July 1847, along with her maid and several layers of bathing costumes into which she changed before being run down into the sea. She wrote:

> Drove down to the beach with my maid, & went into the bathing machine, where I undressed & bathed in the sea (for the first time in my life), a very nice bathing woman attended me. I thought it delightful till I put my head under the water, when I thought I should be stifled.

> How happy we are here! [Victoria enthused on another occasion]
> And never do I enjoy myself more, or more peacefully when I can
> be so much with my beloved Albert & follow him everywhere!

Not quite everywhere, perhaps, especially when she was pregnant, for Albert spent many happy hours supervising the farm, of which he was inordinately proud. The previous owner had taken little interest in the fields but Albert fancied himself as much of a farmer as an architect and interior decorator.

> We shall go [he writes to the Dowager Duchess of Coburg] on the 27th to the Isle of Wight for a week, where the fine air will be of service to Victoria and the children; and I, partly forester, partly builder, partly farmer, and partly gardener, expect to be a good deal upon my legs and in the open air.

Nothing gave Albert greater satisfaction than to improve Osborne farm (with help and advice) from the run-down condition in which they found it, into healthy profit.

Victoria's ideal activities at Osborne were picking strawberries (when in season) with her children, or relaxing on the beach or the garden terraces, perhaps with a book or with her children playing around her, watching her fleet at sea. There were constant movements of men-o'-war in the Solent or off Spithead, and she had a bird's-eye view of them. Sometimes a great seventy-four would slip away into the Channel, all sails set and sometimes smoke belching from a single funnel amidships, for the Royal Navy was in the throes of its long transition from sail to steam propulsion.

Queen Victoria never lost her love for Osborne, and was to die there more than half a century later. The main reason for her affection was that the place offered in equal measure security and freedom. 'Are you not amused at the difference between Windsor and Osborne?' the Hon Eleanor Stanley, one of the Queen's maids of honour, once wrote to her father. 'Here we may pleasure about in every direction, even along the public roads, they are so quiet, and we think nothing of *tête-à-tête* walks, a thing that would make everybody's hair stand on end at Windsor.'

Victoria's capacity for conceiving children never seemed to falter in the early years of her marriage: there were four in the first five years. After Bertie came Alice, on 25 April 1843. The children attracted the usual nicknames or abbreviations. In Alice's case, it was Fatima. She was also the first of the children to be vaccinated. The birth was straightforward. 'Thank God I am stronger and better this time,' Victoria noted, 'than either time before. My nerves are *so well* which I am most thankful for. My adored Angel has as usual, been *all* kindness and goodness, and dear Pussy a very delightful companion. She is very tender with her little sister, who is a pretty and large baby and we think will be the beauty of the family.'

For no particular recorded reason, Fatima's birth coincided with Pussy becoming Vicky, and The Boy, Bertie. Sixteen months later, another boy was born, to the Queen's immense satisfaction. She liked neatness, and two boys and two girls were tidy figures. His birth date was 6 August 1844, and he was named Alfred – or, inevitably, Affie.

The year 1845 proved to be a rest year from the birth of children, and it was not until May 1846 that a third girl, Helena (Lenchen), was born. Another 'rest year' followed and then on 18 March 1848 the Queen produced her sixth child, another girl, and a fine big one at that, who gave her mother a painful time. Victoria was not to know it, but there was to be only one more birth without the comfort of chloroform. At the christening, at which the baby was named Louise, the Duchess of Gloucester shocked all those present ('Imagine our horror!') by getting up in the middle of the service in order to kneel at the feet of the Queen.

Three weeks after the birth of Louise, a Chartist crisis hit London, with nine thousand soldiers on the streets and artillery at strategic points. A revolution as formidable as that in France was feared. The royal family was the obvious first target for the violence of these republicans, and on 8 April the newly-opened Waterloo station was cleared of passengers while the entire royal family embarked on a train. It headed without delay for Gosport, where the party embarked for Osborne. Never were Victoria and Albert more thankful for their decision to choose the Isle of Wight for their retreat. (In the event, by tactful government handling and the good sense of Chartist leadership, the massive demonstration dispersed in pouring rain later that day.)

The key figure in the upbringing of Victoria and Albert's early children was Lady Lyttelton. She had survived all the changes in the ladies of the Queen's bedchamber, and, with the Duchess of Sutherland, was the closest to the Queen of all the members of the court. She was utterly reliable, loyal and good humoured, and in 1842 was the obvious choice to manage the royal nurseries. Lady Lyttelton fully justified the confidence placed in her.

'Had Pussy with us for nearly an hour,' wrote the Queen in January 1842, 'and she was so funny and amusing. She is so fond of her dear Papa, running up to him and calling to him in such an endearing little way. My dearest Albert is so fond of her too.'

The reason for the special closeness between this father and his first child was Albert's belief that he could never be accepted as an Englishman until he had fathered a child. It is possible that Victoria was unconsciously jealous of the intimacy between father and daughter and that this bright little girl sensed it. Certainly, almost until Vicky married there was a lack of communication between mother and daughter. 'I was often such a plague to you,' she wrote after her wedding, expressing surprise that her mother missed her so much.

If Vicky was the Princess Royal, with much to live up to, Bertie as heir to the crown was made to feel that he carried all the burdens of the world on his shoulders. From his birth, his parents' expectations were unreasonable. His mother's insistence that he should resemble his father *in every particular*, and his father's severity and refusal to see anything but the worst in the boy, were hard to bear. Fortunately Bertie had a cheerful and optimistic disposition and suffered the penalties of his position philosophically.

At the same time he had a sensitive nature with a great need for love. This was provided by the woman closest to him during his nursery years, Lady Lyttelton. When he was six, she reported on his

> kindness and nobleness of mind. His sister [Alice] had been lately often in disgrace and his little attentions and feeling on the sad occasions have been very nice – never losing sight of her, through a longish imprisonment in her own room, and stealing to the door to give a kind message, or tell a morsel of pleasant news – his own toys quite neglected, and his lovely face quite pale, till the disgrace was over.

Although there were no hard feelings between the first two children, even if Vicky with her superior intellect sometimes teased Bertie and mocked his stammer, the bond between Bertie and Alice was very marked.

Alice was also close to her father, who described her as 'an extraordinarily good and merry child'. This only emphasised further Bertie's feeling of isolation, especially as these two favourite daughters were both ahead of him in lessons.

There were many comparative accounts of the merits of Victoria and Albert's first three children. Albert even conceived the notion of charging a notable phrenologist of the time, Mr George Combe, to study the children's cerebral qualities. In spite of the later discrediting of phrenology, there is no doubt of the accuracy of his conclusions about the first two girls. Alice was nine, Vicky twelve when he wrote that Alice

> will be less apt in learning the details of knowledge from observation and instruction, but she will, in time, go deeper and further than the Princess Royal in discovering the causes and consequences of actions and events. She may at present appear more dull in intellect than the Princess Royal; but, in time, she will

become intelligent in her own way, and may advance further, in a higher sphere of knowledge than her sister.

Gerard Noel in the only biography of Princess Alice, perceptively noted:

If the Princess Royal got her way through a combination of charm and the exercise of strong feelings, Alice had a quieter and often more subtle way of making herself appealing to others. She had the almost waif-like quality of one who was as merry as any at games and larking, but there was a certain sadness in the fine lines of her angular face, and her deep-set dark eyes.

Of the first four children, Prince Alfred stands out the least vividly. Because it became clear that Duke Ernest would have no children, and Bertie would inherit the British crown, under the complex rules of primogeniture Albert's second son would inherit the Coburg dukedom. For this reason, Albert decreed that Alfred 'shall from his youth be taught to love the dear country to which he belongs in every respect as does his Papa'. Victoria found the boy 'attentive and intelligent' and 'easier and pleasanter to teach than any of the others'. Affie joined the navy, rose to the highest rank, and finally inherited the dukedom in 1893.

Never in the history of the British monarchy had so much time and thought been invested in the education of the royal children. This was just as well. Victoria and Albert produced nine children and the complications in bringing them up were almost infinite. The Queen expressed her wishes thus: 'A good, moral, religious but *not bigoted* or narrow-minded education is what I pray for, for my children.' But their destinies were bound to be different. The Princess Royal was likely to go to Prussia, to marry the heir to the throne. Bertie as heir to the British throne required a different emphasis in his education – constitutional history for example, and fluency in at least two foreign languages. Alice, too, was almost certain to marry into some kingdom, princedom or dukedom. Alfred, almost from birth, had his future mapped out.

As governess, Lady Lyttelton managed her increasing

number of charges for their early years, and very good she was, too. But from the beginning she found it difficult to handle Bertie. His concentration span was negligible, and the more difficulty he experienced in keeping up with Alice, not to mention Vicky, the more riotous he became, 'getting under the table, upsetting the books and sundry other *anti-studious* practices', as his governess noted. As some sort of compensation, Lady Lyttelton admired his drawing, his charm and 'lovely mildness of expression'.

After much consultation with Stockmar, it was decided, in the words of his mother, that Bertie should be 'taken *entirely away* from the women'. A male tutor was therefore found for this troublesome heir to the throne – Mr Henry Birch from Eton. He reported on his charge that he was 'wilful, recalcitrant, extremely disobedient, impertinent and unwilling to submit to discipline'. However, Birch made some progress, and most notably earned the reward of Bertie's affection and respect.

This growing compatibility between man and boy was viewed with deep suspicion by Albert. Although he had loved his own tutor, Herr Florschütz, the serenity of his son's relationship with Birch suggested that insufficient work was being done. To Bertie's dismay, Birch was despatched back to Eton, to be replaced by Frederick Gibbs, who was ordered to raise the study hours to seven a day, six days a week. Bertie loathed him from the beginning: there were terrible rows and little learning.

One of the reasons for Bertie's tantrums and obstreperous behaviour, completely unrecognised by his mother, father, or by Stockmar, was that he rarely mixed with any boys of his own age by whom to set his standards of both behaviour and attainment, and there was no healthy competition. Occasionally, a few carefully chosen boys were invited over to Windsor from Eton. These meetings became confrontations in which Bertie sought to establish his superiority – often with his fists. This led to complaints and the cessation of the short-lived arrangement. But at least one lifelong friendship was formed with one of these boys, Charles Carrington, later Marquis of Lincolnshire, who wrote perceptively of his observations of the two oldest princes:

> [they] were strictly treated and brought up – Prince Alfred was the favourite, but I always liked the Prince of Wales far the best. He had such an open generous disposition and the kindest heart imaginable. He was a very plucky boy and always ready for fun, which often got him into scrapes. He was afraid of his father, who seemed a proud shy stand-offish sort of a man not calculated to make friends with children – individually I was frightened to death of him.

Charles Carrington should have confined his strictures to Albert's inability to make friends with boys. With girls it was quite a different story; Albert lavished attention on his first-born. In the early days of babyhood he spent so much time dandling Vicky on his knee that he could rightly claim to have witnessed her first smile and discovered her first tooth. Yet Vicky could be as rebellious as Bertie and, like him, had inherited the passionate feelings and emotions of their mother.

Stockmar was among those who tried to tame Vicky's emotional extremes. 'Know thyself' this well-intentioned old bore used to reiterate to her, with little effect. Vicky remained highly strung all her life. She was cleverer than her younger brother, but not much, and not deserving of the doting affection of her father in contrast to his unfeeling treatment of Bertie.

The one person who thoroughly understood the Princess Royal was Lady Lyttelton. From her earliest talking days Pussy called Lady Lyttelton 'Laddle', and was herself called Princessy.

The Queen encouraged Vicky's talent for drawing, and mother and daughter could be found side by side, mixing paints together. Albert inspired her talent for music and appointed a one-time concert pianist to give her formal lessons. Vicky loved to watch and listen to her father play on his great organ, later turning the pages of the music for him. Her biographer, Daphne Bennett, wrote that,

She heard Mendelssohn play on that very organ, but was too young at the time to appreciate him, although by a curious trick of memory she could remember her father showing the great musician how to work the stops and could even recall the tune of the few chords he played ... Later she came to enjoy Mendelssohn's oratorios as much as her father.

Inevitably, Vicky developed beyond the range of Laddle's capacity as a teacher, and a Miss Hildyard arrived as a full-time governess. Vicky responded to this clever teacher and grew fond of her. Tantrums became rarer.

Vicky was an interesting girl, short in stature, but prettier than her mother. 'A child with strong feelings', as one of her relations described her. Others spoke of a half-hidden element of melancholy in her dark eyes, as if she suffered portents of tragedy in her life.

Alice soon lost her unseemly nickname of Fatima, conceived by her father, who attempted to compensate by referring to her as 'the favourite' in a letter to Stockmar. He did not add whose favourite, and it is difficult to imagine any of his daughters attracting love and admiration equal to what he felt for Vicky.

Although to a lesser degree than Bertie, Alice felt deeply a sense of intellectual inferiority to her elder sister, who was inclined to flaunt her success at lessons. Alice was of a gentler disposition altogether. Gerard Noel cites a typical tale, told by a dresser to the Queen:

> I remember well meeting the Royal children in the corridor, and, as I passed on the Prince of Wales making a joke about my great height, the Princess [Alice] said to her brothers, so that I should hear it: 'It is very nice to be tall...' Whenever she in the least suspected that anyone's feelings had been hurt, she always tried to make things smooth again.

Alice's affection for her elder brother remained throughout her life, and when Bertie was close to death in 1871, it was Alice who took control of the nursing, found a more suitable doctor for his typhoid fever and may well have saved his life.

She early developed a natural talent for nursing the sick, and when the wounded came back from the Crimean War, she would accompany her mother on visits to the hospital wards.

Prince Alfred showed every sign of being the least inhibited of the first four children. He was also the most cheerful, and exhibited two strong characteristics: his love and admiration for his elder brother, and complete fearlessness. He loved sliding down banisters, regardless of danger. At the age of only five he practised tremendous slides at Buckingham Palace, falling off the banister and immediately trying again. This activity terrified his father, and Affie once concussed himself quite badly.

Affie was as unsatisfactory in his lessons as Bertie. Albert, worried that the younger boy would pick up what he thought were Bertie's wilful tantrums, had them separated in the schoolroom and as far as possible outside it, too. This greatly angered both his sons, and was seen by some critics as evidence of Albert's failure to understand his boys while over-sentimentalising his girls.

There is a case to be made for this view, as many biographers have claimed. Daphne Bennett reveals herself as an exception in this summarising paragraph:

> Albert's love for his children, and particularly for the Prince of Wales, has often been denied; most recently, for instance, Mrs Woodham-Smith* has written that Bertie would have bloomed had he been reared in 'an atmosphere of affection, warmth and admiration'. There is, however, a large amount of reliable evidence that he was brought up in just such an atmosphere: Lady Lyttelton, Lady Bloomfield, Eleanor Stanley, Baron Bunsen, Mr Gladstone and Lord Broughton all testify to the love which both the royal parents bore their children and to the children's close rapport with them.

Roger Fulford is another biographer who takes a similar sympathetic view of Albert's relations with his children, also

---

* Cecil Woodham-Smith, *Queen Victoria*, Vol 1, 1972 Daphne Bennett, *King without a Crown*, 1977

citing comments by Lady Lyttelton of his romping with them and playing hide and seek with Vicky and Bertie. 'He is so kind to them,' noted Victoria, 'and romps with them so delightfully, and manages them so beautifully and firmly.'

There is no reason to doubt these sources, highly prejudiced though they must be. Both Victoria and Albert discovered (like most mothers and fathers) that parenthood grows more difficult and complicated in step with age. No one can doubt that these royal parents were loving, but equally it cannot be denied that they both made some terrible errors of judgement, especially with their boys, and in particular with Bertie for whom they felt the greatest responsibility.

The royal family at home: a peep into the private apartments.
Queen Victoria holding Princess Alice, Prince Albert
playing with the Prince of Wales (*left*) and the Princess Royal

CHAPTER SEVEN

The Great Exhibition

Early in Victoria and Albert's marriage, Melbourne once shrewdly observed to Albert's secretary, Anson, 'The Prince is bored with the sameness of his chess every evening. He would like to bring literary and scientific people about the Court, vary the society, and infuse a more useful tendency into it. The Queen however has no fancy to encourage such people. This arises from a feeling on her part that her education has not fitted her to take part in such conversation; she would not like conversation to be going on in which she could not take her fair share, and she is far too open and candid in her nature to pretend to one atom more knowledge than she really possesses on such subjects . . .'

But as the astute old Melbourne added, the Queen was fluent in German and French, and wrote both languages well. Besides understanding Italian, she had learnt Latin. 'The rest of her education,' he concluded, 'she owes to her own natural shrewdness and quickness, and this perhaps has not been the proper education for one who was to wear the crown of England.'

Although they differed over after-dinner conversation, they were both incorrigible romantics. One of the features that had drawn them to Osborne was the view of the sea, which reminded Albert of the bay of Naples. The Solent even displayed great British men-o'-war as a reminder of Admiral Nelson's days at Naples after the battle of the Nile. Osborne House remained a loved private home for all their lives, but it did lack the inaccessibility and isolation after which Victoria always hankered. Nor was the sea air as bracing as they had both expected.

They often talked about north Britain after their first visit to Scotland in 1842, and determined on a second expedition. So two years later in June 1844 they boarded the *Victoria and Albert* and sailed for Dundee. They had been invited to the castle of Blair Atholl in the heart of the Highlands. The Queen wrote in her Journal that 'the scenery is lovely, grand, romantic, and a great peace and wildness pervades all, which is sublime.' As before, Albert totally agreed.

'Romantic' was also applied to the view from the top of a high hill which they both ascended, escorted only by a Scotsman 'in his highland dress'. Scotland was suddenly seizing them in a grip even more tenacious than that of the Isle of Wight. 'Not a house, not a creature near us, but the pretty Highland sheep with their horns and black faces . . .' The Queen's uplifted spirits lasted even when she was on her way home. Highlanders, she exclaimed, are 'such a chivalrous, fine, active people'.

Three more years passed before Victoria and Albert could find time from affairs of state and childbirth to visit Scotland again. During this period, their minds and conversation often returned to the Highlands. Victoria, who had always enjoyed the novels of Walter Scott, re-read several of them. Then at last, in the summer of 1847, they managed to get away, this time intent on visiting the west coast. In stormy conditions they sailed in their yacht up the Irish Sea, landing at Fort William, to be guests of Lord Abercorn in a large fishing lodge at Ardverikie on the south shore of Loch Laggan.

It was raining when they arrived and the rain continued almost non-stop for the next two weeks. Victoria had never minded getting wet, but Albert hated it and became depressed. They did learn during this visit that only fifty miles to the east, on the other side of the highest mountains, the sun was out and there had been hardly any rain that summer. Deeside was saved from the torrential rain of the west by the Central Highlands, which attracted it. By an astonishing chance, just at this time Sir Robert Gordon, the leaseholder of a Deeside property – an imitation castle called Balmoral – dropped dead over his breakfast. Balmoral was inherited by Lord Aberdeen, recently Foreign Secretary and well known to the Queen. He was fully aware of Victoria and Albert's search for a suitable Scottish property.

Victoria and Albert had recently returned from sodden Ardverikie, and when told of Balmoral – graphically and in detail with some paintings – they precipitately made an offer for the remainder of the leasehold.

Thus, by early 1848, while Europe burst into the flames of revolution, Victoria and Albert became the owners of a Scottish property about as far from those troubles as could be imagined.

Leaving behind a host of unresolved problems, most concerning foreign policy, the Queen with Prince Albert and their first four children, set out in the *Victoria and Albert*, north to Aberdeen to inspect the new property. They arrived at Balmoral early in the afternoon of 8 September 1848. What the children made of the spectacular landscape was not recorded, although from this time they were all eager to go north. The boys, even little Alfred, donned kilts in the 'Balmoral tartan' designed by Albert, and worn by the royal family to this day.

After a late, light lunch, Victoria and Albert climbed a nearby hill to look down on the castle. She later wrote in her Journal, 'To the left you look towards the beautiful hills surrounding Loch-na-Gar [the highest point for many miles], and to the right towards Ballater, to the glen along which the Dee winds, with beautiful wooded hills ... It was so calm, and so solitary, it did one good as one gazed around; and the pure mountain air was most refreshing...'

Victoria's letter to Uncle Leopold a few days later was equally lyrical:

This house is small but pretty ... the scenery all around is the finest almost I have seen anywhere. It is very wild and solitary, and yet cheerful and *beautifully wooded* . . . Then the soil is the driest and best known almost anywhere, and all the hills are as sound and hard as the road. The climate is also dry, and in general not very cold . . . There is a deer forest – many roe deer, and on the opposite hill . . . grouse. There is also black cock and ptarmigan . . . The children are very well, and enjoying themselves very much.

Albert as instantly and completely fell in love with Balmoral and Deeside. 'We have withdrawn for a short time into a complete mountain solitude where one rarely sees a human face,' he wrote, 'where the snow already covers the mountain tops, and the wild deer come creeping round the house.' It was not long before Albert had stalked and shot one of those deer, and much else besides.

In an equally short time, Albert was planning first to improve and enlarge their property, after purchasing the free-hold, and then, as at Osborne, to demolish the whole edifice and build a new castle. He also had his eye on the forest of Ballochbuie and the Abergeldie and Birkhall estates. His ambitions were not diminishing with the passing years, as his brother Ernest noted sardonically when he visited Balmoral. Albert's claim that the hills and forests would remind Ernest of Thuringia was predictably pooh-poohed.

The building works at Osborne, and later at Balmoral, were strictly domestic. The public had the opportunity of seeing and admiring them, especially the more accessible Osborne House, but they made no impact on the nation as a whole. But Prince Albert, an Englishman for ten years by the middle of the century, had far broader ambitions. In that decade a great deal had happened to him personally. Where he had once been the object of suspicion as an impecunious foreign prince, he was now respected by the greater part of the people. Only the aristocracy remained suspicious and mocking, although they had reluctantly to concede that he was a fair shot and fearless on the hunting field.

At a more serious level he was soon in demand as a public speaker. His first speech was made as early as 1 June 1840, at a meeting of the Society for the Abolition of Slavery. Although slavery had been abolished in British possessions since 1833, it still flourished in many parts of the world. 'I sincerely trust that this great country,' Albert appealed to his audience, 'will not relax in its efforts until it has finally, and for ever, put an end to a state of things, so repugnant to the spirit of Christianity, and the best feelings of our nature.'

By 1848 he was president of a number of worthy organisations, many of them – too many argued his critics – in support of the underdog. Albert gladly became first president of the Society for Improving the Conditions of the Labouring Classes, which had very practical aims and achievements. In much of his philanthropic activities, he worked closely with Lord Ashley, the future Earl of Shaftesbury, for whom he had the highest regard.

Albert's causes were widespread and by no means restricted to charitable and philanthropic enterprises. His speeches reflect the diversity of his activities: to a conference on National Education, at the opening of the Exhibition of Art Treasures, at Birmingham 'On the Occasion of Laying the First Stone of the Birmingham and Midland Institute'; at the Exhibition of Art Treasures of the United Kingdom at Manchester; at the opening of the Clothworkers' Hall in the City of London; or the opening of the International Statistical Congress. It was not always easy to be lively and fluent on some of these occasions, but Albert did his best to introduce a challenging note even if there were not many laughs.

The speech for which Albert is best remembered and for which he deserves the most credit was delivered on 21 March 1850 at the banquet given by the Lord Mayor of London for, among others, foreign ambassadors and 'The Mayors of one hundred and eighty Towns'.

My Lord Mayor –
I am sincerely grateful for the kindness with which you have proposed my health, and, to you, gentlemen, for the cordiality with which you have received this proposal.
It must indeed be most gratifying to me to find that a

suggestion which I had thrown out, as appearing to me of importance at this time, should have met with such universal concur-
rence and approbation ...

The proposal to which Albert referred was for a Great
Exhibition of the contemporary arts, industry and science of
the time, an exhibition open to all nations, a celebration of the
industrial revolution, of which Britain was the world leader by
a wide margin.

During the space of the Queen's lifetime, the face and
wealth of the nation had been transformed by the enterprise,
inventiveness and industry of the people. In the field of transport, even before the elaborate canal network had been completed, the first main line railways had been constructed,
providing industry with communications and the priceless
advantage of swift mobility. New machines and the ease of
transporting the products resulted in a great rise in agricultural
prosperity. Thanks to ever-more efficient steam power, the
textile and iron and steel industries doubled and redoubled
their production. Surplus agricultural labour was encouraged
to leave the land and find work in the growing industrial
towns. The population increased rapidly. The nation's financial system was geared to cope with the prosperity from all
this new enterprise.

In short, for the first time in the nation's history, every
aspect of its life converged, from the limitless overseas demand
for the products of British industry, to the people's buoyant
spirit of optimism and enterprise. Was there not cause
for celebration? It was an irony of the Victorian age that
the positive answer to this notional question was uttered
most firmly by a German prince in an adopted country. Or
perhaps it was his detachment as a foreigner that led him to
appreciate the immensity of British achievement. The genesis
of the Great Exhibition lay, ironically enough, in earlier
German and French exhibitions. The Paris *Exposition*
of 1849, following so soon after the troubles of 1848, was
greatly admired, but it was purely national in its nature. Albert

1 Victoria's father, Edward, Duke of Kent.   2 Victoria's mother, Victoria, Princess of Saxe-Coburg, Duchess of Kent.   3 Albert's father, Duke Ernest of Saxe-Coburg-Saalfeld.   4 Albert's mother, Princess Louise of Saxe-Gotha-Altenburg

5 Albert at the age of 13.
6 Victoria at the age of 14.
7 Victoria is now Queen: she is
brought the news by the Lord
Chamberlain, Lord
Conyngham, and Archbishop
Howley

8 Queen Victoria's coronation.
9 Sir Edwin Landseer's portrait
of Victoria on horseback, the
one place where her diminutive
height was concealed

10 The wedding: Albert looked 'splendidly handsome'; Victoria 'wore a dress of rich white satin, trimmed with orange flower blossoms and with a broad flounce of lace'

11 Victoria, twenty years old, sketched in her wedding dress

12 The Queen's sketch of Lord Melbourne

13 The handsome William Lamb, 2nd Viscount Melbourne, upon whom the Queen so depended, especially before her marriage

14 A romantic if improbable rendering of Albert as a medieval knight. Victoria loved it

15 Albert sketched by his wife in the year of their marriage

16 Portrait of the royal family by
Winterhalter, 1846. Children (left to
right): Alfred, Albert Edward, Prince
of Wales, Alice, Baby Helena,
Victoria
17 Photograph by Roger Fenton of
the children at Windsor on
10 February 1854, Victoria and
Albert's 14th wedding anniversary, at
which they gave their parents a
rendering of James Thomson's The
Seasons. (Left to right): Princess
Alice as Spring; Victoria and Arthur
as Summer; Helena as the Spirit of
the Empress Helena; Alfred as
Autumn; Louise and Albert Edward
as Winter

18 Photograph of
Victoria and Albert with
their nine children at
Osborne

Life in the Highlands:
19 Bringing the stags home to Balmoral
20 A view of Balmoral rebuilt in 1855

21 Victoria and Albert in early middle age

22 The blue room at Windsor
Castle, where Albert died on
14 December 1861
23 Queen Victoria and her
daughters Alice and Louise
with Albert's portrait
24 Victoria planting a memorial
oak to Albert in Windsor Great
Park in 1862
25 The Royal Mausoleum,
Frogmore

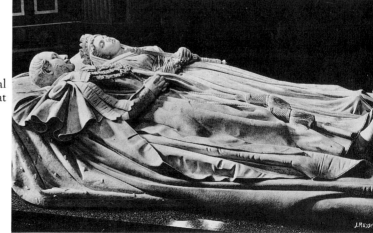

himself recalled from his childhood the excitement of the German Frankfurt Fairs, but these, too, were national and on a much smaller scale than what he envisaged for London.

For several years Albert had worked with the assistant keeper of the Public Records, Henry Cole. A man of affairs much respected for his acumen, Cole was a typical product of his time, enterprising and with wide-ranging interests. His official title concealed a host of other activities. He was greatly influential in the introduction of the penny post by Sir Rowland Hill in 1840, and was one of those men who recognised the ludicrous incongruity of developing the railway system with two different gauges of line.

Albert and Cole probably first met as co-members of the Society of Arts soon after Cole was accepted for membership in 1846. They found they had numerous common interests, and between them organised a series of exhibitions on design in industry, which attracted much admiring attention.

Cole visited the French *Exposition* of 1849, and returned bursting with enthusiasm and a desire to create something even more exciting for Britain. He at once inspired an equal passion in Prince Albert. Cole can rightly claim to co-sponsorship of the Great Exhibition, but it was Albert who shaped the concept by insisting on its *international* nature – a 'great exhibition of industry of *all* nations'.

The Royal Society of Arts (it had just received its royal charter) embraced the idea with tremendous enthusiasm. But would industry? We must find out, insisted Albert; and despatched Cole and the secretary of the society on an extensive tour of the industrial districts of Britain 'in order to collect the opinions of the leading manufacturers'. To add weight to their survey they were armed with a personal letter from Albert. The ever-ebullient Cole returned to London with, he claimed, pledges of support from '5,000 influential persons'.

By the autumn of 1849 it was clear that the envisaged size and scope of the exhibition had gone far beyond the capacity of the Royal Society of Arts. Albert therefore approached the

Prime Minister, Lord John Russell, and his Cabinet with a view to setting up a royal commission. This was agreed. Moreover, the Prime Minister and several of his ministers were prepared to serve on it, along with Gladstone and Cobden, and great figures in civil engineering and architecture, like Sir Charles Barry whose new Palace of Westminster – the Houses of Parliament – had recently been completed.

The commission met for the first time on 3 January 1850. They had no more than eighteen months to prepare, design and construct the venue for the exhibition. At a time when railway lines, great bridges and tunnels and large factories were commonly completed within two years or less, this was not considered all that remarkable an undertaking. Nor would it have been had not an opposition been mounted to the whole enterprise.

The size of the original venue, Leicester Square, was soon seen to be entirely inadequate for what Cole and Prince Albert had in mind. It was Cole who made the daring suggestion that the exhibition should be held in Hyde Park. Albert agreed and the Queen, who had been following the progress of Albert's enterprise with keen interest, gave her permission for the use of this royal park. Covering 340 acres, it was the setting for numerous parades and duels, public celebrations and the daily fashion of riding in Rotten Row. Hyde Park was traditionally a place of relaxation for the common people while the *haut monde* used it to show off their presence, their carriages and *equipages*.

When the commission's plans were made known, there was a great outcry. Questions were asked in Parliament and *The Times* struck a hostile attitude. 'I doubt if London will be *habitable*,' complained one opponent. Vagrants, thieves, pickpockets and prostitutes would haunt the park. The opposition intensified when plans were made public of the building proposed to house the exhibition. It was to be an immense edifice made from no fewer than 19 million bricks, topped by a gigantic dome designed by the railway engineer Isambard Kingdom Brunel. Colonel Charles Sibthorpe, an old adversary of Albert, pronounced in Parliament that it would be 'one of the greatest frauds, greatest humbugs, greatest absurdities ever known ... that accursed building'.

One of the prime purposes of the exhibition was to improve industrial design, and the hideous appearance of the proposed building did nothing to further this aim. The plans also gave an impression of permanence and would require the destruction of numerous mature elm and other trees. *Punch* contributed a quatrain:

> Albert! Spare those trees,
> Mind where you fix your show;
> For mercy's sake, don't please,
> Go spoiling Rotten Row.

No fewer than 245 designs were submitted in all. Only one or two, including one French submission, were considered seriously. Then there arrived at the commission's offices a set of drawings of a structure unlike any of the others, striking rather than eccentric, breathtakingly graceful in its configuration. The plans came from forty-nine-year-old Joseph Paxton, gardener to the Duke of Devonshire at his Chiswick and Chatsworth estates. At Chatsworth Paxton had designed and built a remarkably beautiful and outsize conservatory, or lily house, for *Victoria Regina*, an enormous species of water lily from British Guiana. He had the good sense to send a duplicate set of his submitted plans and drawings to the *Illustrated London News*, the widest read weekly magazine, which published them eagerly.

The materials, as for Paxton's conservatories, were simply iron and glass, columns and girders of cast-iron, each set forming a square of twenty-four feet. These could be extended upwards or sideways, all prefabricated and lifted into position, which provided for rapid construction and disassembly when required. The centre or transept section, above the main entrance, was raised and topped by a semi-circular tube of the same material. The structure covered eighteen acres, was 300 feet long and 64 feet high, the transept high enough to clear all the trees, which would remain embraced, untouched and unpruned, like giant shrubs.

Paxton's plans created a sensation, and his name ranked with Cole's and Albert's in the credits for the exhibition. *Punch* named the building the Crystal Palace.

Albert's committee unanimously accepted the Paxton design, terms were agreed on 26 July, and the materials immediately ordered. The first column was standing two months later, and it took just three months to complete the entire Palace. Some 4,500 tons of cast-iron, 300,000 panes of glass, and many acres of wooden flooring were used in the construction. All criticism had long since died. 'The Times has had to back out of the position it took up about the Park,' wrote Albert triumphantly to Stockmar.

Victoria and Albert with all of their children arrived to inspect the Crystal Palace on 18 February 1851. The Queen was amazed and enchanted, and never more proud of her beloved Albert. She described it, for once without hyperbole, as 'one of the wonders of the world, which we English may indeed be proud of'.

The Duke of Devonshire was equally impressed. 'Fancy one's gardener having done all this,' he was heard to mutter.

The Queen had heard of one puzzling problem. What about all the sparrows trapped inside, and the mess their droppings would make on the exhibits? This had been anticipated and dealt with, or so it seemed. 'Sparrowhawks, ma'am,' came the Duke of Wellington's succinct reply. It was true, and it worked.

The galleries were divided into four categories, by Albert personally: raw materials, mechanical inventions, manufactures and works of art.

The Queen, with Albert in attendance, made several more visits to the Crystal Palace as the last touches were made and more and more exhibits arrived from near and distant parts of Britain, the Continent, and farther afield, especially the United States and Canada.

May Day – 1 May 1851 – had been chosen as the day of

the opening ceremony, leaving the whole summer ahead for the arrival of visitors from home and abroad. The Queen in a dress of pink watered silk, alongside Albert in the full dress uniform of a field marshal, flanked by their two eldest children, drove out from Buckingham Palace at 11.30 a.m. It was drizzling, but not enough to cool the ardour of some 200,000 people between Buckingham Palace and the Crystal Palace a mile or more distant. On arrival there were already 300,000 paying customers under the glass, making close to a half million spectators cheering their heads off – 'one densely crowded mass of human beings in the highest good humour and most enthusiastic,' wrote the Queen that night. 'Just as we approached the Crystal Palace the sun shone and gleamed upon the gigantic edifice, upon which the flags of all nations were floating, while inside the fresh green of the new leaves of the fully-grown elm trees added a background touch of colour.'

It was an event which neatly matched William Makepeace Thackeray's 'May Day Ode' published only that morning:

> As though 'twere by a wizard's rod
> A blazing arch of lucid glass
> Leaps like a fountain from the grass
> To meet the sun.

Once inside the transept Albert became the leading host to the Queen, along with all the grandees of the commission, shiny top hats and the jewellery of the wives glinting in the sun.

After a brief speech of welcome, and the inauguration ceremony, the royal party proceeded around the galleries. Not all the products from abroad were unpacked and mounted, but they could examine admiringly the 'tastefully ornamented' sleigh of M'Lean and Wright of Montreal, the gold and silver products of Sazikoff of Moscow, more prosaically Geiss of Berlin's zinc castings, and Bottinelli of Milan's carved marble chimney piece. Clocks with cherubs were numerous, as were Scottish deer hunters, horn to lips, with horse, dog and victim beneath, all rendered in silver.

Cornelius and Baker of Philadelphia showed an immense gas chandelier, Leclercq of Brussels an even bigger and more elaborate sculptured chimney piece. Nearer home, Yates & Haywood of Rotherham displayed an ornamental stove featuring numerous carved cherubs, fruit and other decorative work. There were ornamental carriages from Birmingham, ornamental iron bedsteads from Paris, a threshing machine from the United States, and several locomotives including Daniel Gooch's magnificent new *Lord of the Isles* broad gauge.

To our eyes a hundred and fifty years later, the only features in tolerable taste were the numerous fountains, some of the statues dotted about the galleries, the elm trees in fresh spring leaf, and the Crystal Palace itself. But that was not the contemporary judgement. There was an essay competition with hundreds of entries. The first prize went to the author of 'The Exhibition as a Lesson in Taste'.

The Queen evidently agreed with such sentiment. Two days later she wrote to her Uncle Leopold:

> I wish you *could* have witnessed the 1st *May* 1851, the *greatest* day in our history, the *most beautiful* and *imposing* and *touching* spectacle ever seen, and the triumph of my beloved Albert. Truly it was astonishing, a fairy scene ... It was the *happiest, proudest* day in my life, and I can think of nothing else. Albert's dearest name is immortalised with this *great* conception, *his* own, and triumph is *immense*.

Perhaps 'the *greatest* day in our history' was something of an exaggeration: the past fifty years alone had seen Nelson's victory at Trafalgar in 1805, and ten years later, on 18 June, the victory of Waterloo had changed the course of history – and there, rather old and bent now, was the man who had made that victory possible, the Duke of Wellington himself. But it was certainly a *great* day in Britain's history, attested to by the tears of pride shared by many as they entered the Crystal Palace for the first time. The Home Secretary and many others wept unashamedly and so did several other ministers. The Colt Company of the United States displayed a number of its guns and revolvers, but that was the only sign of violence along the galleries, for above all this was, as Albert intended it to be, a celebration of peace. The revolutions of the past few years were over; at home there had been no more Chartist riots, peace and prosperity, reflected by the sun through Paxton's glass, seemed to have settled over the western world. The Prime Minister, Lord John Russell, wrote a letter of congratulation to Albert when he returned to his office. The prince replied,

My dear Lord John,
    Many thanks for your letter and congratulations upon the wonderful success of yesterday. The sight was ample repayment for any trouble during the last two years, but most I hope from the beneficial effects which the contemplation of the works brought together will have upon the different nations who contributed them.

During the five summer months of 1851, over six million people entered the Crystal Palace. The great majority of them were British, and they noticed that the great majority of the exhibits were British or imperial. Albert had intended the Great Exhibition to be an international demonstration of the advance of man in the arts and science, industry and invention. A deserved success it certainly was. At the time Albert did not see it, as did Victoria's subjects, as a demonstration of national self-aggrandisement, a demonstration to the world of British superiority and leadership, and a celebration of the British industrial revolution.

It soon became clear that there would be a profit, and a considerable one – in the event £180,000, which to this day subsidises scholarships for young students in the arts and science. It is hard to judge what the prince would have thought of the Albert Memorial designed by George Gilbert Scott after the prince's death. He would probably have approved. He certainly did not underrate his contribution to the Great Exhibition, or any other of his achievements for that matter.

He would certainly have approved of the Albert Hall on the other side of the road, though not of the famous 'echo' discovered by the conductor of the first concert, but now substantially cured.

On the other hand, Prince Albert never failed to give credit when it was due. He knew how great was his debt to Paxton, and this rough diamond of a gardener who dropped his aitches, to the amusement of the Queen, received a knighthood. To Henry Cole, who became a KCB, Albert wrote, 'You have been one of the few who originated the design, became its exponent to the public, and fought its battles in adversity, and belong now to those who share in its triumphs.'

Apart from the scholarships, which have benefited so many students over the past century and a half, under the guidance of Albert and with the profit derived from the exhibition, land was acquired south of the Albert Hall for the construction over the years ahead of a complex of buildings, of varying architectural quality, but fulfilling the prince's dream of great museums. He did not live to see any of them but the Natural History Museum, the Science Museum, the Imperial College of Science and Technology and the magnificent Victoria and Albert Museum all owe their existence to the Great Exhibition and its chief founder.

It had been agreed from the start that the sacred acres of Hyde Park would be restored when the exhibition was over. Enamoured of his own achievement, Paxton fought a brief battle to keep the Crystal Palace where it was as a permanent conservatory and aviary. But the commissioners were obliged to fulfil their promise. The government sold the building to the highest bidder. The Crystal Palace was therefore disassembled with the same facility as it had been erected, and moved to Sydenham in south London. Here in enlarged and modified form it became the centre of an amusement park, serving at different times as menagerie, concert hall, theatre, opera house and exhibition hall – again.

With the removal of the Crystal Palace from central London, Albert was deprived of the tangible evidence of his greatest achievement. Something was lost to him, some spark of inspiration was drained away. He continued to espouse new causes and throw himself into campaigns, but they exacted a higher price. Both his nerves and his physical condition deteriorated and were never completely regained.

The Crystal Palace mysteriously burnt down on the night of 30 November 1936. People were puzzled how an erection of iron and glass could burn so freely.* But all the floors and much else were dry timber, and there were many coats of paint on the ironwork and other flammable material.

---

* As a Brighton citizen, the author was among the crowds who hastened to the summit of the South Downs to witness the remarkable blaze forty miles distant.

CHAPTER EIGHT

'More dead than alive from overwork'

Prince Albert was a worrier and had always found it hard not to succumb to the first hints of fatigue. Victoria had recognised this in the early days of her love for him. All the contests in his married life, all the new responsibilities with which he had so eagerly burdened himself, had taken their toll. The Queen had observed it all, and had endured anxiety every time she noted the familiar signs of stress in her husband.

No event had so seriously stretched Albert's nervous and physical resources as the organisation of the Great Exhibition. Two weeks before the formal opening, he appeared to be weary almost beyond bearing. He wrote to his grandmother, the Dowager Duchess of Coburg:

> I am more dead than alive from overwork. The opponents of the Exhibition work with might and main to throw all the old women into a panic, and to drive myself crazy. The strangers, they give out, are certain to commence a thorough Revolution here, to murder Victoria and myself, to proclaim the Red Republic in England. The plague is certain to ensue from the confluence of such vast multitudes, and to swallow up those whom the increased prices of everything had not already swept away. For all this I am to be responsible, and against all this I have to make sufficient provision.

Like many people with limited reserves of nervous strength and uncertain health, Albert was a deep-dyed hypochondriac, even in his twenties; and it was no help at all that he enjoyed only a negligible sense of humour, and that of a satirical nature.

Stockmar was one of the first to recognise Albert's poor health and nervous constitution. Being a hypochondriac himself, he was also quick to recognise the same weakness in his protégé. When the two men visited Florence in the winter of 1838–9, their carriage became stuck in a snowdrift for several hours in bitter temperatures. On arrival Albert went down not with a cold, but an abscess in a tooth. He took to his bed for *five days*, apparently distraught with pain. Stockmar kept to his room 'as a precaution', he explained, without adding what it was he feared.

Stockmar also learned from Albert himself how in the early days of his marriage when Victoria gloried in dancing the nights away before she began her succession of pregnancies, Albert was deprived of his much-needed sleep. 'Lack of sleep is making me weary,' he complained to his grandmother. 'It is difficult to bear.' Late nights led to late breakfasts. These in turn led to stomach upsets and 'a feeling of lassitude'.

The Queen made many sympathetic references in her Journal to Albert's 'delicate stomach'. It was true that life was much less healthy at Buckingham Palace or Windsor than at the Rosenau. The German kitchens, for example, were immaculately clean, the food healthy and well-cooked, and the style of living, much of it out of doors, with plenty of exercise, kept Albert much fitter than in England.

At both Windsor and London, Albert discovered that drains were blocked, cesspools unemptied, one of them directly beneath their bedroom window at Windsor. All this was bad enough, but when Albert examined the kitchens, he was horrified to find them filthy dirty, running with mice, rats and cockroaches and every kind of infection-carrying insect. In summer, bluebottles made free with cooked and uncooked joints of meat. In winter, you needed a broom to sweep the mice and rat droppings from the larders. Unlike the Queen, Albert had no opportunity in childhood to build up natural defences against all the consequent infections. No wonder that he was constantly suffering from minor ailments, colds and swollen glands.

Albert took it upon himself to reform both kitchens and drains, the storage of fresh food and the emptying of cess-pools. Stockmar, while agreeing with the need for these reforms, warned of trouble in what would be seen by the staff as meddling in long-established practices. As usual, Albert took note of these warnings and went about the reforms slowly and carefully. Although she supported him, Victoria had to conceal her puzzlement. She had, after all, grown up under the present conditions and had hardly ever suffered illness.

During the first ten years or so of their married life, certainly until the Great Exhibition of 1851, Queen Victoria watched her husband's health closely like a mother with an ailing child, at the same time observing with equal keenness and anxiety Albert's own attitude to his sick spells and nervous exhaustion. She had recognised his hypochondria from their earliest days together; but she also saw that there was good cause for it. She tried to protect him when she could, usually without success. His determination to stand by his commitments and do what he obstinately regarded as his duty was too strong. Once when they were enjoying a brief spring break at the old Balmoral in 1849, Albert caught a chill while out deer-stalking. He was due at Grimsby in a day or two to open the new docks. Victoria begged him not to go, but among Albert's weaknesses was a failure to delegate. Anyway, he had promised, and it was important to him personally, for the new docks had been built for trade with Germany, something close to his heart. The Queen persisted, unwisely, for it only hardened his resolve. 'If you will not do your duty,' he snapped at her, 'I must do mine.' And so he did.

Baron Stockmar, too, did his best to persuade Albert to reduce his self-imposed commitments. He, better than anyone – even the Queen – knew that Albert sought out tasks and responsibilities beyond the capacities of his nervous constitution. Stockmar had thought at one time that the Great Exhibition would be Albert's undoing. He begged him, in August 1851 at the height of the exhibition, to take a rest after it was over. Albert replied, 'I promised you, no doubt, not to embark on anything new after the close of the Exhibition, and I have, moreover, made up my mind to retreat into my shell as quickly as possible.' Even this promise was qualified, for there was still much to do, in particular deciding how to use the financial surplus gained by the success of the project.

The Great Exhibition had so preoccupied Albert that for several months there were simply not enough waking hours to give attention to the perennial stress subject, the nursery and the schoolroom. Even with the departure of Baroness Lehzen and the advent of Lady Lyttelton, Prince Albert in particular (especially after the discovery of young intruders in the palace), was deeply concerned about the security of the nursery wing at night. Lady Lyttelton recalled, 'The last thing we [Prince Albert and herself] did before bedtime was to visit the access to the children's apartments, to satisfy ourselves that all was safe. And the intricate turns and locks and guard-rooms and the various intense precautions, suggesting the most hideous dangers . . . made one shudder.'

Both the Queen and Prince Albert fussed about their children to an unusual degree, stretching the patience even of Lady Lyttelton. First it was their diet and health, and later, in the schoolroom, their progress and behaviour. In mitigation it has to be remembered that Victoria and Albert were both very young. When only twenty-five they already had four children. There was no family tradition on either side of bringing up children. Victoria was an only child with the terrible example of the Hanoverians to guide her; Albert's experience was little wider. They certainly had no access to guide books on the subject, and people were loath to offer advice.

Victoria and Albert loved their children and in the early days liked to romp with them in the gardens or the nursery. At the same time, Victoria resented their all-too-ready intrusion into her life with Albert. As for the prince, there was no less love for his children, but he still found it hard to be at ease with his sons. It did not help that the first boy was the most intractable and caused most worry, for Albert assumed too readily that the others might follow Bertie's example.

Unlike his mother, Bertie was conscious from early childhood that he had been singled out for special responsibilities. To train him to meet these, his parents instructed his tutor to apply a degree of work pressure. Bertie responded to the mind-bending seven-hours-a-day regime with tantrums. 'A very bad day,' his tutor once recorded. 'The P. of W. has been like a person half silly. I could not gain his attention. He was very rude, particularly in the afternoon, throwing stones in my face.'

It did not require much psychology to recognise that the boy wanted someone to love and care for him in a kindly way. Both his mother and father failed to respond to this need. Once Bertie could look to Lady Lyttelton for the love for which he ached; then it was Henry Birch. Each, in turn, was taken away.

For Albert, his eldest son was by far the greatest source of domestic stress. And this situation was to continue until the end.

Relieved to some degree of the pressure of the Great Exhibition, Albert involved himself even more deeply in politics, almost as if he feared the risk of a lessening of tension in his life. He had become embroiled in a controversy with Lord Palmerston, the Foreign Secretary, and a difficult man at the best of times, who now treated Albert roughly. On 17 February 1852 Victoria wrote a long letter to Uncle Leopold, covering a number of worrying subjects, from the threat from the newly installed Louis Napoleon and a consequent risk of attack from France to the extension of the suffrage (previously limited to land and property owners), and a surprising reference to Albert.

Albert becomes really a *terrible* man of business; I think it takes a little off from the gentleness of his character, and makes him so preoccupied. I grieve over all this, as I *cannot* enjoy these things, *much* as I interest myself in *general* European politics; but I am every day more convinced that *we women, if* we *are to be good* women, *feminine* and *amiable* and *domestic* are not *fitted to reign* ... However, this cannot now be helped, and it is the duty of everyone to fulfil all that they are called upon to do, in whatever situation they may be!

Balmoral was the one place where Victoria could be confident that Albert would relax and forget all the 'business' and political trials and tribulations. Osborne House was too close to the centre of events, too accessible for ministers and others. There was by no means the same peace and tranquillity at Osborne as at Balmoral. They managed to get a short break in Scotland in September 1852. In fact they were staying at a neighbouring estate, Alt-na-Giuthhasach, when they embarked with several servants on a climb and ride, their favourite occupation. It was 16 September, the weather was fine, the scenery beautiful. They were resting and sketching 'the wild and picturesque' Dhu Loch when the outside world intruded in the form of a messenger with a pile of letters. 'Amongst them,' wrote Victoria later, 'was one from Lord Derby [Prime Minister], which I tore open, and alas! it contained the fatal news: that *England's* or rather *Britain's* pride, her glory, her hero, the greatest man she ever had produced [Field Marshal the Duke of Wellington], was no more. Sad day! Great and irreparable national loss!'

The days when Victoria's admiration for Wellington was conditioned by regret that in politics he was a Tory had long since been forgotten. Albert was equally shattered by the news. 'The death of the Duke of Wellington,' he wrote from Balmoral to which they had hastily returned, 'has deprived the Country of her greatest man, the Crown of its most valuable servant and adviser, the Army of its main strength and support ...'

Two years before he died, the duke had suggested to Albert that he should succeed him as C-in-C of the army. Albert wisely refused. Not only had he no experience of soldiering, but what would be the result if Chartist riots were renewed, the army called out to suppress them, and more deaths occurred? The monarchy itself would be held responsible. It could lead to a British repeat of the 1793 events in France.

If Albert would not take on this heavy responsibility, he certainly put himself, heart and soul, into the organisation of the duke's funeral, which was to be a magnificent affair. Albert did not himself design the bronze funeral car, but he approved the design, which was almost as blameworthy. It was an enormous construction, twenty-one feet long, surmounted by a coffin almost seven feet long (although the duke was only five feet eight inches tall). The decorations were elaborate almost beyond belief, and very heavy, too, causing the vehicle to stall twice in the mud on its long journey down the Mall, through St James, past the law courts to St Paul's cathedral. The Queen, tears coursing down her cheeks, watched from the new balcony on the front of Buckingham Palace, Albert at her side. The dirges played by successive bands, including the Dead March from *Saul*, caused renewed sobbing, the culmination of grief represented by Wellington's charger carrying only his master's boots, reversed in keeping with tradition.

Tennyson, now Poet Laureate, wrote a long 'Ode' beginning

> Bury the Great Duke
> With an Empire's lamentation,
> Let us bury the Great Duke
> To the noise of mourning
> Of a mighty nation.

A few weeks later, Lord Derby's government fell. Victoria had no Wellington to turn to for guidance. She wrote in distress to King Leopold, 'We shall soon stand sadly alone; Aberdeen is almost the only personal friend of that kind we have left. Melbourne, Peel, Liverpool – & now the Duke – *all* gone!'

The Earl of Aberdeen formed the new ministry. By chance, an architect from Aberdeen, William Smith, had been summoned to Balmoral by Albert a week before the death of Wellington. The purpose of the visit was to discuss the site for the new Balmoral Castle. This, they decided, was to be some 100 yards north-west of the existing house. Smith drew up plans in co-operation with Albert, in the Scottish baronial style. It was very much bigger than the existing house, which continued to be used while the work was carried out. The building was to be dominated by a 120-foot square tower, from which, of course, the royal standard would fly whenever the Queen was in residence. Local stone from a nearby quarry was to be used in the construction. As at Osborne, Thomas Cubitt was placed in charge of the building work.

The Queen took the closest interest in their new home, and on 28 September 1853, just a year after the initial discussions with Smith, she laid the foundation stone. Her Journal for that day begins:

> A fine morning early, but when we walked out at half-past ten o'clock it began raining, and soon poured down without ceasing. Most fortunately it cleared up before two, and the sun shone brightly for the ceremony ... Mama and all her party arrived from *Abergeldie* a little before three ...

A bottle, a sheet of parchment and coins of the realm had been made ready. Victoria and Albert dated and signed the parchment, following by the signatures of their children and the Duchess of Kent. The parchment was then sealed in the bottle and lowered into a prepared cavity.

Victoria was handed in turn a trowel for spreading the mortar and a mallet for striking the stone. She then declared the stone laid, and poured oil and wine. Bagpipes were played.

> The workmen and people all gave a cheer when the whole was concluded [Victoria's Journal continued]. In about three-quarters of an hour's time we went in to see the people at their dinner;* and after this walked over to *Craif Gowan* ...
>
> We dressed early, and went for twenty minutes to see the people dancing in the ballroom, which they did with the greatest spirit.

* A temporary village of wooden buildings housed the 2,000 workmen and their families.

The spirit was in part inspired by the local spirit. There was always plenty of it on Deeside.

Prince Albert had always hankered after some academic status. His early marriage had deprived him of any degrees or honours in Germany, and it was not until 1851 that an opportunity occurred to gain significant academic recognition in his adopted country. On 12 February, the Duke of Newcastle, Chancellor of Cambridge University, failed to rise from his bed. He had died in his sleep. (Four years earlier the duke had granted Albert an honorary degree, which had pleased him, but Albert had had no other connection with the university or the city since then except as an occasional visitor.)

Albert was therefore amazed and delighted to receive a letter the following day from Dr William Whewell, master of Trinity College wondering if Albert would allow his name to go forward as a candidate for election to the chancellorship of the university in succession to the duke. Victoria was equally enthusiastic about the offer but agreed with Albert that they should consult Stockmar before accepting. The baron thought it was an excellent idea, and so did Lord Lansdowne, an old Trinity man himself and now Lord President of the Council.

Everyone so far, including Dr Whewell, had presumed that Albert would be the sole nominee. It would surely be improper to become involved in a contest. Albert's reply, as a precaution, made this a condition of acceptance. But matters, as so often in university life, did not proceed predictably. Another college, St John's, proposed an old man and member of the college, Lord Powis. 'A deaf old woman' he might be, as one of Albert's backers described him, but he was a Cambridge graduate, a noted Tory and as English as a Kent apple.

According to Albert's biographer, Sir Theodore Martin:

'Here, in so far as the Prince was concerned, his candidature came to an end. But his supporters ... were not in a temper to accept the triumph of a rival college … They accordingly determined to go to the poll, "being persuaded that a large majority of the University agree with them in thinking His Royal Highness the most proper person to be the Chancellor of the University".'

Albert found himself being carried along on a tide of enthusiasm by his supporters, while at the same time he wanted the chancellorship very much. So, on his behalf, they fought the good fight in a short but very sharp campaign. 'It is true that Prince Albert was not educated at Cambridge,' charged one of his supporters, 'but Lord Powis has not been educated anywhere.'

> The fiery cross was sped across the kingdom, [wrote Martin] and from every side members of the University flocked to Cambridge in unprecedented numbers to record their votes. Of these no fewer than 1,790 were given, of which 953 were for the Prince, and 837 for Lord Powis.

The majority of 116 was just comfortable enough for Albert to accept the chancellorship. In a statement from Buckingham Palace he concluded:

> I have resolved to accept the trust, which the University is willing to confide in me. In forming this decision I have been influenced by a respectful deference to the wishes of a majority of its members [and] by an earnest hope that through a zealous and an impartial discharge of the trust which I undertake, I shall succeed in establishing a claim on the confidence and goodwill of the whole Academical body.

Albert was delighted by the outcome and soon put out of his mind the risks involved in the contest with Lord Powis.

Victoria succeeded in avoiding childbirth in 1847, choosing instead the turbulent year of '48. Karl Marx in collaboration with Friedrich Engels was preparing in London the *Communist Manifesto*; the Prince of Prussia and Louis-Philippe of France had sought shelter in England. But nowhere was safe, and the Queen could hear the distant rumble of the mob in the Mall while in labour with Louise on 18 March 1848, 'a spot of light on the gloomy scene,' as Albert wrote. 'I have good news for you today . . . and though it be a daughter, still my joy and gratitude are very great, as I was often full of misgivings because of the [political] shocks which have crowded upon Victoria of late.'

Lady Lyttelton added, 'Our new baby is right royal; very large, extremely fair, with white satin hair, large, long blue eyes and regular features, a most perfect form from head to foot. The Queen is extremely proud of her; hitherto she is as placid and happy as possible, cries very little and begins to laugh and even crows, which at six weeks is early.'

Little more than two years later, on 1 May 1850, the eighty-first birthday of Arthur Wellesley, the Duke of Wellington, another boy was born, and named Arthur in his honour. The old duke agreed to stand as godfather, but alas died within less than two years. Arthur was to become the Duke of Connaught and never wished to be anything but a soldier. He enjoyed a distinguished military career, attaining the rank of field marshal. Arthur was not the brightest of the children but, compared with Bertie, gave his mother little anxiety.

These first seven royal children got on well together under the steady eye of Lady Lyttelton. They were happiest at Osborne, where they had the free run of the grounds, playing for hours in their Swiss Cottage. All the children were given garden plots, and the head gardener gave them basic instructions in growing flowers and vegetables. To encourage them further, Albert bought any successful stock at proper market prices.

Here at Osborne they learned to swim and follow all kinds of outdoor pursuits. It always seemed to be sunny on the Isle of Wight, the sea full of traffic, from trans-Atlantic steam passenger vessels, great fighting ships, to pleasure yachts and fishing boats. 'How happy we are here!' the Queen would often exclaim.

Osborne House was exactly right for the children while

they were still young, just as Balmoral Castle with its more demanding occupations suited them in later childhood.

Even when Osborne House and Balmoral Castle were in active commission, the children spent the greater part of the year at Windsor or in London at Buckingham Palace. Their timetable varied little for both Victoria and Albert believed that children benefited from a regular routine. Children and parents rose at six thirty in the summer, seven-thirty in the winter, though they did not meet until after breakfast. This was a plain meal and not at all German: coffee or tea, bread and butter, cold meat or hot eggs.

At Windsor, Victoria and Albert would then visit the home farm, if the weather allowed; at Buckingham Palace they simply took a walk in the spacious garden. Next, the Queen went to her office while Albert read the newspapers before attending to his papers. At some point during the morning the Master of the Household visited Victoria to receive his orders for the day, according to the activities and number of guests.

Then came the morning visit by Victoria and Albert together to the nurseries, where they were received by Lady Lyttelton and told about the lessons of the day and any notable progress, or the reverse – which usually meant Bertie, who dreaded these visits. If there were any cause for praise, it usually concerned Vicky. Written reports on the schoolroom activities invariably arrived at Albert's study before luncheon.

Before changing for dinner with the household, Victoria and Albert made a last visit to the nurseries to say good night. Once they arrived in the middle of prayers, presided over by Lady Lyttelton. Albert was astonished to see his children kneeling, a practice he found 'stiff and cold – a peculiar feature of English religion. In Germany kneeling went out with the Reformation.'

Victoria felt puzzled and unsettled. She had been brought up by a German mother and had always knelt. She took advice and talked the matter over with Albert. In the end they decided

133

to follow Lady Lyttelton's example as the children were being brought up in England, and the subject was dropped.

For the children, the other meals were as plain as their breakfast: much bread and milk, their main midday meal being often boiled beef and carrots or potatoes, followed by rice pudding or semolina. They were none the worse for this diet, and if they had upset stomachs, then castor oil was the usual remedy.

All the children were brought up under this austere regime. Fires were lit only when absolutely necessary, and then kept small – Queen Victoria detested hot rooms. Similarly, windows were kept closed only when it was *really* cold. But the children kept wonderfully fit. At a time when child mortality was still high (and not only among the poor) and rickets and bad teeth commonplace, their growth rate, good health and complexion were a fine reflection on the good sense of their mother and Lady Lyttelton.

In contradiction to Victoria and Albert's apparent near-obsession with routine for their family, certain of the children could find themselves whisked out of the schoolroom and taken to the circus, or to the zoo, or, later, to the theatre or opera 'for a treat'. Bertie's enthusiasm for the theatre and actors and – especially – actresses in later life stemmed from this early familiarity with the theatre.

These sudden absences from the classroom did not at all please Lady Lyttelton, but there was nothing she could do, or even say.

CHAPTER NINE

War and Mutiny

On 27 March 1854 France declared war on Russia. Britain added her declaration on the following day. The Crimean War had begun, one of the most unpleasant, bloody and unnecessary wars in western history. Its origins lay chiefly in Russian aggression against Turkey and determination to occupy Constantinople. The Turks had been fighting for a year already and had lost the greater part of their fleet in the Black Sea at the battle of Sinope. British and French first action was to secure the Turkish capital, and then besiege and occupy Sebastopol in the Russian Crimea.

The British people, and the Queen herself, had whipped themselves into a state of war fever. Albert was doubly shocked by the turn of events and declaration of war. He was amazed that some of the blame for the crisis was heaped upon his shoulders. The press attacked him by name, accusing him of having secret communication with Russia. It was widely but incorrectly believed that the people's hero, Lord Palmerston, had been forced by Prince Albert to resign in 1851.

Albert's mood was reflected in a letter to his brother two months earlier:

> You are right to look into the near future with fear. It looks very black for the whole world. Here the hue and cry for war has grown to a degree that I should never have thought possible. The people have generously made me their scapegoat.

There were also those who were jealous of Albert's popularity following the success of the Great Exhibition. A strong proportion of the army hierarchy were anti-Albert, believing as they did that he was responsible for Lord Hardinge rather than Lord Raglan being promoted C-in-C in succession to the Duke of Wellington.

Rumours flew. *The Spectator* reported on 24 January 1854, 'The story, not only told in all parts of England a day or two ago, but by some believed, was, that Prince Albert was a traitor to his Queen, that he had been impeached for high treason, and, finally, that on a charge of high treason he had been arrested and committed to the Tower.'

In all his fifteen years in his adopted country, Albert had never been so low and depressed. Victoria was outraged by these press attacks, which seemed daily to become more scurrilous. But she reserved a fair part of her fury for Albert for not defending himself and fighting back. To answer this charge Albert determined to take legal action against one newspaper, the *Morning Advertiser*, which was attempting to recover its falling sales by printing all kinds of fabricated and libellous stories.

Albert called in the Lord Chancellor, Lord Cranworth, to discuss how best to proceed. The Chancellor did not beat about the bush, advising Albert to drop all ideas of going to court, which would only bring him down to the low level of those who were attacking him. It was not until later, when the turmoil had settled, that Albert recognised the wisdom of this advice.

In a bitter and self-pitying response to an unhelpful letter from Stockmar, Albert wrote:

> A very considerable section of the nation had never given itself the trouble to consider what really is the position of [the Consort of] a Queen Regnant. When I first came over here, I was met by this want of knowledge and unwillingness to give a thought to the position of this luckless personage. Peel cut down my income, Wellington refused me my rank, the Royal Family cried out against the foreign interloper, the Whigs in office were only inclined to concede to me just as much space as I could stand on . . .

Punch was among representatives of the press to advocate counter-attack. On 26 November 1853, the editor printed a poem called 'Prince Punch to Prince Albert', the last verse advocating:

> Then silence your civic applauders
> Lest better men cease from applause,
> He who tribute accepts from marauders,
> Is held to be pledged to their cause;
> Let no corporate magnates of London,
> An honour presume to award:
> Their own needs, till ill-doings be undone,
> Little honour to spare can afford.

Two months later, John Delane, respected editor of *The Times*, took a strong line against his fellow editors for their attacks. *The Spectator* agreed and went further in demanding that every libel should now be the subject of a printed apology.

The real turning of the tide for Albert, however, was the speech by the Prime Minister after Victoria reopened Parliament on 30 January 1854. He declared that '... the result of the calumnies, base as they are, and of these delusions, blind as they have been, will be to attach the crown still more strongly to the realm and to give a firmer and stronger foundation to the throne ...'

Not another word of criticism of Albert was uttered or printed after that.

There was more sharp domestic division when two months later war with Russia was declared. Albert had always been a strong anti-militarist. He had long accepted the xenophobia of these strange islanders among whom he lived, but he had been seriously shocked by the fervour for war which had swept the country, including his wife, like some plague. In addition to Albert's ethical and moral objections to war with Russia, he was fearful of the military outcome, in spite of the support of the French. He knew better than the Secretary of War, Lord Panmure, how weak and ill-equipped the army was.

For the Queen, however, these were stirring, if anxious, times. On 28 February 1854, with war now inevitable and the fleet on its way to the Bosporous, she wrote to King Leopold:

> The last battalion of the Guards (Scots Fusiliers) embarked today. They passed through the courtyard here at seven o'clock this morning. We stood on the balcony to see them – the morning fine, the sun rising over the towers of old Westminster Abbey – and an immense crowd collected to see these fine men, and cheering them immensely ... They formed line, presented arms, and then cheered up *very heartily*, and went off cheering. It was a *touching and beautiful* sight ...

The opening days of the war were marked by political disturbance at home, with unseemly jockeying for power between Lord John Russell and Lord Palmerston, a situation which exasperated Albert. Surely, this was a time to present a united front to the nation and to the enemy. The Anglo-French armies moved at a snail's pace, and the Queen and her people had to wait some six months before there was a landing on the Crimean coast. At the same time, Albert favoured a cautious approach to keep casualties down to a minimum. In spite of his recent plea of inexperience in military matters when offered the post of C-in-C of the army, he now began to bombard the War Office with opinions and recommendations. As many of them were sensible they might have been listened to with interest, but such was not the case. In anticipation of heavy casualties, Albert advocated the strengthening of the Militia at home, in order to release trained regulars for the fighting front. Later, when cholera broke out among the troops, he proposed the setting up of a convalescent home on Corfu, instead of sending the survivors straight back into the fighting.

Good news was received at last towards the end of September when the French and British forces defeated the Russians at the battle of Alma. Indecision led to the allies failing to press home their advantage. They now surrounded Sebastopol. The Russians counter-attacked at Balaclava, which led to the charge of the Light Brigade – when 'into the valley of Death rode the six hundred', immortalised in Tennyson's poem. In spite of the victory at Inkerman, Sebastopol held out, committing the ill-equipped besieging troops to a winter of cold, and even hunger.

The scandals exposed by *The Times* war correspondent, William Russell, led to the downfall of the Aberdeen government, and the accession to the premiership of Palmerston. Victoria found this 'personally not agreeable to me, but I think of nothing but the country, and the preservation of its institutions, and my own personal feelings would be sunk if only the efficiency of the Government could be obtained'.

Through the first three months of 1855, while the troops besieging Sebastopol died of disease or wounds and Lord Raglan, commanding the expedition, lived in splendid luxury on shipboard, the politicians quarrelled amongst themselves in and out of Parliament. One person who took the initiative on behalf of the fighting men was Florence Nightingale, a nurse with great organisational powers. 'Such a *head*!' exclaimed the Queen after their first meeting. 'I wish we had her at the War Office.' Florence Nightingale became the premier figure in nursing history when she took a party of nurses to Scutari to tend the wounded and improve the terrible conditions which prevailed there.

It would have been seen as a fine attempt to raise morale if Prince Albert had sailed with them and visited the troops in the fighting line, but there is no record of his even considering such a course. Albert's one remembered contribution to the Crimean War was to propose a decoration for exceptionally valorous deeds – the Victoria Cross.

At a dinner in London in June 1855, the very month Raglan died, he made a scarcely camouflaged attack on newspapers which reported the bad news from Russia. Unlike his son, the Prince of Wales, he was afraid of the British free press, and affected to despise it. In a reference to Russell's revelations in *The Times*, he once exclaimed to the Secretary of State for War, 'The pen and ink of one miserable scribbler is despoiling the country of all the advantages which the hearts blood of 20,000 of its noblest sons should have earned.'

War was still raging in the Crimea and Sebastopol had not yet fallen, when Victoria and Albert went to Paris on 18 August 1855 at the invitation of Emperor Napoleon III. It was the Queen's first visit, and the centre of Paris had been largely rebuilt since Albert was last there. 'I never saw anything gayer and more beautiful!' exclaimed the Queen to Uncle Leopold. 'Our reception is *most* gratifying – for it is enthusiastic and really kind in the highest degree.' The Parisians were fascinated and enraptured by the little English Queen. There were parades and banquets and receptions. Albert suffered horribly from indigestion.

The crises of the Crimean War were matched domestically and on a small scale by those of Balmoral. Albert had planned to follow the building at every stage, but it seemed neither right nor practical that he should be seen supervising the construction of a family house amidst the turmoil of war. In his absence progress was slow and there were numerous setbacks – strikes for higher wages by the migrant workers, many of whom left to join the gold rushes in California and Australia; one night a fire swept through the wooden huts housing the workers, who lost all their possessions. Victoria and Albert had to pay for a replacement village out of their own pockets.

At last in early September 1855 the building work had advanced far enough for the entire family, the staff and household to come to stay, although the old house had not yet been demolished. Victoria was delighted. 'The view from the windows of our rooms ... of the valley of the *Dee* with the mountains in the background – which one never could see from the old house, is quite beautiful. We walked about, and alongside the river, and looked at all that has been done.'

Two evenings later there arrived a telegraphic despatch which read 'From General Simpson – Sebastopol is in the hands of the Allies'.

God be praised for it! [wrote the Queen] Our delight was great
... Albert said they should go at once and light the bonfire which
had been prepared when the false report of the fall of the town
arrived last year ... The new house seems to be lucky, indeed;
for, from the first moment of our arrival, we have had good news.
In a few minutes, Albert and all the gentlemen, in every species
of attire, sallied forth, followed by all the servants, and gradually
by all the population of the village – keepers, gillies, workmen –
up to the top of the cairn. We waited, and saw them light it;
accompanied by general cheering. The bonfire blazed forth brilli-
antly, and we could see the numerous figures surrounding it –
some dancing, all shouting ... About three-quarters of an hour
after, Albert came down, and said the scene had been wild and
exciting beyond everything.

Bertie and Affie were awakened and insisted on climbing
up to the cairn, where drams of whisky were circulating, and
'the people in great ecstasy'.

The Queen completed her account of that memorable
evening:

We remained till a quarter to twelve; and, just as I was undressing,
all the people came down under the windows, the pipes playing,
the people singing, firing off guns, and cheering – first for
me, then Albert, the Emperor of the French, and the downfall
of *Sebastopol*.

The wonders of that autumn of 1855 seemed uniquely abund-
ant. The Russian war might not be over – the peace agreement
was not finally signed until 30 March 1856 – but the worst
was behind them and Victoria and Albert could turn their
attention back to domestic matters. Victoria had given birth
to another boy on 7 April 1853. For the first time she accepted
gladly the use of chloroform to ease her suffering during
labour, '& the effect was soothing, quieting & delightful
beyond measure'. Conservative elements in the medical profession were profoundly shocked, regarding it as a dangerous
example to her subjects. As so often before, Uncle Leopold
was one of the first to hear about the birth, Victoria's eighty,
when on 18 April, she addressed him in Brussels:

I can report most favourably of myself, for I have never been better or stronger. Stockmar will have told you, that Leopold is to be the name of our fourth young gentleman. It is a mark of love and affection, which I hope you will not disapprove. It is the name which is dearest to me after Albert's, and one which recalls the almost only happy days of my sad childhood. To hear 'Prince Leopold' again will make me think of all those days! . . .

'Little Leo' was underweight, even sickly, unlike all Victoria's previous children. Certain members of the court contended that the baby's weakness stemmed from the use of chloroform, in their eyes an unnatural and possibly improper means of diminishing childbirth pain. What did the Good Book command? 'Be in pain, and labour to bring forth, O daughter of Zion, like a woman in travail.'

Sir James Clark, almost as concerned as the Queen herself, carried out some medical detective work. It could be the weakness of the wet nurse's milk, he surmised. Victoria made enquiries at Balmoral, which she regarded as the source of every panacea. A Mrs Macintosh was found, and brought south 'in cap and plaid shawl without a word of English'. A month later, there was still no improvement. Next, Victoria made similar enquiries at Osborne. Appropriately at nearby Cowes, another wet nurse was found. The improvement was swift and wonderfully effective and Victoria's delight and relief knew no bounds. Alas, it was only temporary. The finest, richest breast milk could not relieve the infant from the congenital disease with which he had been born. Prince Leopold suffered from 'the bleeding disease' – haemophilia.

Victoria was distraught when she learned of this condition afflicting her child, at the same time vehemently denying that it was 'in our family'. Then whose family was responsible? There was no record of haemophilia among the Saxe-Coburgs any more than the Hanovers. However, in the past the death of sufferers may have been wrongly attributed to other causes, and it was a disease that could and often did strike young, and remain dormant for generations. As a result of the utmost care, Leopold lived to thirty years. He married and had children, one of them, Alice,* being a carrier and losing a son from the disease. Vicky, her younger sister, Alice and (the yet unborn) Beatrice were all carriers, spreading the disease throughout the royal houses of Europe, even to Russia and to the little Tsarevitch.

For Queen Victoria it was mortifying to see her children spreading the bleeding disease like a defacing stain across Europe. She never came to terms with the guilt she experienced, and it was no coincidence that the dreadful diagnosis was immediately followed by a tearing emotional row with Albert, which left them both exhausted and with intensified guilt.

Although Leopold predeceased his mother by almost seventeen years, following a fall in Cannes, he had given his parents much joy as well as anxiety. He was a highly intelligent young man, tall and good-looking. 'The dearest of my dear sons', was how Victoria always referred to him after his death.

The onset of winter 1855 marked the beginning of the end of childhood for their first born. Even at the christening of her younger brother, Alfred, in 1844, Albert had decided with Victoria that Vicky's future lay in Prussia. The heir to the King of Prussia, Prince Frederick, was invited to the christening as Affie's godfather. Prince Frederick had a twelve-year-old son, Prince Frederick William, Fritz. Vicky was then three.

The future of these two royal children was further secured at the 1851 exhibition. The Prussian prince's mother Crown Princess Augusta brought young Fritz with her. Victoria thoroughly approved of the boy, with his handsome features and keen blue eyes. He was by no means a typical Junker, and seemed to hold liberal views. He also enjoyed the company of Princess Vicky, and the two children toured the exhibition time and again, clearly delighted with one another's company. This intimacy was reflected by their mothers' plotting and planning for their future. Albert, equally approving, visualised the coming romance and marriage in more dynastic terms, a

---

* Princess Alice, Countess of Athlone

strengthening of the ties between the two great nations.

The political need for closer relations between Britain and Prussia had been highlighted by Prussia's failure to support the Anglo-French allies in the Russian war. As it happened, Fritz joined the family at Balmoral shortly after the news arrived of the fall of Sebastopol. Victoria faced the prospect of the following few days with desperate anxiety and excitement. 'The visit makes my heart break, as it *may* and probably *will* decide the fate of our dear eldest child,' she wrote.

Fritz had matured greatly, and not only because he had grown a moustache. After breakfast one morning, he approached Victoria and Albert and asked if he might talk to them about 'belonging to our family'. Victoria held and squeezed his hand, saying how happy she would be. She did, however, impose one condition: there was no question of marriage before Vicky was seventeen. Vicky was then fourteen, Fritz twenty-four. Could the realistic Albert seriously believe that they could remain unmarried for three years? His own engagement to Victoria had lasted only a few weeks.

Meanwhile, an informal betrothal would be in order, and Victoria described the circumstances from Balmoral a few days later:

> September 29, 1856
> Our dear Victoria was this day engaged to Prince Frederick William of Prussia, who had been on a visit to us since the 14th . . . We were uncertain, on account of her extreme youth, whether he should speak to her himself, or wait till he came back [to Britain] again. However, we felt it was better he should do so; and during our ride up *Craig-na-Ban* this afternoon, he picked a piece of white heather ('the emblem of good luck'), which he gave to her; and this enabled him to make an allusion to his hopes and wishes, as they rode down *Glen Girnoch*, which led to this happy conclusion.

Albert could flatter himself that he had tied the first important knot in the great alliance of which he had dreamed for so long.

*   *   *

Domestic events continued to march in step with national crises. In May 1857, Fritz arrived at Osborne to stay with the family and see as much as was permitted of Vicky. Both Vicky and Fritz had grown more mature in the intervening seven months. Fritz demonstrated much greater self-confidence now that his future was certain, though he suffered from surprise, even shock, at the light-heartedness of family relations compared with the heavy, Teutonic atmosphere of the Berlin court. Everyone seemed to show their feelings without restraint. Fritz was very proprietorial of Vicky, expecting to have every dance with her, and to have her alone for at least one hour every day. This was arranged, the Queen acting as chaperon, much to her chagrin, by sitting in the adjoining room with the door open. 'Such a *waste* of time!'

For her part Vicky was delighted to see Fritz again and to be openly engaged. In Fritz's eyes she had not only grown in height, but in beauty too as Vicky's biographer, Daphne Bennett, pointed out. A portrait by Winterhalter of this period is, however, not very different from one by Ross when she was a child. The features are much the same, the large, slightly hooded eyes and the upward curve of the lips giving the face a most pleasing expression. Only the hair style is changed: in 1857 she wore it parted in the middle, slightly bouffant at the sides and drawn back from her face.

Vicky had been confirmed since her last meeting with Fritz, and was remarkably adult in her views and manners. The wedding date was fixed for 20 January 1858, when she would be seventeen, and Fritz twenty-six.

While the celebrations continued in fine weather at Osborne, news arrived of a major outbreak of violence in India. There had been little or no warning of trouble in this vast area of the British Empire, and the shock to the nation and the government – to say nothing of Victoria and Albert – was severe.

We are in sad anxiety about India [Victoria wrote to Uncle Leopold], which engrosses all our attention. Troops cannot be raised fast or largely enough. And the horrors committed on the poor ladies – women and children – are unknown in these ages, and make one's blood run cold. Altogether, the whole is so much more distressing than the Crimea – where there was *glory* and honourable warfare, and where the poor women and children were safe. Then the distance and difficulty of communication is such an additional suffering to us all. I know you will feel much for us ... There is not a family hardly who is not in sorrow and anxiety about their children, and in all ranks – India being *the* place where every one was anxious to place a son.

The manner of British rule over India was complicated and ripe for challenge. Much of the country had for years been under the control of the mighty East India Company. The rest, except some surviving pockets belonging to Portugal, consisted of feudatory states ruled by native princes under British supervision.

In recent years, many of these states had been brought under direct British rule. The annexations were accompanied by a consolidation process, including the construction of a network of railways and roads, the formation of a telegraph system, a civil service on a national basis, and a postal system to emulate the one in the United Kingdom.

These plans and annexations aroused strong resentment in parts of the sub-continent. The Crimean War had hinted at British military weakness, and some 80 per cent of the Indian army was Indian, many British regiments having been posted away to the Crimea. In Bengal especially, the native regiments were unsettled by the rumour that rifle cartridges were being coated with the grease of cows or pigs, or both. As the first animal was sacred to the Hindus, and the second unclean to the Moslems, this caused outrage, although it was only a subsidiary cause of the uprising.

Although euphemistically called a mutiny, it was in fact a full-scale revolutionary war, in which many British soldiers and their families were massacred. The first news to arrive at Osborne was from the garrison at Meerut where the Indian soldiers shot their English officers and then occupied the city of Delhi.

The garrison at Cawnpore was besieged for several weeks. Then water and ammunition failed and General Sir Hugh Wheeler was obliged to negotiate a safe conduct with the Indian prince commanding the Indian warriors. The women and children survivors were herded on to barges on the Ganges. These were then set on fire and any who attempted to swim ashore were sabred. Others were hacked to pieces and thrown down a well.

The news of the outrage was sent back by the commander of the relieving army. 'The horrors of shame & every outrage which women must most dread,' wrote the Queen, 'surpass all belief, & it was a great mercy *all* were *killed*!'

The revolution spread rapidly. 'It is impossible to speak of the horrors taking place,' Albert wrote to his brother, 'but the heroism of the English and the calmness, the confidence and the endurance being shown are remarkable and uplifting to see.'

There was, alas, nothing uplifting about English counter-measures spurred on by the fury of revenge. As the Indian troops and irregulars were beaten back, few prisoners were taken and there were reports of torture and the notorious practice of shooting ringleaders tied over the mouths of cannon. William Russell of *The Times*, fresh from the Crimean War, told readers of these outrages. As a result Lord Canning, the governor-general, issued an order denouncing 'rabid and indiscriminate vindictiveness', and thus earned for himself the sobriquet 'Clemency' Canning. Other newspapers applauded the hard line taken by officers and demanded Canning's recall.

Victoria and Albert were shocked by the people's 'lust for revenge'. Insisting on a conciliatory line after the suppression of the mutiny, both they and others pointed out that if Britain were to continue to govern the sub-continent, kindness, justice and Christian tolerance must be the guiding policy. This could only be achieved, in the first instance, by the government taking over from the East India Company all the territory previously under its control.

Victoria, though she never visited India in all her long life, had a deeply romantic attitude to this jewel in her crown, employed a number of Indian servants, and in 1875 was proclaimed Empress of India.

Less than a year before the wedding of their eldest daughter, Victoria gave birth to what was to be her youngest child, a daughter. It was a delayed birth but satisfactorily handled. All fear of the labour had dissolved now that she could rely upon chloroform. Albert, of course, was by her side all the time, and the first words she recognised were spoken by him: 'It is a fine child, and a girl!' It was 14 April 1857, and she was named Princess Beatrice – 'Baby'.

Beatrice took on, unasked, the responsibility of consoling her mother for the loss of Vicky. Victoria described this last and particularly beautiful baby as 'the flower of the flock'. Sir James Clark warned Victoria that she should not have any more children, but failed to explain that it was her mental rather than physical condition that concerned him. It was true that she had felt very anxious and nervously upset during this last pregnancy, but the thirty-eight-year-old mother of nine said she longed for more children. Her melancholy question addressed to her doctor, 'Can I have no more fun in bed?' suggests that she had received no instruction on the avoidance of pregnancy.

The Queen faced three tasks in the twelve months after the birth of Baby. They all required effort and it was fortunate that she was so well after the delivery: 'I have felt better and stronger this time than I have ever done before,' Victoria claimed.

It had rankled that, since Melbourne's failure to authorize a royal title for Albert, her beloved husband still lacked one fifteen years after their marriage. The influences which had worked against him then had largely disappeared with the death of so many of the 'old family'. Lord Palmerston, Prime Minister since February 1855, was consulted, and indicated his support. But the Lord Chancellor, Lord Cranworth, after diligent search, discovered that it would be illegal for Albert to be made Prince Consort by Act of Parliament. Unamused, the Queen took the matter in her own hands and created her husband Prince Consort by letters patent. The change dated from 25 June 1857.

The next and even more unpleasant task also concerned Parliament – the settling of a marriage dowry on her eldest daughter. She had always *hated* this begging-bowl feature in her life, especially since the mean cutting of Albert's allowance. This time Palmerston did not let down his sovereign. He sounded out the opposition and promptly got through a decision to settle a dowry on Vicky of £40,000, plus an annuity of £4,000. The vote was 328 to 14 against.

This vote greatly eased one aspect of the wedding for Victoria and Albert. Like every mother before the wedding of a daughter, Victoria spent much enjoyable time choosing items for the trousseau. Less pleasant were the rumours from Prussia that the Emperor and the Crown Prince were about to embark on a campaign to move the venue of the wedding from England to Prussia. The Queen at once called for the Foreign Secretary and instructed Lord Clarendon to despatch a message to the English ambassador in Berlin 'not to *entertain* the *possibility* of such a question as the Princess Royal's marriage taking place at Berlin. The Queen *never* could consent to it,' she continued, 'and the assumption of its being *too much* for a Prince Royal of Prussia to *come* over to marry *the Princess Royal of Great Britain* IN England is too *absurd* to say the least . . . Whatever may be the usual practice of Prussian Princes, it is not *every* day that one marries the eldest daughter of the Queen of England. The question therefore must be considered as settled and closed.'

There was a price to be paid for winning this contest. Elizabeth Longford explains: 'Eight days before the ceremony a redoubtable army of Hohenzollern relatives began to descend on Buckingham Palace. The Queen could get along well enough with the older princes but the huge, hideous young ones with their ferocious moustaches and sharp, sarcastic remarks about England set her teeth on edge.'

Overall there was for the Queen much more pleasure than pain during the interval before the wedding. Victoria remained a gregarious woman and enjoyed the fact that Buckingham Palace resembled an extremely luxurious hotel in which most of the guests knew one another, the state rooms and wide corridors embracing much of the *Almanach de Gotha*. During the day Albert took his heartier male guests out shooting, the ladies and youngsters were taken round the sights of London, including the Crystal Palace at its new site in Sydenham. In the evenings there were intimate little supper parties where families who rarely saw one another met, listened to music – there were orchestras all over the place – or played whist.

The Queen loved it all, and was flattered by her brother-in-law Ernest's remark that she looked far too young to have a married daughter. On one evening she gave a state dinner for a thousand people, scarcely one of them lacking a title. As the state dining-room filled with guests, it was reported that the shimmer of jewellery and silk dresses reflected in the giant gas candelabra, became almost painful to the eyes.

When the Queen entered with her daughter, their short stature only seemed to emphasise their exalted rank – the two grandest women in Europe, far above mere Prussians and Hessians, Gothas and Brandenburgs. The sheer authority and indomitability of Queen Victoria was recognised by every guest standing behind their chair, waiting for her to take her seat. She was covered in diamonds and other priceless jewels, and then, as if to show their unimportance, had decorated both hair and dress with grass and haphazardly chosen flowers.

As the day of the wedding approached, parents and daughter increasingly dreaded the imminent separation. They had recently been living almost as a *ménage à trois*, and though Victoria looked forward to having Albert to herself again, she knew she would desperately miss her clever, interesting, loving daughter. As for Albert, perhaps the relationship was even more intimate. He had been giving Vicky lessons in statecraft and European politics in preparation for her life and responsibilities in Berlin.

The day before the wedding, 'poor dear Vicky's last unmarried day', was mainly given up to present-giving. Three tables had been set up in the large drawing-room. On two of them were Vicky's gifts. The Prussian prince, determined not to be outshone, had given his bride some enormous pearls. 'Fritz's pearls are the largest I ever saw,' noted the Queen. The third table was mounted by three huge candelabra, Victoria and Albert's gift to Fritz. Vicky gave her mother a brooch containing her hair. She embraced her mother, saying, 'I hope to be worthy to be your child.' It sounded like an echo of Victoria's vow of long ago, 'I will be good.'

Late that evening the three of them bade a last good night in Vicky's room. Victoria and Albert embraced her and gave her their blessing. 'She was much overcome,' Victoria recounted. 'I pressed her in my arms, and she clung to her truly adored papa with much tenderness.'

Little consideration has been given to the feelings of Vicky's sisters and brothers. These children formed a tight community of their own, seeing little of other families. Bertie, closest to Vicky in age, and Alice, would miss her most. Bertie shed many tears, and Alice dreaded the loss of her most intimate friend. Both children not only loved but admired Vicky for her cleverness. Alfred too would miss Vicky, but the other children, down to little Beatrice, formed almost another generation and might scarcely notice her absence after a time. For the wedding the girls wore pink satin trimmed with Newport lace, cornflowers and marguerites in their hair; the boys were in Balmoral tartan kilts, unfamiliar even to the uniform-conscious Prussian junkers.

The marriage procession formed in the forecourt of Buckingham Palace, some thirty carriages in all. Victoria and Albert with the bride had been daguerreotyped before mounting their carriage. All three looked solemn, the Queen blurred as well from her nervous shaking. 'It was the second most eventful day of my life as regards feelings,' she wrote later. 'I felt as if I were being married over again myself, only much more nervous.'

The procession moved slowly down the Mall, and then turned left into St James. The Chapel Royal was the venue for the ceremony as it had been for Victoria and Albert.

The bride's dress was of white moiré silk trimmed with Honiton lace; Fritz wore the uniform of a Prussian general. Vicky's grandmother, the Duchess of Kent, looked amazingly young in purple velvet and ermine.

Vicky, very composed, walked between her father and great uncle, King Leopold. They were preceded by the three elder of Vicky's sisters. Princess Alice could not entirely conceal her tears. Dr John Bird Sumner, the Archbishop of Canterbury, conducted the service. It was not a very efficient performance mainly because he failed to conceal his nervousness.

When the married pair emerged from the chapel they were greeted with a deafening sound of cheers from some 100,000 spectators, the music of a band, and the crash of artillery.

Vicky held back her tears until it was time to leave in the carriage for Windsor where they were to honeymoon. There the reception was as enthusiastic as in London. A rumbustious group of Eton boys unhitched the horses and dragged the carriage up to the castle.

The final departure for Berlin was from Gravesend on 2 February. It was a foul, chill morning with high winds and scudding clouds, reflecting the agony of separation. Earlier, Vicky had told her mother, 'I think it will kill me to take leave of Papa.' Now the time had come, in their day cabin on board the royal yacht *Victoria and Albert*. Vicky clung to Albert, the tears coursing down her already swollen cheeks. Then it was Victoria's turn, the tall soldierly figure of Fritz standing aside in embarrassed unease. The newly-weds' love was as deep as that between Victoria and Albert, but there were many storms ahead, beginning symbolically with the rough seas of the Channel, which Albert had once had to face before his own wedding.

CHAPTER TEN

What to do with Bertie?

On 26 June 1857, just as the first reports of the Indian Mutiny were coming in, an unprecedented military ceremony took place in Hyde Park. There were 4,000 troops present, many of them mounted, and a band played martial music. A semi-circle of seats had been constructed for spectators. In a special enclosure there waited sixty-two veterans of the Crimean War, all of whom had participated in some desperate action and conducted themselves with singular bravery. They were to be the first holders of the Victoria Cross, each medal carrying simply the two words, 'For Valour'.*

To the sound of cheers and firing guns, Victoria and Albert rode into the centre of this semi-circle, Victoria in black skirt and scarlet jacket, the Prince Consort, the instigator of the award, in field marshal's uniform. Prince Frederick William of Prussia, soon to be a member of the family, rode with them, followed by the suite in splendid uniforms.

The heroes were brought to the Queen in turn, some of the wounded requiring assistance. She exchanged a few words with each man, then bent down from her horse and pinned the medal to the man's left breast – 'a most moving and memorable moment'. More private soldiers than officers were honoured, for the award was open to all ranks, and carried with it an annuity of £10 a year.

* Some 1,360 VCs have been awarded, many of them posthumously; 633 were awarded in the First World War.

153

Victoria was deeply moved by the occasion. She wrote to Uncle Leopold:

What a *beautiful* and *touching* sight and ceremony (the first of the kind ever witnessed in England) the distribution of the medals was. From the highest Prince of the Blood to the lowest Private, all received the same distinction for the bravest conduct in the severest action, and the rough hand of the brave and honest private soldiers came for the first time in contact with that of their Sovereign and Queen! Noble fellows! I own I feel as if they were *my own children*; my heart beats for *them* as for my *nearest and dearest*. They were so touched, so pleased; many I hear cried . . . Several came by in a sadly mutilated state . . .

Whether or not influenced by the nation's preoccupation with militarism and jingoism during the Crimean War, or even the VC presentations, Victoria and Albert's oldest son and Prince of Wales, Bertie, chose this year of 1858 to express a strong wish to become a soldier. It could hardly have come as a surprise to his parents. He had always been fascinated by military ceremonies and parades – and he witnessed plenty of them – and above all military uniforms. Latterly, with the dismissal of Gibbs as his tutor for failing to improve Bertie academically, Victoria and Albert had appointed a colonel in the Grenadier Guards as 'Governor' – a new style of appointment even though his task was similar to Gibbs'. 'I have great confidence in Colonel Bruce,' Victoria wrote to Vicky in Berlin; and promoted him to major-general.

This appointment coincided with Bertie's seventeenth birthday, which in turn coincided with the surprise decision of his parents to give him a clothing allowance. Victoria warned him, 'We do *expect* that you will never wear anything *extravagant* or *slang*.' Soon she was complaining to her eldest daughter that Bertie 'took no interest in anything but clothes'. 'Oh! dear, what would happen if I were to die next winter: it is too awful a contemplation.'

Albert determined to press ahead with Bertie's cultural development, ordering Bruce to take the young man round art galleries in London and Italy. In Rome he had a specialist to instruct him on the famous busts. At dinner in the evening, there were not many laughs, all the guests being chosen for their cultural knowledge and achievements. There was never a military figure to be seen.

To Bertie's relief and satisfaction, this interminable cultural tour was cut short by the outbreak of war involving Austria-Hungary, Italy and France. A sloop, HMS *Scourge*, was sent to collect the prince, the general and their party. On the way home they called in at Lisbon, where at last Bertie had 'plenty of larking' with the happy-go-lucky King Pedro of Portugal. Victoria and Albert were not amused by this frolic.

What to do with Bertie? His parents discussed this problem ardently and took widespread advice. He was a most amiable young man, concerned to please everyone, especially his mother and father, yet he showed no sign of responsibility, serious interest in the arts or politics or anything much except shooting, hunting and clothes, some of these, alas, rather 'slang'. He was quite good at languages, German of course, and especially French which he loved. But soldiering remained his first interest.

Then, in an inspired moment, Victoria decided Bertie should become a royal ambassador. She agreed with Albert that it was risky but that the young man had to be given his head at some time. Canada had contributed substantially to the Crimean War and the British government thought it right and proper to make some acknowledgement of the sacrifice the Canadian people had made – a royal visit, in fact. Victoria shuddered at the thought of the journey, the stress on her nerves, the unfamiliarity of strange places. She summoned Lord Palmerston, the Prime Minister, and suggested, 'What about the Prince of Wales taking my place?'

Palmerston agreed, and Bertie could do nothing but welcome the idea, although he hoped he could get in plenty of shooting. So in July 1860 he was packed off in an enormous ship-of-the-line, accompanied by General Bruce, several political grandees, two amiable equerries, and his own doctor.

At the last minute before sailing, at the earnest pleading of President Buchanan, a short visit to the USA was added to the programme. Bertie was delighted at the prospect.

Bertie's serious duties included the laying of the foundation stone of the Federal Parliament building in Ottawa and the opening of a new railway bridge across the St Lawrence river. There was plenty of time for shooting during the day and dancing at night. Reports addressed to Victoria and Albert were read anxiously: they were wholly favourable. 'His manners with the people are frank and friendly without any mixture of assumed study to gain popularity by over civility.' Bruce told his employers that Bertie acquitted himself 'admirably'.

More ominous were some of the newspaper reports, which did not find their way to Buckingham Palace. Of one dance: 'He talked away to his partner . . . he whispered soft nothings to the ladies as he passed them in the dance, in short was the life of the party.' Another report told that the prince 'was more pleased with a pretty girl than all the state ceremonies and reception addresses of which he has been the honoured object.'

New York City was the high point of the American leg of this tour. There were levées and balls, and very few duties. Bertie loved the place, and the Americans loved him. President Buchanan wrote to the Queen that the Prince of Wales:

> has passed through a trying ordeal for a person of his years, and his conduct throughout has been such as become his age [nineteen] and station. Dignified, frank and affable, he has conciliated, wherever he has been, the kindness and respect of a sensitive and discriminating people.

Victoria welcomed home her son with great relief. Bertie in his ship had been much delayed by ferocious Atlantic storms, and his mother's nerves were in tatters. Albert's nerves were similarly affected, but for a different reason. He was concerned that Bertie's work timetable had been disrupted; nor did he take much account of the messages of praise at his son's performance, even General Bruce's account of Bertie's reception. All these favourable reports, Albert contended, even the one from President Buchanan, were calculated to ingratiate the young man's mother and father. To Bertie, Albert wrote bitterly, 'You appear to be under the delusion that the tumultuous welcome was for *you*. It was nothing of the kind. It was simply an expression of loyalty to the Queen.' At the same time he brushed aside Bertie's suggestion that now was the time to join the army. Certainly not: your education has to be completed.

Albert's failure to understand his eldest son and lack of generosity towards him, were his least attractive characteristics. Father and son were leagues apart in outlook and tastes, and seemed almost to talk a different language on points of duty and morality. Victoria was much closer to Bertie than Albert but never failed to support her husband in any discussion or action he recommended, and there was never the least hint that in troubled times she might provide protection from Albert's wrath. She knew that on the question of Bertie especially, they must speak as one.

It is possible to feel sympathy for all three of this ill-matched trio, but in particular for Bertie who remained affectionate towards both his parents while puzzled that he never seemed to earn any credit, no matter how hard he strived.

One reason for Prince Albert's lack of sympathy for Bertie throughout the 1850s was his own poor health and hypochondria, the one fuelling the other. The organising of the Great Exhibition, with all its accompanying anxiety and frustration seems to have set the pattern for a mode of living that fed on overwork and its accompanying nervous tension. 'The things of all sorts that are laid on our shoulders, i.e. on *mine*, are not to be told,' he once wrote to Stockmar, who remained his first confidant. The truth was not that all sorts of things were laid on his shoulders: he went out in search of responsibilities and then at once began to worry about them. Alas for Bertie, who was one of his father's main concerns, and Albert could not contemplate life without worry.

'I am tired to death with work, vexation and worry,' Albert wrote, again to Stockmar, after visiting Bertie at Oxford, where he found nothing satisfactory to report.

'We have been a good deal plagued lately with tiresome and annoying business, which unfortunately dear Papa will take too much to heart,' Victoria told Vicky in Berlin, 'and then it makes him unwell always – and affects his sleep. He really ought not to do so,' she continued, 'because it makes one's life so difficult if one minds things so much.'

If Baron Stockmar had been more of a doctor and less of a toady, he might at least have attempted to shake Albert out of his nervy hypochondria and unnecessary overwork. Only wise old Palmerston, who had by no means always enjoyed Albert's favour, begged Victoria to make her husband work office hours, learn to relax and cease from 'endlessly harassing himself'.

Albert complained about almost everything, most vehemently about the state of his health, and specifically about the state of his stomach and his sleeplessness. Gastric attacks could last for weeks, when only the plainest of food in small quantities was acceptable. Cramp in the stomach, bad teeth, and heavy catarrh also plagued him.

In the early months of 1860 Victoria conceived the idea of accompanying Albert on a visit to Vicky and Fritz in Coburg, staying with his brother and visiting the Rosenau. The prospect of this journey cheered Albert up no end. Victoria noticed how his health improved and certain contemporary worries (the worst of which was his concern at the expansion of the French navy and the threat of invasion) diminished in importance. They discussed their plans in detail and he wrote many letters to Vicky and also to his brother in Coburg.

Albert and Victoria were due to leave for Coburg in September, but his ill-health threatened to lead to a cancellation. His chief complaint was by now an old one – stomach cramps, shivering and aching limbs. Sir James Clark, bland as ever, tried to reassure Victoria and Albert that it was due to overwork and that all would be well as soon as he started his holiday. Still feeling weak and unwell, Albert embarked in the royal yacht on 23 September 1860 and after a comparatively calm passage, steamed up the Scheldt to Antwerp. Here they were met by King Leopold, seventy years old but looking fit, which was more than could be said of Albert.

For his part, Albert noted the unhealthy appearance of Wilhelm, Prince Regent of Prussia and Vicky's father-in-law. With the King himself very frail, it looked as if Fritz and Vicky were nearer to the throne than they had expected when they married. In the train between Antwerp and Coburg Victoria and Albert also learned of the recent death of the Dowager Duchess Marie who had been a stepmother to Albert when he was young. All this gloom and tragedy, Albert could reflect, made a doleful start to the holiday to which he had looked forward for so long.

Although the family was in full mourning when they reached Coburg, Vicky and Fritz were well and in high spirits, thankful to see Albert again, who in turn was enchanted to have sight at last of his first grandson. Little Willie was in a white dress decorated, for mourning, with black bows, the withered arm, from a bungled delivery, well concealed.

Victoria was equally moved by the occasion. 'Such a little love!' she wrote. 'He came walking in at [his nurse's] hand … He is a fine fat child, with a beautiful soft white skin … He has Fritz's eyes and Vicky's mouth and very fair curly hair. We felt so happy to see him at last!'

At the other end of the age scale, they met Stockmar the following day. Until four years earlier the baron had been such an important part of their daily lives; and now he 'looked quite himself,' Albert commented, 'though a little weak'. It was not surprising that he was 'showing signs of age' for the old doctor was now well over seventy and had relinquished many of his responsibilities.

On the following day Albert arranged for a visit to the Rosenau, something he had looked forward to for so long. Victoria travelled in a carriage with Ernest and Fritz, while Albert shared the second carriage with Vicky. When Albert's carriage was a short distance from the old castle, he ordered the coachman to halt, and taking Vicky by the hand led her along a secret path he had known as a child.

Later, Albert claimed that he had dreamed of doing this since the day Vicky, his first child, was born. Now that it was happening, he found he was not strong enough to face the emotional ordeal. He paused and might well have fallen but for Vicky's firm grip on his hand. Somehow he pulled himself together and struggled along the overgrown path until they were in sight of the Rosenau.

In a voice that was only just steady, Albert pointed out to Vicky the features of the castle, describing the different rooms where he had spent so much of his boyhood. Then they walked on and joining the other party went inside.

On the last day of the month, and almost the last planned day of their stay, they all visited another castle called the Kallenberg. Ernest had some new guns which he was anxious to try out, so the brothers shot over the hills for a while and then returned to lunch with the others. Afterwards, Victoria and Vicky settled down to some sketching while Albert excused himself, explaining that he had to see some people back at Coburg.

He departed alone in a carriage drawn by four horses. After several miles some sound, perhaps of a distant train whistle, caused the horses to shy. They bolted, out of the coachman's control. Ahead of them appeared a railway crossing, with the bar up and a wagon already waiting.

A horrible collision seemed inevitable. Albert acted promptly, opened the carriage door and leaped through the air into the ditch at the side of the road. He landed heavily and was cut about the face by the thorn bushes which grew freely at the roadside. Bleeding and badly shaken, he pulled himself clear. The carriage had been thrown on to its side and the horses had wrenched themselves clear of their traces. One horse lay dead in front of the now stationary train, the other three had made off up the road to Coburg. The coachman lay on the road verge, badly hurt.

Coincidentally, the three fleeing horses were recognised on the streets of Coburg by Colonel Henry Ponsonby, equerry to Prince Albert. He hastened to the scene where Albert, who was doing what he could for the coachman, instructed him to go to Kallenberg to inform the Queen of the accident 'but on no account to alarm her'. The tactful Ponsonby told the Queen that Albert had only scratched his nose. 'This prevented my being startled or *much* frightened. That came later,' Victoria recounted:

> I went at once to [Coburg] to my dearest Albert's rooms and found him lying quietly on [his valet's] bed with lint compresses on his nose, mouth and chin. He was quite cheerful, had not been in the least stunned, there had not been any injury and the features would not suffer. Oh! God! What did I not feel! I could only, and do only, allow the feelings of gratitude, not those of horror at what might have happened, to fill my mind. Everyone in such distress and excitement in Coburg. I sent off many telegrams to England, etc.

Albert came down to dinner that evening, heavily bandaged but putting on a show of cheerfulness which he did not really feel. Only Vicky among those at the table knew of her father's fear of carriage accidents since the death from this cause of both the Duke of Orleans and the King of Saxony in the same year. Only Vicky knew that before setting out for Coburg that day, Albert had half joked that he hoped that he would survive the journey. And from his recovery bed, it was to Vicky that her father confessed that as he faced imminent catastrophe, he had positively welcomed the thought of death.

Increasingly, as her father approached middle age and relations between him and her mother became more nerve-racked, the sensible but sensitive Vicky seemed to become closer than ever to her father. This feeling of affinity was fully reciprocated by Albert, who dreaded the end of this visit, although it had been only a qualified success.

One final melancholy act had to be played out, and on the last day at Coburg. His brother suggested a walk in the woods to some of their old haunts where they had played as boys. At one of the most beautiful spots, Albert paused, his handkerchief to his face. At first Ernest thought that his accident injuries might have reopened but, on looking closer, saw that it was tears not blood that were troubling his brother. 'He persisted in declaring,' Ernest wrote later, 'that he was well aware that he had been here for the last time in his life.'

The court was back at Windsor by the third week in October 1860, after another rough crossing of the Channel in the *Victoria and Albert*. Both the Queen and the Prince Consort wrote without delay to Vicky, who had now returned to Berlin. Victoria wrote:

Windsor Castle, October 20, 1860
Dearest Child,
    From this dull old prison, which however I was not sorry – once we had left Coburg and parted from you – to arrive at . . . Alice has I think told you all about our voyage – which was not pleasant – but which – all things considered – was better than might have been, and most fortunate we did come over when we did – for I don't think we could have crossed since!
    . . . The parting from you was indeed very sad! I saw how upset you were to see us go – and felt much so myself! Here we have found all well, Beatrice is my darling, but she is fast, alas! growing out of the baby – is becoming long-legged and thin. She is still however most amusing and very dear . . .

A few days later, Victoria wrote again to her beloved Vicky, prompting Albert to rebuke her for the frequency of the correspondence. It seemed that even after the children were safely married their parents continued to bicker about them. They agreed on the awfulness of Bertie, but there were rows about their next son, Alfred. Affie was as determined to join the navy, as was Arthur, later, to become a soldier. But Albert took it upon himself to arrange for Affie to go to sea at the tender age of thirteen.

I have been shamefully deceived about Affie [Victoria complained to Vicky] it was promised to me that the last year before he went to sea, he should be with us, instead of which he was taken away . . . Papa is most cruel upon the subject. I assure you, it is much better to have no children than to have them only to give them up! It is too wretched.

Affie's frigate *Euryalus* sailed to Malta, where she was welcomed with a royal salute. Outraged, Affie's fellow midshipmen bumped him on the deck in time with every gun shot. Such robust treatment did not seem to do him any harm, however. The Queen found her sailor son 'much improved' when he eventually came home on leave.

No one, least of all Victoria and Albert, could discern any sign of improvement in the Prince of Wales. He was still at Oxford, working sullenly and rarely, managing to evade his tutors and spend most of his time on the hunting field. Albert became seriously ill in December 1860, recovering only just in time for Christmas. This was spent in the now-traditional manner, with a great illuminated tree, fireworks, cards, presents, a great deal to eat (though not for Albert) and almost all the family there. As an added bonus, there was snow and enough ice for skating. Albert pushed Victoria in a chair with renewed youthful vigour and figure-skated beautifully. It was just like Frogmore twenty years earlier, a 'dear happy Christmas' as the Queen described it to the one missing member of her family.

On the same day Albert wrote to his brother in Coburg to wish him a happy new year – 'though I don't expect much good of it'.

Lord Palmerston had a more cheerful message for his Queen and her Consort. Quoting the poet Pope, he wrote:

> May day improve on day, and year on year
> Without a pain, a trouble, or a fear.

Within twenty-four hours, Albert's message of gloom proved to be the more accurate. From Prussia came a telegram informing them that the King, Frederick William IV, had died. He had looked so awful the last time they had seen him, that the news should have come as no surprise.

Victoria replied to the anguished letter from Vicky which followed:

What a dreadful New Year's day you must have spent! While we were surrounded by all the children and . . . all was gaiety – you were watching the flickering lamp of life gradually going out of the poor King whose memory will ever be remembered with gratitude and affection by us!

I trust, dearest child, this sad and to you so novel scene, (I have never even yet witnessed a death bed) will not be too much for your warm and feeling heart!

Fritz and Vicky were now only one step from the throne and Fritz's father, the new King, was not in good health. For Albert, deeply preoccupied with his own ill-health and weakness, there occurred now another savage blow with the death of his new doctor, William Bayly. For too long Sir James Clark had treated lightly Albert's well-nigh non-stop complaints. Bayly was due to replace old Clark and had already proved himself an exceedingly skilled physician. His death was caused by a railway accident, in which he was the only fatal casualty. Clark became seriously ill himself at the same time; he was over seventy-five and Victoria and Albert feared the worst.

Concern for Albert's health threatened to become the first consideration not only of the Queen but of all members of the court. On a tour of the Midlands, which included many appointments and engagements, Victoria was awoken in the middle of the night by the sound of retching. Albert was lying across the bed, doubled up in agony, his face pouring with sweat. She was about to call for help when he recovered enough to reassure her that the pain would pass, as indeed it did. He also managed to get through the next day's engagements, though Victoria feared for him. Back in London, Clark, now recovered, could make no diagnosis but, as usual, told him to ease up on his work.

The worst blow among the agonies of early 1861 occurred on 16 March. On that day, Victoria wrote from Frogmore, her mother's home, to 'my dearly beloved Uncle [Leopold]:

> On this, the most dreadful day of my life, does your poor broken-hearted child write one line of love and devotion. *She* is gone! That *precious, dearly beloved tender* Mother whom I never was parted from but for a few months – without whom *I* can't *imagine life* – has been taken from us! It is *too* dreadful! But she is at peace – at rest – her fearful sufferings at an end! It was quite painless – though there was very *distressing*, heartrending breathing to witness. I held her dear, dear hand in mine to the very last, which I am truly thankful for! But the watching that precious life going out was fearful!

So Victoria had now 'witnessed a death bed', like her daughter. She had not always been as kind to her mother as she might have been, especially in the Conroy days, but she had truly loved her and would indeed miss her dreadfully. Albert had kept from Victoria Clark's diagnosis some weeks earlier of cancer of the arm. It was in fact erysipelas, curable today with one shot of penicillin, but in the 1860s a frequent cause of death.

Albert shared her grief to the full, as he shared all her sufferings. This time the suffering was hysterical, almost to the point of a nervous breakdown. Vicky came over from Germany for the funeral and to console her mother. But Victoria was inconsolable, as she made clear in a letter to Vicky after her return home a month after the Duchess of Kent's death:

> You are right, dear child, I do not wish to feel better. My head has been tiresome and troublesome and I can still bear little or no noise. The relief of tears is great – and though since last Wednesday night I have no very violent outburst – they come again and again every day, and are soothing to the bruised heart and soul ... The more distant the dreadful event becomes, and the more others recover their spirits – the more trying it becomes to me!

Albert, suffering additionally from a tooth abscess, sleeplessness, coughing and his usual intestinal problems, decided with Victoria to seek comfort from 'Doctor' Osborne. This doctor failed, too, partly because there was no will in the two patients to get better – from grief or toothache. On 25 April they returned to London – 'I dread it so much,' the Queen remarked.

Through all this misery, Albert had taken upon himself the task of sorting out the affairs of his late mother-in-law, which were in a chaotic state. Nor was the work helped by the sudden death of Sir George Couper, the duchess's comptroller, or by Albert's refusal to call in any professional assistance.

Stories about the unstable condition of the Queen had spread widely around the courts of Europe. Some of them reached Vicky, who was greatly alarmed, although when she made a brief visit to London, it was the condition of her father that worried her more. His latest concern was that Bertie must be found a bride, and Vicky was supposed to find a suitable one. Her mother had earlier made her own appeal. 'Oh, if you would find us one!' she begged. 'We must look out for princesses for Bertie,' she continued, 'as his wife ought not to be above a year or 2 younger than him, therefore 14 or 15 now, pretty, quiet and clever and sensible.'

Victoria had also without any apparent reason changed her mind about the army as a career for the boy. She suddenly conceived the notion that the army's discipline combined with personal independence might be the making of the young man. He was certainly wasting his time at university. Albert did a reverse turn, too, possibly by now for the sake of peace. Anyway, three days before the death of the Duchess of Kent, he confronted his troublesome son at university. He was backed up by General Bruce, who also, and equally suddenly, changed his mind.

Facing these two men, who had made life such a misery for him for so long, Bertie could scarcely believe his ears when he heard his father tell him that he was to proceed at once to Ireland, to the Curragh Camp, east of Kildare, to be attached to a battalion of the Grenadier Guards. He was not, however, to lead the life of an ordinary guards officer. Bertie was, in effect, to go on an amazing crash course in order that within a few weeks he would be capable of manoeuvring a brigade in the field – and 'to learn the duties of every grade from Ensign upwards'. He would have his own quarters where he could entertain his fellow officers. Everything had been worked out in the smallest detail. The programme had been prepared by the military for only one purpose, to satisfy the Queen and the Prince Consort.

To Bertie it all sounded wonderful and romantic in the first degree. He hurried from the meeting, murmuring his thanks, and called for his tailor. He already knew every detail, every shade of colour, of a Grenadier Guards officer's uniform. He had never been so happy in his life, and he by no means led an isolated life: all around him platoons marched on the parade ground, swords flashed in the summer sun and the barking of orders was like sweet music to Bertie's ears.

Some five weeks into his training, Victoria and Albert, with the Duke of Cambridge, the army's C-in-C, turned up in Dublin to see their new soldier son. They had hoped to see Bertie leading a battalion. But 'You are too imperfect in your drill, sir,' his colonel had told him. 'Your word of command is indistinct.' Albert, who knew nothing about army practice (even though a field marshal) was very disappointed, and doubted that Bertie could ever make a soldier.

The Grenadier Guards officers were a rich and raffish lot, some of whom kept mistresses in their quarters as well as hunters in the stables. They were by no means unfriendly or disrespectful to Bertie, but they were very high spirited, and amused by the Prince of Wales's sexual innocence. One night after a mess party, when doubtless a great deal of champagne had been drunk, some of them persuaded 'a vivacious young actress', Nellie Clifden, to occupy Bertie's quarters and slip into his bed before he returned. Bertie's loss of innocence that night had the profoundest effect on the young man.

In that sort of company, the news of this prank spread rapidly and reached London society in no time, though no one dared to recount the story to Victoria and Albert.

Fortunately they were up at Balmoral, far removed from sources of gossip.

Victoria and Albert and their party had taken to travelling by night to Scotland in the newly introduced sleeper-cars, which Victoria found so much more relaxing than daylight travel. The journey out of London started ominously, in a real August summer storm. 'A cloudburst with thunder and lightning accompanied us to the station,' the Queen recalled, 'and as we drew out of St Pancras the night sky was covered with eerie blue light.' The turbulent night evidently soon settled down, and on the following morning Deeside looked its noblest and best.

Balmoral was the one place where Albert seemed able to throw off both gloom and ill-health. Friends said that he became a new man as soon as he began breathing fresh Scottish air. Victoria had given him for his birthday a new set of guns, breech-loading rifles, and he was soon out on the hills with his ghillie and loader. On his first expedition he shot no fewer than three stags, and repeated the score the following day. He immediately wrote to Palmerston to recommend that the infantry be re-equipped with breech-loaders forthwith.

Day after day the weather was clear and cold, and there was a special happiness in the air, too. Numbered among the party were Princess Alice and the handsome (but penurious) Prince Louis of Hesse,* who was the nephew of the reigning grand-duke. Alice's elder sister had brought about the intro-duction, and to the satisfaction of both families, an engage-ment was soon announced. The young couple were as ardently in love as Vicky and Fritz, and as Victoria and Albert, for that matter. A few months earlier Albert had written to Stockmar, 'Tomorrow our marriage will be twenty-one years old! How many a storm has swept over it, and still it continues green and fresh and throws out vigorous roots.' Alice enjoyed a special frail beauty, unmatched by any of her sisters. She also

---

* He became the grandfather of Admiral of the Fleet the Earl Mountbatten of Burma.

had a sweet temperament. What was to be Albert's last visit to his Scottish castle was filled with happiness. The Queen was greatly refreshed by it, and even Albert could complain only of a cold.

They went out for long expeditions through the Highlands, travelling on foot, horseback or in traps, according to the roads. They travelled hundreds of miles, putting up at inns or lodges belonging to neighbours. Of the second of these tours Victoria noted, 'This was the pleasantest and most enjoyable expedition I ever made, and the recollection of it will always be more agreeable . . .' She loved travelling incognito, concealing her identity, among her most humble subjects. To this end, their escorting policeman was sent ahead around midday to seek lodgings for the night. These were not always readily available, as the area was sparsely populated, and in any case the accommodation was plain by their usual standards. But none of them worried about that.

In late September, Alice and Louis, Lady Churchill and General Grey, Albert's private secretary, five ghillies led by Jo Grant and John Brown, who was to become an important figure in the Queen's life, set out with Victoria and Albert for an expedition deep into the Grampians. They headed first for a place called Fettercairn, set at the foot of Cairn o' Mount, near the fast-flowing River North Esk, and forty miles from Balmoral. The Queen takes up the narrative of a typical informal outing:

> A little further on we came to a wood, where we got out and walked along Major McInroy's Burn. The path winds along through the wood just above this most curious narrow gorge, which is unlike any of the other lynns; the rocks are very peculiar, and the burn very narrow, with deep pools completely overhung by wood. It extends some way. The woods and grounds might be in Wales, or even in Hawthornden. We walked through the wood and a little way along the road, till the carriages overtook us. We had three miles further to drive to Fettercairn. We came upon a flat country, evidently much cultivated, but it was too dark to see anything.

At a quarter-past seven o'clock we reached the small quiet town, or rather village, of Fettercairn, for it was very small – not a creature stirring, and we got out at the quiet little inn, 'Ramsay Arms', quite unobserved, and went at once upstairs. There was a very nice drawing-room, and next to it, a dining-room, both very clean and tidy – then to the left our bed-room, which was excessively small, but also very clean and neat, and much better furnished than at Grantown. Alice had a nice room, the same size as ours; then came a mere morsel of one, (with a 'press bed,') in which Albert dressed; and then came Lady Churchill's bed-room just beyond. Louis and General Grey had rooms in an hotel called 'The Temperance Hotel', opposite. We dined at eight, a very nice, clean, good dinner. Grant and Brown waited. They were rather nervous, but General Grey and Lady Churchill carved, and they had only to change the plates, which Brown soon got into the way of doing. A little girl of the house came in to help – but Grant turned her round to prevent her looking at us! The landlord and landlady knew who we were, but *no one else* except the coachman, and they kept the secret admirably.

The evening being bright and moonlight and very still, we all went out, and walked through the whole village, where not a creature moved; – through the principal little square, in the middle of which was a sort of pillar or Town Cross on steps, and Louis read, by the light of the moon, a proclamation for collections of charities which was stuck on it. We walked on along a lane a short way, hearing nothing whatever – not a leaf moving – but the distant barking of a dog! Suddenly we heard a drum and fifes! We were greatly alarmed, fearing we had been recognised; but Louis and General Grey, who went back, saw nothing whatever. Still, as we walked slowly back, we heard the noise from time to time, – and when we reached the inn door we stopped and saw six men march up with fifes and a drum (not a creature taking any notice of them), go down the street, and back again. Grant and Brown were out; but had no idea what it could be. Albert asked the little maid, and the answer was, 'It's just a band,' and that it walked about in this way twice a week. How odd! It went on playing some time after we got home. We sat till half-past ten working, and Albert reading, – and then retired to rest.

Soon after Victoria and Albert returned to Balmoral, their fortunes reverted to their earlier condition. Their first disappointment was over Bertie again. He had ostensibly gone to Germany to observe the army manoeuvres, but that was only a cover for meeting a Danish princess in Baden. Vicky negotiated this delicate rendezvous because she thought Princess Alexandra would make a fine wife for her brother. He did quite like her but not with the fire and enthusiasm Vicky had hoped for. He was equally lukewarm when he returned to Balmoral. Additionally, as his mother reported to Vicky, he had conceived 'a sudden fear of marrying and above all of having children (which for so young a man is so strange a fear) seems to have got hold of him.' What could they do about Bertie? they asked themselves again. There was worse to come.

Before returning to London, John Brown, Victoria's favourite ghillie, 'hoped we should all be well through the winter and return all safe . . . and above all that you may have no deaths in the family'. That was not to be. Almost their first news was that typhoid fever had struck the Portuguese royal family, with whom they remained very close. Prince Ferdinand was the first to succumb. A few days later King Pedro himself, only twenty-five years old, died. This second loss was deeply felt by Albert: King Pedro was an old friend to whom he was not only adviser and surrogate father, but also a first cousin once removed.

CHAPTER ELEVEN

The Conflicts of Mature Marriage

In 1860 Victoria and Albert's marriage had lasted for twenty years. No one doubted its success, though very few knew how precious the emotional relationship was. High words and tantrums may have been overheard by the domestic staff but these were not discussed – even among themselves, and certainly not outside the palace.

Certain members of society, however, notably the Duchess of Bedford, believed they knew about the quarrels between the monarch and her consort from the early days of their marriage. This duchess also declared that Albert had never been in love with Victoria and had married her only for the position and wealth. Few heard this theory and even fewer believed it.

In this early period of marriage, no one understood better than Lord Melbourne the complex strains and conflicts which beset the relationship between Victoria and Albert. Melbourne was not only highly intelligent; he was also Victoria's first confidant. He alone understood the difficult Lehzen affair, sympathising with both sides, foreseeing the inevitable outcome and sharing Albert's relief.

The child-bearing years brought Victoria and Albert many joys, many changes and many new stresses. They greatly enlarged Albert's responsibilities, which was excellent for him, but led to resentment in Victoria. She did not care for delegating the powers she had enjoyed and was soon complaining about the 'unreasonable' amount of time which Albert's business took up.

172

How much these strains and stresses were caused by pregnancy depression no one will ever know. The process of childbearing occupied so much of their marriage and was unusually onerous for the Queen. True, with every pregnancy Albert increasingly stood in for her, especially during the last weeks, but there were certain duties she could never delegate.

In addition the wide range of the children's ages meant that Victoria was simultaneously tackling infants and adolescents with all their problems, and in particular Bertie's. Her unhappiness was further increased by the guilt she suffered from her jealousy of Albert's closeness to the two eldest girls, Vicky and Alice.

The Queen was at times at her wits' end to know what to do about Albert. She could not open her heart to her eldest son. The only person she could confide in was Vicky in Germany, and the long letters raced to and fro by special messenger. 'You say no one is perfect but Papa,' the Queen wrote. 'But he has his faults too. He is very often very trying – in his hastiness and over-love of business – and I think you would find it very trying if Fritz was as hasty and harsh (momentarily and unintentionally as it is) as he is!'

The explosions of anger over some trifling disagreement were mutual, and prolonged, like some verbal artillery exchange. After these appalling exchanges came the letters, mostly ill thought out and hastily written. Albert wrote to Victoria:

You have again lost your self-control quite unnecessarily. I did not say a word which could wound you, and I did not begin the conversation, but you have followed me about and continued it from room to room. There is no need for me to promise to *trust* you, for it was not a question of trust, but of your fidgety nature, which makes you insist on entering, with feverish eagerness, into details about orders and wishes which, in the case of a Queen, are commands, to whoever they may be given. This is your nature; it is not against Vicky, but is the same with everyone and has been the cause of much unpleasantness for you. It is the dearest wish of my heart to save you from these and worse consequences, but the only result of my efforts is that I am accused of want of feeling, hard heartedness, injustice, hatred, jealousy, distrust, etc. etc. I do my duty towards you even though it means that life is embittered by 'scenes' when it should be governed by love and harmony. I look upon this with patience as a test which has to be undergone, but you hurt me desperately and at the same time do not help yourself.

There is no record of Victoria's reply to this outburst, but elsewhere there is evidence that such tumultuous rows were followed by expressions of deep love – 'My love and sympathy are limitless and inexhaustible,' Albert once wrote. Her messages of peace were equally ardent. These disputes were at their worst after the birth of their last child and may well be associated with a radical change in their sexual relations, but that, of course, will never be known.

Another and equally hysterical outburst occurred shortly after the birth of the frail last boy on 7 April 1853. A fire had broken out at Windsor only three weeks earlier, when the Queen and her ladies were forced to take shelter in the Green Drawing-Room while the servants, soaked and choking, attempted to remove furniture and pictures. The Queen was calm throughout but there is evidence of something like a nervous breakdown in this quotation from a letter from Albert to Victoria:

Dear Child. I have reread your letter over several times. Now it will be right to consider calmly the facts of the case. The *whole* offence which led to a continuance of hysterics for more than an hour, and the traces of which have remained for more than 24 hours more, was: that I complained of your turning several times from inattention the wrong leaves in a Book which was to be marked by us as a Register & test the completeness of a collection of Prints. This miserable little trifle produced the distressing scene. In which, in case I am accused of making things worse by my false method of treatment, I admit that my treatment has on this occasion as on former ones signally failed, but I know of no other. I either try to demonstrate the groundlessness and injustice of the accusations which are brought against me, then I increase your distress. You undervalue your own capacity & are unnecessarily diffident on that account. I never intend or wish to offend you. If you are violent I have no other choice but to leave you. I leave the room and retire to my own room in order to give you time to recover yourself, then you follow me to renew the dispute and have it *all out*. Now don't believe that I do not sincerely and deeply pity you for the sufferings you undergo, or that I deny you do suffer really very much, I merely deny that I am the *cause* of them, though I have unfortunately often been the *occasion*. I am often astonished at the effect which a hasty word of mine has produced. In fact in your candid way you generally explain later what was the real cause of your complaint ... It appears now that the apprehension, that you might be made answerable for the suffering, perhaps the loss of health, of the Baby (occasioned by the milk of the Wet nurse not agreeing on account of your having frequently expressed a wish to have a Nurse from the Highlands of Scotland) was the real *cause* of your distress which broke out on the occasion of the Registration of the prints. Your letter now contains a hint about something concerning Stockmar which you have treasured up!

Their relationship may have changed over the past twenty years, punctuated as it was by nervous outbursts, and their appearance had certainly aged, yet they still made a handsome regal couple.

When Victoria was twelve, Lady Wharncliffe, wife of the statesman, described her as 'very much grown though short for her age, with nice countenance and distingué figure, tho' not very good; and her manner the most perfect mixture of childishness and civility I ever saw. She is born a Princess,' she concluded, 'without the *least* appearance of art or affectation.'

Victoria's Uncle Leopold was only one of many who were concerned about her height, but even when fully grown she was barely five feet tall. This same uncle also showed early concern about her plumpness. He knew she took little exercise beyond riding, but he advised her 'to force herself to take exercise'. Moreover 'a certain little princess,' he noted archly, 'eats a little too *much*, and almost always a little *too fast*.' Like most Hanoverians, she seemed unable to contain her appetite all through her life, and her plumpness increased accordingly.

Melbourne took up the same refrain when Victoria became Queen. He was always telling her to eat less, emphasising that it was 'a family failing'. 'Only eat when you are hungry,' he once advised her; to which she neatly retorted, 'I should be eating all day, then, because I am always hungry.' But she was 'horrified' when, at the age of nineteen, she was found to weigh eight stone thirteen pounds, 'an incredible weight for my size'.

Melbourne never carped about his Queen's plumpness and once sought to reassure her by suggesting that she had 'a good chance of getting very fat'. As for her height, he considered that, far from this being a misfortune, it added to her queenly appearance. This was true but Victoria never quite believed it and remained sensitive about her height, though comforted that her shortness was unobserved when she rode.

Melbourne did, however, carp about the Queen's hair. From childhood fairness, of which he had approved, it tended to grow darker and there was nothing to be done about that. Victoria thought her eyebrows inadequate and proposed to shave them to encourage growth. Melbourne discouraged this, declaring that they were 'very nice' as they were.

At the time of her declaration of intention to marry Albert, the Irish-born politician John Wilson Croker while admitting she was not beautiful, asserted that the flush on her cheeks and her clear eyes, soft without being downcast, made her 'as interesting and handsome as any young lady I ever saw'.

The Queen never quite lost her fear of going blind. She believed she had inherited her eyes from the blind George III and complained of soreness in them from childhood. As is common, they weakened with age, and she was almost blind at the end, but her eyesight lasted better than she feared, though her eyes' protuberance tended to increase in old age. She could not alter that, any more than she could conceal her receding Hanoverian chin. The smallness of her hands, of which she was also conscious, she sought to camouflage by wearing an unusually large number of rings. In spite of this there are numerous reports of their remarkable softness.

No such qualifications were voiced about the appearance of Prince Albert. Everyone remarked on his fine figure and regular features. He was the *beau idéal* of a prince, made more splendid when beside his unhandsome brother. On his second and decisive visit to London, with Ernest, Victoria, it will be recalled, first caught sight of him, travel weary and forlorn, from the top of a staircase at Windsor. 'It was with some emotion that I beheld Albert, who is *beautiful.*'

The following day, when she could observe him at leisure, Victoria wrote of 'such beautiful blue eyes, an exquisite nose, and such a pretty mouth with delicate moustachios and slight but very slight whiskers: a beautiful figure, broad in the shoulders and fine waist.'

Albert began to suffer from a receding hairline quite early in his marriage and, like Victoria, put on weight, though not through over-eating. We get an unexpected and brief picture of him in November 1854, at the age of thirty-five, from Thomas Carlyle. The latter was searching for pictures in the Print Room at Windsor for his life of Frederick the Great, when the librarian warned him of Prince Albert's approach:

> There was a soft step to the door – and there was the handsome young gentleman, not advancing until I bowed. Well-built figure of near my own height, florid *blond* face (with fair hair) but the eyes much better than I fancied; a pair of strong steady eyes, with a good healthy briskness in them. He was civility itself, and in a fine simple fashion; a sensible man withal.

There seems no evidence of the stress and worry which Albert was alleged to be suffering from the absence of an end to the Crimean War.

CHAPTER TWELVE

Tragedy in the Blue Room

The news of Bertie's seduction by Nellie Clifden would inevitably have reached the ears of Prince Albert in time, but it took that old mischief-maker and sanctimonious toady Baron Stockmar to ensure that the scandal was not delayed in its telling. On 12 November 1861, three days after Bertie's twentieth birthday, Albert received a letter from the baron. All Europe was agog, he wrote, over the story that the Prince of Wales was having an affair with an actress in Ireland, and had even brought her to stay at Windsor Castle.

Albert was stunned by the news and for three days did nothing except to enquire of Lord Torrington whether there was any truth in the story. Torrington was known as 'that arch gossip of all gossips', a member of the court for many years, and sometimes also described as '*The Times* correspondent at Windsor Castle'. 'Stockmar's information is perfectly true,' Lord Torrington answered. 'Everyone knows.'

Rather than face his young son, Albert typically wrote him a letter: page after page of dismay and horror, predictions of disaster and mortification. How *could* he have done such a thing? The letter, dated 16 November 1861, began:

> I write to you with a heavy heart on a subject which has caused me the deepest pain I have yet felt in this life, having to address my son, in whom we had during twenty years fondly hoped to rear a Prince, and an ornament to a great and powerful and religious nation, as one who has sunk into vice and debauchery ...

'Vice and debauchery' and, later, 'depraved'. Such words seem somewhat excessive and naïve, considering the standards of morality among the rich and raffish of a Guards regiment. It was commonplace, even thought desirable, for such young men to be introduced to the techniques of sex before marriage. The sexually inhibited Albert knew nothing of this. Moreover this woman, Albert pointed out, frequented the lowest dance halls, and was already dubbed 'the Princess of Wales'. She was very likely diseased, she would probably become pregnant, even arrange to become so, and ensure that everyone would know the identity of the father. Albert continued:

> If you were to try and deny it she can drag you into a Court of Law to force you to own it & there with you in the witness box, she will be able to give before a greedy Multitude disgusting details of your profligacy for the sake of convincing the Jury, yourself cross-examined by a railing indecent attorney and hooted and yelled at by a Lawless Mob!! Oh horrible prospect, which this person has in her power, any day to realise! and to break your poor parents' hearts!

Albert judged it time to inform Victoria of this grave turn of events, and perhaps even show her his letter.

The Queen was dismayed but not entirely surprised. 'Oh! that boy – much as I pity him I never can or shall look at him without a shudder as you can imagine . . .' 'The Queen never forgot her husband's woebegone face as he came into her room carrying the letter,' Elizabeth Longford wrote of this moment. Victoria also recognised that, once again, Albert did not look at all well, and a feeling of dread overcame her. Many a time Albert had told her that, happy as he had always been in his marriage and life, if he were to be attacked by serious illness, he would submit himself to the will of God. By Friday 22 November he knew only too well that he was indeed seriously ill. 'I do not cling to life,' he told the Queen. 'You do: but I set no store by it. I am sure if I had a serious illness I should give up at once, I should not struggle for life. I have no tenacity of life.'

What he still retained, however, was his tenacious sense of duty. Suffering as he was from toothache, insomnia, pain in the bowels, shivering and sickness, and above all despair about his son, he fulfilled a commitment to inspect buildings for the new Staff College and Royal Military Academy at Sandhurst. The rain poured down all day and he returned drenched and tortured by rheumatic pains.

Nevertheless, there was one further duty he felt obliged to perform. Although he had received a prompt and contrite letter from his eldest son, now at Cambridge, he knew that he must talk to him for what he almost certainly believed would be the last time. None of Albert's doctors appear to have advised him against such an expedition, although their patient had written in his diary (24 November), 'I am full of rheumatic pains and feel thoroughly unwell. Have scarcely closed my eyes at night for the last fortnight.'

Albert took the 10.30 a.m. train to Cambridge on 25 November. It was a cold and stormy day. Nevertheless, he insisted on taking a walk round the city with his son. They were recognised by many people on the streets: the Prince of Wales the shorter of the two, the Prince Consort bent towards him in earnest conversation, both wrapped up well against the raw weather. Bertie, unused to navigating on his own, lost his way and made the long walk even longer.

Albert spent another more or less sleepless night in Cambridge, and was back at Windsor shortly after midday on 26 November. The pains in his back and legs were worse than ever, but he felt that he had done all he could to save Bertie from further moral degradation. Dr William Jenner, the great authority on what was euphemistically called 'the fever', visited Windsor the next day, examined Albert, and remained.

Jenner offered no diagnosis and Albert needed none. He knew he was dying. In a brief exchange with Alice who was playing the dual role of loving daughter and nurse, and occasionally, when requested, pianist and vocalist (she had a sweet voice), he asked her, 'Have you told your sister [Vicky] anything?'

'Yes, I told her you are very ill,' she replied.

'You did wrong,' answered her father. 'You should have told her that I am dying. Yes, I am dying,' he repeated.

The effect of this statement on his daughter and the Queen, who was also present, was dreadful. Victoria was hardly sleeping at all and was wearing herself out dashing needlessly from room to room pausing only to wipe her tears and fall into a chair sobbing.

In the midst of this appalling domestic crisis there occurred an international crisis between Washington and London. Almost a year earlier, and shortly after Bertie's return from North America, civil war broke out in the USA. The southern states refused to abolish slavery, believing their economy was at stake, but the causes of the conflict were much more complex than that alone. South Carolina was the first of the southern states to secede from the Union, and nine more rapidly followed, forming a Confederacy. The first shots were fired in December 1860, and the civil war intensified with the election as President of Abraham Lincoln, who determined that unity must be restored.

The fighting became savage and outrages were committed by both sides. The Union was superior in numbers and industrial strength. The Confederacy enjoyed a solid sense of righteousness and political and moral tenacity. It was the first 'modern' war, with novel weaponry, trenches and barbed wire, and with steamships and railways a consideration in strategy.

The British naturally tended to back the underdog, but mainly because of the threat to the British cotton industry which imported most of its raw cotton from the southern states and was unable to make up the loss of these supplies from elsewhere. The Unionists were well aware of this prejudice and were sensitive to any hint of material support that might be offered to the enemy. Besides, the Unionists were, after half a century, still smarting from the British burning of Washington in the war of 1812.

This was the background to what became known as 'the *Trent* affair'. The essence is summed up in the diary entry

Albert managed to write, although very ill, on 28 November 1861:

> An American warship holds up our mail packet *Trent* on the high seas and boards her, and removes by force four gentlemen from the Southern States, who were to have gone to London and Paris as envoys. They are carried off to New York. General indignation. The Law Officers declare the act as a breach of international law.

The envoys, it seems, had earlier succeeded in getting as far as Cuba, where they were given passage in the British ship. The *Trent* had been halted by a shot across her bows, an armed party then boarding her. Prince Albert was right about the 'general indignation' in the country, up to the highest level. The American minister in London, Charles Francis Adams, was warned of the dire consequences of this act of piracy. There was the hum of imminent war in the air through-out Britain. The First Lord of the Admiralty, the Duke of Somerset, was ordered by Prime Minister Lord Palmerston, to activate the fleet. 'The act of wanton violence and outrage which has been committed, makes it not unlikely that other sudden acts of aggression may be attempted.'

At the Foreign Office, Lord John Russell, the Foreign Secretary, drafted a bellicose and threatening memorandum for the British ambassador in Washington. In effect, this threatened withdrawal of 'our man in Washington' unless there was total acceptance of the British demands. A declar-ation of war must then inevitably follow.

A copy of this draft memorandum was received by Albert at Windsor, regardless of his weakening condition. It was 30 November.

Although 'I could hardly hold my pen' as he described his condition to the Queen, Albert forced himself out of bed at his usual hour of 7 a.m. It was Sunday morning, the Prince Consort had only a few more days to live, but the new draft prepared for the Queen, although firm, lacked the crude belli-cosity of the Foreign Secretary's effort.

[the Queen] should have liked to have seen the expression of a hope, that the American captain, did not act under instructions, or, if he did that he misapprehended them, that the United States Government must be fully aware that the British Government could not allow its flag to be insulted, and the security of her mail communications to be placed in jeopardy; and Her Majesty's Government are unwilling to believe that the United States Government intended wantonly to put an insult upon this country . . .

It was a long memorandum, but there was a softening in language and construction in every line. Washington was not to know it, but it was the Prince Consort himself who had taken the sting out of the message and made war between the two nations now improbable.

All the amendments were accepted and later in Washington all the requests were met, the apologies made, and it was conceded that the American captain was acting on his own initiative. The envoys were 'cheerfully liberated'. Relations between Washington and London returned to normal. The Queen in her own hand had written in the margin, 'This draft was the last the beloved Prince ever wrote . . .' He ate no breakfast, she further noted. He forced himself to attend chapel with Victoria but afterwards could eat no luncheon; nor, later, any dinner. Sir James Clark and Dr Jenner both visited Albert that evening and expressed their disappointment. Their patient suffered another dreadful night of shivering and pain.

The activities of the court were now concerned exclusively with the Prince Consort, his welfare and condition. When she was not consumed by anguish, Victoria was short and tetchy. When Palmerston, for the second time, begged her to take further opinion of the medical profession, she wrote an admonishing reply:

The Queen is very much obliged to you for the kind interest displayed in your letter received this day. The Prince has had a feverish cold the last few days, which disturbed his rest at night, but Her Majesty has seen His Royal Highness before similarly affected and hopes that in a few days it will pass off ... Her Majesty would be very unwilling to cause unnecessary alarm, where no cause exists for it, by calling in a Medical Man who does not upon ordinary occasions attend at the Palace.

More forcefully, in her Journal, Victoria wrote, 'Dreadfully annoyed at a letter from Lord Palmerston suggesting Dr Ferguson should be called in as he heard Albert could not sleep or eat. Very angry about it ...'

No one has written more movingly about the next period than Lytton Strachey:

The restlessness and acute suffering of the earlier days gave place to a settled torpor and an ever-deepening gloom. Once the failing patient asked for music – 'a fine chorale at a distance'; and a piano having been placed in the adjoining room, Princess Alice played on it some of Luther's hymns, after which the Prince repeated 'The Rock of Ages'. Sometimes his mind wandered; sometimes the distant past came rushing upon him; he heard the birds in the early morning, and was at Rosenau again, a boy. Or Victoria would come to read him *Peveril of the Peak*, and he showed that he could follow the story, and then she would bend over him, and he would murmur, 'liebes Frauchen' and 'gutes Weibchen', stroking her cheek ...

The day after Albert had effectively saved the nation from war, 2 December 1861, the Queen wrote that she was 'terribly nervous and depressed' partly because Albert had risen from his bed at 7 a.m. and sent for Dr Jenner. After the doctor had arrived and examined Albert yet again, he told the Queen 'that there was no reason to be alarmed; but that one might fear its turning into a long feverish disposition ...'

On most days Albert had insisted upon dressing. Not on that Monday, however. In dressing-gown and slippers, he moved restlessly from room to room as he had done earlier, stretching out on a sofa one moment and then sitting in an armchair in the sitting-room. His only nourishment during the day was 'some soup with brown bread which unfortunately disagreed with him'.

Victoria derived some comfort from writing to her 'Dearest Uncle' in Laeken.

> Windsor Castle, 4th December 1861
> I have many excuses to make for not writing yesterday, but I had a good deal to do, as my poor dear Albert's rheumatism has turned out to be a regular influenza, which has pulled and lowered him very much. Since Monday he has been confined to his room. It affects his appetite and sleep, which is very disagreeable, and you know he is always *so* depressed when anything is the matter with him. However, he is decidedly better today, and I hope in two or three days he will be quite himself again. It is extremely vexatious, as he was so particularly well till he caught these colds, which came upon worries of various kinds ... Ever your devoted Niece,
> Victoria R.

Two days later her news was more reassuring:

> Windsor Castle, 6th December 1861
> My Beloved Uncle, – I am thankful to report decidedly better of my beloved Albert. He has had much more sleep, and has taken much more nourishment since yesterday evening. Altogether, this nasty, feverish sort of influenza and deranged stomach is *on* the mend, but it will be slow and tedious, and though there has *not* been one alarming symptom, there has been such restlessness, such sleeplessness, and such (till today) *total* refusal of all food, that it made one *very, very* anxious, and I can't describe the *anxiety* I have gone through! I feel today a good deal shaken, for four nights I got myself only two or three hours' sleep. We have, however, every reason to hope the recovery, though it may be *somewhat* tedious, will not be *very* slow. You shall hear again to-morrow. Ever your devoted Niece,
> Victoria R.

Alice, too, felt more hopeful on the evening of 5 December. After reading to him, 'He was most dear and affectionate when I went in with little Beatrice whom he kissed. He quite laughed at some of her new French verses which I made her [Beatrice] repeat. Then he held her little hand in his for some time and she stood looking at him. He then dozed off, when I left, not to disturb him.'

In spite of Dr Jenner's reassurances, the Queen was beside herself with alarm, especially at night. She had been told by the doctors not to sleep in the room with him. She needed, almost as much as Albert, a good night's sleep. But she found it 'a terrible trial to be thus separated from him & see him in the hands of *others*, careful and devoted as they are.'

On the morning of 7 December she found him again delirious. 'I went to my room,' she wrote, '& cried dreadfully & felt oh! as if my heart must break – oh! such agony as exceeded *all* my grief this year. Oh God! help me to protect him!'

Dr Jenner, as the world authority on typhoid – he had established the difference between typhus and typhoid fever ten years earlier – knew that the Prince Consort had typhoid fever; and he must have known, weak as the patient was, that there was only a small chance of his survival. But he determined not to use the dread word 'typhoid' to the Queen. It was 'gastric or bowel fever' he told her, 'the thing they had been watching all along'. They knew exactly how to treat it, he reassured her. It would take two weeks longer before a recovery could be expected. If these white lies were intended to reassure Victoria, Jenner might as well have told the truth.

Sir Charles Phipps, Albert's equerry, brought a note of good sense into the crisis, and was concerned about the deception. On 7 December he wrote to Palmerston, telling him that the illness had been identified as 'gastric'. He did not explain why that should make the fever worse than all the many others, like low fever or slow fever or bowel fever. 'The Queen is at present perfectly composed,' he continued, 'but I must tell you, *most confidentially*, that it requires no little management to prevent her from breaking down altogether. What would particularly try her would be any public Alarm about the Prince, which coming back to her through the Public Prints would make Her fancy that the truth was concealed from her . . .'

Meanwhile, the concerned and affectionate correspondence continued between Windsor and Laeken:

> Windsor Castle, 9th December 1861
>
> My Beloved Uncle, – I enclose you Clark's report, which I think you may like to hear. Our beloved invalid goes on well – but it *must* be tedious, and I need not tell you *what* a trial it is to me. Every day, however, is bringing us nearer the end of this tiresome illness, which is much what I had at Ramsgate, only that I was much worse, and not at first well attended to. You shall hear daily.
>
> You will, I know, feel for me! The night was excellent; the first good one he had. Ever your devoted Niece,
>
> Victoria R.

To which King Leopold replied:

> Laeken, 11th December 1861
>
> My Beloved Victoria, – *How I do feel for you from the bottom of my heart*; that you should have this totally unexpected tribulation of having dear Albert unwell, when not long ago we rejoiced that he was bearing this time of the year so well. Now we must be very patient, as an indisposition of this description at this time of the year is generally mending slowly. The great object must be to arrange all the little details exactly as the patient may wish them; that everything of that description may move very smoothly is highly beneficial. Patients are very different in their likings; to the great horror of angelic Louise, the moment I am ill I become almost invisible, disliking to see anybody. Other people are fond of company, and wish to be surrounded. The medical advisers are, thank God! excellent, and Clark knows Albert so well. Albert will wish you not to interrupt your usual airings; you want air, and to be deprived of it would do you harm. The temperature here at least has been extremely mild – this ought to be favourable. I trust that every day will now show some small improvement, and it will be very kind of you to let me frequently know how dear Albert is going on. Believe me ever, my beloved Victoria, your devoted Uncle,
>
> Leopold R.

*   *   *

On 7 December Jenner had told the Queen that a light rash had appeared, confirming the nature of the fever. He explained again in what the Queen called 'the kindest, clearest manner' that the fever must run its course.

On the following day, 8 December, Victoria wrote to 'my first born' in Germany:

> Dearest Papa is going on as favourably as we could wish – and please God! we shall have no drawbacks and then we shall patiently submit to the tediousness of it. But it is all like a bad dream! To see him prostrate and worn and weak, and unable to do anything and never smiling hardly – is terrible.
>
> I am well but very tired and nervous for I am so constantly on my legs – in and out and near him. I sleep in my dressing room, having given up our bedroom to dear Papa . . .
>
> I know, my darling, how anxious you will feel – but all is favourable and you shall hear daily. God bless you.

Prince Albert spent the day in his dressing-gown, the Queen beside or near him. 'Sir James assured me I need *not* be alarmed,' the Queen wrote later, 'but I seem to live in a dreadful dream. My angel lay on the bed & I sat by him watching him & the tears fell fast.' Later she saw Sir James and Dr Jenner, and 'talked over what could have caused this. Great worry and far too hard work for long! *That must* be stopped . . .'

It was Sunday 8 December, and the Queen repaired to St George's Chapel and listened to Charles Kingsley preaching. Because the patient was no worse than the previous day his doctors saw no harm in telling her that there was some improvement in his condition. Alice had remained behind to nurse her father. This sensible, sweet-natured eighteen-year-old seems to have had fewer illusions about the real condition of her father than anyone at Windsor, with the possible exception of Jenner. She kept her fiancé in Darmstadt daily informed about events:

> Poor Mama . . . has no idea how to nurse him although she would so gladly do everything . . . I only hope I am really useful to them, for I do want to do everything for them, if it were possible . . .

Her work of comfort and nursing was fully appreciated, as one member of the household wrote:

The Princess Alice's fortitude has amazed us all. She saw from the first that both her father's and mother's firmness depended on her firmness and she set herself to the duty ... He could not speak to the Queen of himself, for she could not bear to listen, and shut her eyes to the danger. His daughter saw that she must act differently, and she never let her voice falter, or shed a single tear in his presence. She sat by him, listened to all he said, repeated hymns, and then when she could bear it no longer, would walk calmly to the door, and rush away to her own room.

On this Sunday, the last of his life, he again asked Alice to play for him. She played *Ein' feste Burg ist unser Gott.*

He next asked for his sofa to be pushed closer to the window; he wanted to watch the clouds billowing across the sky. Then he appeared to fall asleep, and Alice covered him with a rug. Her father opened his eyes, and she asked him, 'Were you asleep?'

'No,' he replied, smiling. 'But my thoughts were so happy that I did not want to drive them away by moving.'

With his eyes open he could see the sun shining – a low, winter sun, giving the trees long shadows, but pleasing after days of rain. Victoria was cheered, too, when she visited him after her dinner. 'When I went to him,' she wrote, 'he was so pleased to see me, stroked my face and smiled, and called me *Weibchen* [dear little wife].'

For the first time since Albert had been struck down, a bulletin was issued. There was to have been a shooting party in a few days' time and the guests had to be put off. The newspapers added their own view that the illness was likely to be a long one.

In spite of his earlier rebuff, Palmerston persuaded the Queen to call in other opinions. Writing of this decision, Sir Charles Phipps warned:

The measure had been made very difficult, first by the Queen being disinclined to it, and secondly by the fear of alarming the

Prince himself. He is *extremely low* about himself – there is no doubt that the death of the King of Portugal not only grieved him very deeply, but would make him exceedingly nervous if he had any idea that his illness bore any similarity to that of which the King died. Any alarm or further depression might have a *very injurious* effect upon the Prince in his present state, and it will therefore require some tact and judgement to announce the arrival of fresh medical advice ... The Queen's cheerfulness is beyond all praise. It seems quite possible to see a person under circumstances which must cause anxiety maintain self-command, and act more reasonably. But if she were alarmed and broke down, I think the reaction would be very great.

Two of those summoned to Windsor were the specialist, Dr Watson, and the Physician-in-Ordinary, old Sir Henry Holland. The younger man was shocked at the advanced condition of the prince, and reported to Phipps, who passed the message on to Palmerston, that 'the malady is very grave and serious in itself – and that even the Prince's present weakness is very great: in short I say that it is impossible not to be very anxious.'

Palmerston replied to Phipps:

Your telegram and letter have come upon me like a thunderbolt. I know that the disorder is one liable to sudden and unfavourable turns, but I had hoped that it was going on without cause for special apprehension. The result which your accounts compel me to look forward to as at least possible is in all its bearings too awful to contemplate. One can only hope that Providence may yet spare us so overwhelming a calamity.

Prince Albert was ratty with the new doctors, but he had been equally impatient with Dr Jenner and old Clark. The doctor he really wanted and frequently called out for was Baron Stockmar, in whom he had never lost faith and trust.

Friday 13 December dawned dark and lowering, reflecting the findings of the doctors. Albert was having breathing trouble, and it was clear that congestion of the lungs had set in. When the Queen made her usual early-visit she found him panting for breath, his eyes open but blank, his body still, as

More bulletins issued which were of course shown to me. I asked if I might go out for a breath of fresh air. The doctors answered 'Yes, just close by, for half an hour!' I went on the terrace with Alice. The military band was playing at a distance & I burst out crying and came home again. Sir James was very hopeful, he had seen much worse cases. But the breathing was the alarming thing – *so* rapid, I think 60 respirations in a minute.

Among those sitting or walking about near the Blue Room in gaunt despair, the person most wanted by the patient and the most frequently at his side, even more than the Queen, was Princess Alice. If she left him, however briefly, Albert aroused himself, even if seemingly unconscious, and called out her name.

On the morning of 14 December, Alice took time off, not to sleep which she desperately needed to do, but to write a letter to her fiancé Louis in Darmstadt. It included the ominous statement, 'In another 24 hours everything will be decided.'

On that evening, at close to six o'clock, Sir Charles Phipps sent a new bulletin to Palmerston. It began, 'Alas! the hopes of the morning are fading away . . . The Prince Consort continues in a very critical state.'

The winter evening and darkness closed about the great castle. At nine thirty the Queen withdrew from Albert's bedside, unable to control her grief but determined not to break down in front of Albert at this critical time. Sobbing uncontrollably, she still managed to ask for the Dean of Windsor, the Hon. Gerald Wellesley. He was nearby and came at once to give comfort.

Lady Augusta Stanley wrote movingly of those last minutes in the life of Prince Albert:

Princess Alice, the Prince and Princess of Leiningen, the Prince of Wales and Princess Helena were in the room, with Miss Hildyard [nursemaid] and me, Robert [General Bruce] and others between the doors. Princess Alice whispered to me with great calm, 'That is the death rattle' and went for her mother. Then in that darkened room they knelt; the Queen and her elder children watching in agonised silence the passing of that lofty and noble soul. Gentler than an infant slumber it was at last. The poor Queen exclaimed 'Oh yes, this is death.'

It was a while before the Queen could write of that evening, but the memory of it, in every detail, lasted for the rest of her life.

I bent over him & said to him 'Es ist Kleines Frauchen' & he bowed his head; I asked him if he would give me 'ein Kuss'* & he did so. He seemed half dozing, quite quiet. I left the room for a moment and sat down on the floor in utter despair. Attempts at consolation from others only made me worse. Alice told me to come in and I took his dear left hand which was already cold, though the breathing was quite gentle and I knelt down by him. Alice was on the other side, Bertie and Lenchen kneeling at the foot of the bed ... Sir Charles Phipps, the Dean and General Bruce knelt almost opposite to me. Two or three long but perfectly gentle breaths were drawn, the hand clasping mine and *all, all was over*. I stood up, kissed his dear heavenly forehead & called out in a bitter and agonising cry 'Oh! my dear Darling!' and then dropped on my knees in mute, distracted despair, unable to utter a word or shed a tear!

Phipps and Prince Leiningen carried her into the Red Room and laid her on the sofa. Between the sobs she was heard to cry out in loneliness and grief, 'There is no one to call me Victoria!'

---

* A kiss from someone dying of typhoid would probably transmit the disease, but Victoria was immune having suffered from typhoid herself.

CHAPTER THIRTEEN

'You will not desert me?'

By 14th December 1861 there was scarcely a citizen unaware of the crisis at Windsor. *The Times* that morning published the mournful bulletin: 'HRH the Prince Consort passed a restless night, and the symptoms have assumed an unfavourable character during the day.' The next morning, its leader column began:

> The nation has just sustained the greatest loss that could possibly have fallen upon it. Prince Albert who a week ago gave every promise that his valuable life would be lengthened to a period long enough to enable him to enjoy, even in this world, the fruit of a virtuous youth and a well-spent manhood, the affection of a devoted wife and of a family of which any father might be proud – this man, the very centre of our social system, the pillar of our State, is suddenly snatched from us.

Phipps and Victoria's nephew, Ernest Leiningen, had carried the limp Queen into the Red Room and laid her on the sofa. Here she remained sobbing for a while, then with a supreme effort, indicated that she wished to see her children. She told them that she promised to live for them. The Prince of Wales was the first to embrace her. 'Indeed, Mama, I will be all I can to you.' And she kissed him repeatedly. 'I am sure, my dear boy, you will.' The household then filed past, some weeping, all bowing or curtseying. The Queen cried out, 'You will not desert me? You will all help me?'

'Indeed we will, Ma'm.'

After a short while, Sir James Clark made an appearance

and guided her firmly back into the Blue Room. Later, much later, the Queen wrote, 'Oh! that I can even now write it – & that I did not go out of my mind! I went in alone with that kind, fatherly old Friend – who so loved us both . . .'

She did not want to look, but forced herself to do so and kissed the cold forehead.

In what must have seemed a counterpoise to the days of sickness, and then death, the Queen headed on her own for the nursery and picked young Beatrice from her cot without waking her, and held her briefly in her arms.

'He went without a struggle,' noted one witness to Prince Albert's death, 'his face calm and peaceful.' Palmerston was told of the end in a hastily composed letter from Sir Charles Phipps:

> The Prince is dead. I hope I had sufficiently prepared you for the dreadful event which took place at ten minutes before eleven this night. The Queen though in an agony of grief, is perfectly collected, and shows a self control which is quite extraordinary. Alas! she has not realised her loss - and, when the full conscious-ness comes upon her – I tremble – but only for the depth of her grief. What will happen – where can She look for that support and assistance upon which She has leaned in the greatest and least questions of her life?

The answer, for the immediate future, was Princess Alice, who had supported her mother through the worst moments of the sickness and death of her father.

It could not be the Prince of Wales, willing though he might be. Initiative and decisiveness had long since been drained from Bertie by his father and mother. 'I will be all I can to you,' Bertie had promised. But it was Alice, aged eighteen, who gently brought her mother back to reality and cared for her with such subtlety that she hardly noticed she was being nursed.

Alice had written to her future mother-in-law, Princess Charles of Hesse:

> My heart is *quite* broken, and my grief is almost more than I can bear. When I think back to the whole dreadful illness, to the

Friday and to the last Saturday, that dreadful, difficult time that I went through with Mama seems like a bad dream, and my aching heart bleeds afresh when I remember the last, painful hours. Oh God that it should have been my beloved, adored father lying there dead, his hands so cold and stiff – I felt as if I had been turned to stone – when I saw him draw his last breath, and saw the pure, great noble soul leave its earthly dwelling . . .

The experience had, indeed, been almost beyond bearing, but the shock had also caused Princess Alice to take a violent and involuntary step into adulthood and mature responsibility at a time when her best qualities were needed to cope not only with the aftermath of her father's death, but with her own imminent marriage. Augusta Stanley wrote that, quite suddenly, Alice seemed to be 'a different creature . . . Her fiancé hurried over from Germany to find an Alice he had never known before.'

Although the Queen was to be almost paralysed with grief for weeks and months to come, there are signs that both Alice, who remained close to her, and Vicky in Germany, were able to bring some small degree of comfort.

In what must have been the Queen's first letter after Albert's death, she wrote, 'God's will be done! A heavenly peace has descended . . . it cannot be possible . . . Oh! God! Oh! God . . . but I feel I can bear it better today . . . I don't know what I feel . . .'

Vicky received a more coherent letter two days later:

Oh! my poor child, indeed 'Why may the earth not swallow us up?' Why not? How am I alive after witnessing what I have done? Oh! I who prayed daily that we might die together and I never survive him! I who felt, when in those blessed arms clasped and held tight in the sacred hours at night, when the world seemed only to be ourselves, that nothing could part us. I felt so very secure . . .

Lacking those clasped blessed arms, Victoria went to bed every night with Albert's nightshirt held tight to her, a cast

197

of his hand within reach. Over the empty pillow beside her hung a portrait surrounded by a wreath of evergreens.

The Blue Room where he had died was to be only one of countless memorials to Albert up and down the country.* The Queen had it comprehensively photographed in order that it could be preserved exactly as it was at the time of his death. Orders were given that his dressing-gown and fresh clothes were to be laid out every evening; a jug of hot water was placed on his wash-stand; the glass from which he had taken his last medicine rested on his bedside table for the remainder of the Queen's life, which she thought would be brief, but was actually to be almost forty years. Full mourning was ordered, extending the existing mourning for Victoria's mother. Bertie was rebuked for using writing paper with too narrow a black border, while her own paper had so wide a border that her writing sometimes disappeared into it, making the letter unreadable.

The Queen's household did not believe that the Queen would stand up to the grief and the stress of a life that had been so dependent in every respect upon her husband. They forecast that she would break down, like her grandfather, George III. Word spread around the courts and chancelleries of Europe that Queen Victoria had already been rendered insane.

The strain was almost intolerable, but her powerful will and resilience saved her. Above all, Albert himself saved her as she determined to do her duty by her family and by her country as if he were still alive. The first evidence that the uncrowned 'King Albert' would continue to reign until the Queen's own death is to be found in a letter she wrote to her Uncle Leopold less than a week after Albert's death:

> 20th December 1861
>
> My *Own* Dearest, Kindest *Father*, – For as such have I *ever* loved you! The poor fatherless baby of eight months is now the

---

* Even as this is being written in 1995, the government is spending £14 million on the refurbishment of the Albert Memorial in Hyde Park.

utterly broken-hearted and crushed widow of forty-two! My life as a *happy* one is *ended*! the world is gone for *me*! If I *must live* on (and I will do nothing to make me worse than I am), it is henceforth for our poor fatherless children – for my unhappy country, which has lost *all* in losing him – and in *only* doing what I know and *feel* he would wish, for he *is* near me – his spirit will guide and inspire me! But oh! to be cut off in the prime of life – to see our pure, happy, quiet domestic life, which *alone* enabled me to bear my *much* disliked position, CUT OFF at forty-two – when I *had* hoped with such instinctive certainty that God never *would* part us, and would let us grow old together (though *he* always talked of the shortness of life) – is *too awful*, too cruel! And yet it *must* be for *his* good, his happiness! His purity was too great, his aspiration *too high* for this poor, *miserable* world! His great soul is *now only* enjoying *that* for which it *was* worthy; And I will *not* envy him – only pray that *mine* may be perfected by it and fit to be with him eternally, for which blessed moment I earnestly long. Dearest, dearest Uncle, *how* kind of you to come! It will be an unspeakable *comfort*, and you *can do* much to tell people to do what they ought to do. As for my *own good*, *personal* servants – poor Phipps in particular – nothing can be more devoted, heartbroken as they are, and anxious only to live as *he* wished!

Good Alice has been and is wonderful . . .

Ever your devoted, wretched Child,
Victoria R.

Leopold was due to arrive in England to stay with his niece immediately after Christmas, to her great relief, but she so much wanted to emphasise her determination to follow Albert's policies and stand by his beliefs that she wrote another heartfelt letter on Christmas Eve:

24th December 1861

My Beloved Uncle, – Though, please God! I am to see you so soon, I must write these few lines to prepare you for the trying, sad existence you will find it with your poor forlorn, desolate child – who drags on a weary, pleasureless existence! I am also anxious to repeat *one* thing, and *that one* is *my firm* resolve, my *irrevocable decision*, viz. that *his* wishes – *his* plans – about

199

everything, *his* views about *every* thing are to be *my law*! And *no human power* will make me swerve from *what he* decided and wished – and I look to *you* to *support* and *help* me in this. I apply this particularly as regards our children – Bertie, etc. – for whose future he had traced everything *so* carefully. I am *also determined* that *no one* person, may *he* be ever so good, ever so devoted among my servants – is to lead or guide or dictate for him; in fact I am only *outwardly* separated from him, and *only* for a *time*.

No one can tell you more of my feelings, and can put you more in possession of many touching facts than our excellent Dr Jenner, who has been and is my great comfort, and whom I would *entreat* you to *see* and *hear* before you see *any one else*. Pray do this, for I *fear much* others trying to see you first and say things and wish for things which I *should not* consent to.

Though miserably weak and utterly shattered, my spirit rises when I think *any* wish or plan of his is to be touched or changed, or I am to be *made to do* anything. I know you will help me in my utter darkness. It is but for a short time, and *then* I go – *never, never* to part! Oh! that blessed, blessed thought! He seems so *near* to *me*, so *quite my own now*, my precious darling! God bless and preserve you.

Ever your wretched but devoted Child, Victoria R.

What a Xmas! I won't think of it.

The doctors, and all those close to the Queen, agreed that the sooner she left the scene of the tragedy at Windsor the better it would be for her spirit. Before that, however, she made a pilgrimage on foot to Frogmore with Alice and there, close to her mother's tomb, she chose the position for a mausoleum 'for us both'. Her one comfort during these early days of grief and mourning was her firm belief that she would soon follow her beloved, certainly by the time the mausoleum was completed. Then, she and her court embarked on the royal train for the first stage of the journey to Osborne.

Osborne. The peace, the sound of the sea and the wind in the trees planted so recently by Albert. Bertie accompanied her as far as Gosport, saw her on board her yacht, and returned to Windsor to complete the preparations for his father's funeral service, at which he would represent his mother. It took place two days before Christmas in St George's Chapel, Windsor. Bertie and all his brothers and sisters present behaved impeccably, and this was widely noted. After the ceremonial, the Prince Consort's coffin was placed in the entrance to the royal vault, to await the completion of the mausoleum, which was accomplished just one year later. The sarcophagus was only a temporary one however, and it was not until 26 November 1868 that the prince was laid at last in his final resting place.

Only one factor tarnished the aftermath of this tragedy. The Queen, from the depths of her grief, sought wildly for the cause of her husband's death. She was not a very religious woman, and could not accept that it was God's will, and leave it at that. She sought a rational explanation why Albert, in the full flower of his manhood at forty-two, should succumb so swiftly to a fever. She discounted, or forgot, his assertion that he would never fight for his life if he were taken seriously ill. The doctors diagnosed the cause of Albert's death as overwork and worry, which so weakened him that he was incapable of fighting off the fever. And he was weak, the Queen reasoned in agony, because of the intolerable pain of learning of Bertie's disgraceful behaviour at the Curragh Camp. She had witnessed, had she not, the depths of Albert's misery and shame, broken-hearted by his failure to instil in his son a sufficiently high standard of respect for honour and decency.

From Osborne Victoria wrote to her eldest daughter in Berlin effectively telling her that Bertie had killed his father. Horrified at this charge, Vicky replied as strongly as she dared, begging her mother to 'be kind, pitying, forgiving and loving to the poor boy for Papa's sake'.

However it would be a long time before Victoria felt able to express any forgiveness. 'All you say about poor Bertie is right and affectionate in you,' she replied to Vicky; 'but if you had seen Fritz [Vicky's husband] struck down, day by day get worse and finally die, I doubt if you could bear the sight of the one who was the cause.'

Wise old Palmerston knew how fruitless it would be to argue about Bertie. He recommended to his Queen that the Prince of Wales should be sent off on a long expedition abroad. Within five weeks he was out of the country, and did not return for five months.

One of the Queen's closest friends, the Marquis of Hertford, visiting her at Osborne, found her 'the most desolate and unhappy of creatures'. When she ascribed the cause of Albert's death to the Prince of Wales and 'the dreadful business at the Curragh', Lord Hertford had the courage flatly to deny this. 'Oh, no, Madam.'

In the first weeks after her bereavement the Queen remained in an unsteady frame of mind. Rumours persisted that the shock had been so great that she had lost her reason. This was hardly surprising when, for instance, she told Lord Clarendon that a political crisis – and one was threatened – would send her mad. Tapping her forehead at the same time, she repeated the words, 'My reason! My reason!'

On another visit to Osborne, Lord Derby reported that 'The Queen talked freely of Albert: he *would* die – he seemed not to care to live. Then she used the words, "He died from want of what they call pluck."'

Prince Albert's life spanned one of the most lethally infected periods in British history. The advance in the industrialisation of the country was not matched by public concern for sanitation. People crowded into the towns and cities to work in the new factories, but there was virtually no drainage. From time to time, Parliament had to rise because of the stench of the River Thames. It was no better up-river at Windsor. When the Prince Consort died of typhoid fever he fell victim to the infectious disease that was responsible for 30 per cent of male deaths at that time. Many more fought it and won the battle for their lives, as Victoria herself had done, and as her eldest son was to do.

Ironically and tragically, it was Albert who convinced Victoria of the dangerous pestilence of undrained cities. One of the reasons why they purchased first Osborne, and then

Balmoral was to escape the fevers raging in overcrowded areas, and the Queen remained notorious for insisting on open windows even in mid-winter. Five years after Albert's death from typhoid, which many people thought was derived from the appalling drains of Windsor Castle, Parliament passed the Public Health Act, which called for main drainage in Britain's cities, a good water supply and 'the prevention and removal of nuisances', such as excessive smoke. During the 1870s conditions began to improve and it is reasonable to claim that by his death Prince Albert brought about the acceleration of the Public Health Act which was soon saving many thousands of lives.

However, the provisions of the Act had not been fully applied when ten years after Albert's death, in December 1871, the Prince of Wales was struck down by typhoid fever. On 13 December, twenty-four hours before that dread anniversary, the Queen was writing, 'There can be no hope.' But Bertie fought back and won against the horrible illness, and at the same time won the praise of the nation.

The Queen, who had been physically robust all her life, had been weakened by the worry and distress of Albert's last months. At the end of 1861 she was damaged physiologically and psychologically. She had lost a great deal of weight and yet found walking an effort. Attacks of neuralgia were frequent, with accompanying depression. She was not suffering from what is loosely defined as a nervous breakdown, although she certainly feared having one, and many people, especially outside the household, suspected that such was the case. They were as wrong in their diagnosis as those who ascribed her condition to her way of life.

For a number of weeks after losing Albert, she suffered from a mental numbness comparable with the physical numbness associated with a deep wound. Such conditions can be life-preserving, and probably saved her from insanity. Her inertia also led to a withdrawal from both public life and her formal duties, like attendance at Privy Councils. A compromise was eventually reached whereby she remained unseen in a room with a door open to the members of the Council. She could hear the items as they were read out and an intermediary at the door related her comments.

But there was one subject from which she not only did not withdraw, but attended to with great zeal. This was the wellbeing and future of her children. Alice's wedding, she decided, must go ahead as arranged in July 1862, though how Victoria would manage without the daily assistance of her oldest unmarried daughter she could scarcely imagine.

On 2 July, when it was all over, the Queen wrote to Vicky, 'Poor Alice's wedding (more like a funeral than a wedding) is over and she is a wife! I say God bless her – though a dagger is plunged in my bleeding, desolate heart when I hear from her this morning that she is "proud and happy" to be Louis' wife!'

As for 'poor Bertie', thanks to his elder sister Vicky, he again met and was soon entranced by the particularly beautiful princess, Alexandra of Denmark. Within some nine months of his father's death, he proposed to her and was accepted, to the delight of the aged King Leopold who helped to bring them together. Bertie wrote home to his mother:

> I cannot tell you with what feelings my head is filled, and how happy I feel. I only hope it may be for her happiness and that I may do my duty towards her. Love and cherish her you may be sure I will to the end of my life. May God grant that *our* happiness may throw a ray of light on your once so happy and now so desolate home. You may be sure that we shall both strive to be a comfort to you.

Despite these good intentions, the great-grandfather of Britain's present Queen did not always do his duty by his wife, nor cherish her on those occasions when she needed it – as after a severe attack of rheumatic fever, for instance.

The marriages of Victoria's other children were of varying success. The loving, pretty and intelligent Vicky suffered most, being treated vilely by the Prussian court, and having the great misfortune to give birth to the future Kaiser, Wilhelm

II, who gave early signs of half-insane jealousy, cruelty and obsessive conceit. His treatment of his father when Fritz succeeded as Emperor was so loathsome that Vicky rightly believed that he accelerated his death. Lord Salisbury once warned Bertie that his nephew was 'a little off his head'.

As Dowager Empress in the dark days of her widowhood, Vicky was thrown from her horse, not badly but awkwardly. Her injuries failed to heal and cancer developed. For four years she was in pain until she died – a few months after her mother.

Nothing could save Princess Alice when a plague of diphtheria struck her family in Darmstadt in 1878. All were infected, the youngest daughter dying, and Alice herself finally succumbing, weakened by nursing her family. It was that black date, 14 December, and a Saturday, too, seventeen years after the death of her father. The last words she spoke were 'Dear Papa'. The coincidence gave Queen Victoria a certain morbid satisfaction, without diminishing her grief – 'I was so proud of my nine [children],' she exclaimed.

Alfred, the next born, the naval officer who became Duke of Edinburgh, married late and to his mother's distress into the Russian royal family. In January 1874 he married Grand Duchess Marie, the Tsar and Tsarina's only daughter. Later, Alfred became Duke of Coburg, as originally intended. The marriage prospered and produced five children, but Affie died in 1900, before his mother.

Helena – Lenchen – married a 'penniless prince', Christian of Schleswig-Holstein, who was also 'pleasing, gentlemanlike, quiet and distinguished'. Older than his wife, this prince lived through the reigns of William IV, Queen Victoria, Edward VII and almost the whole of the First World War. It was a happy marriage with five children, one christened Albert, to the Queen's satisfaction.

Louise – poor LouLou – made the mistake of falling in love with and marrying Lord Lorne, heir to the eighth Duke of Argyll. He was a homosexual and they had no children. He became Governor-General of Canada and jointly with his wife gave needed encouragement to the arts there, the one interest they had in common. Louise, soon Duchess of Argyll, was adept at finding excuses for returning to Europe for long periods.

In the winter of 1880 when she remained in Canada, Louise suffered a serious accident. Her horse-drawn sledge went out of control, dragging her along some distance by her hair. Louise was thrown heavily against a tree, suffering concussion and almost losing an ear. She never fully recovered but had the compensation of convalescing for long periods in Bermuda and then on the shores of Lake Constance.

Victoria's soldier son and favourite, Arthur, Duke of Connaught, rose in the ranks to become Lieutenant-Governor and C-in-C Bombay. At first Victoria was mystified and disappointed when he married Princess Louise Margaret, the daughter of the estranged Prince Frederick and Princess Marianne of Prussia. When they met, however, the Queen was enchanted by her, and later made herself responsible for the couple's three children when their parents were in India. The last of these children, Victoria Patricia – Patsy – married a naval officer who rose to flag rank, the Hon Sir Alexander Ramsay. She did not die until 1974.

'No one knows,' the Queen once wrote of her haemophiliac son, Leopold, 'the constant fear I am in about him.' She was sure that her delicate son would not be able to withstand the pressures of married life, but Leo went his own way and found a sensitive, intelligent and handsome princess, Helen of Waldeck-Pyrmont. 'I am much pleased with his choice,' Victoria conceded, 'for I have heard such high and excellent character of her.' Leo had two children, Alice, who married the Earl of Athlone and was a haemophilia carrier; and a boy, who may have suffered from the disease but lived to be sixty-nine. Leo himself died of the same disease shortly before his son was born.

When 'Baby' Beatrice married Prince Henry 'Liko' of Battenberg there was no apprehension that the dread bleeding disease might strike the Queen's family once again. But, like her mother, Beatrice was also a carrier, and of the three boys she bore, one died of haemophilia. 'This awful disease,' as Victoria lamented '– the worst I know of – it seems to persecute our poor family.'

There was a further tragedy for poor Beatrice in 1896 when her husband died of a tropical fever while engaged, quite unnecessarily, on a minor military expedition in West Africa. Perhaps, had Liko lived, he might have restrained Beatrice from her over-enthusiasm in censoring the Queen's Journal after her death, burning priceless material by the furnace-load.

The death of Prince Henry was also a severe blow to the Queen. Part of the understanding in her granting approval of the marriage was that the couple should live mainly at court. Victoria had from the beginning of her reign been strongly dependent on a man's support – first Melbourne, then for more than twenty years, on Albert. Her one-time ghillie, John Brown, promoted and brought down to England some three years after Albert's death, had filled a curious but vital role.

When Brown also died, Victoria wrote to her friend, the poet laureate, Alfred Lord Tennyson, singing his praises:

> Lately I have lost one who, humble though he was, had no thought but for me, my welfare, my comfort, my safety, my happiness. Direct, speaking the truth fearlessly and telling me what he thought and considered to be just and right, without flattery. He was part of my life and quite invaluable . . .

It was as well that Victoria was to be succeeded by her eldest son and not by any of her daughters. She may have feared that Bertie would be inadequate as sovereign, but he was better fitted for the role than his mother judged, and certainly better equipped than any of his sisters. Vicky might have been a satisfactory queen, though she cannot be judged by her sad record as German Empress, when she was persecuted by her elder son and the whole hateful Prussian court.

All Victoria's daughters had their merits but none had the range of qualities nor the immense strength of will and sense of duty possessed by their mother. Perhaps the last born,

Beatrice, was closest to her mother in positive characteristics as well as defects, though she exhibited greater stoicism than Victoria in the face of misfortune.

In popular memory and history, the Queen – 'the widow of Windsor' – scarcely ever emerged from her dark withdrawal from public life, except perhaps for the two celebrations, her golden and diamond jubilees in 1887 and 1897. There was a time when her failure to appear in public and her apparent neglect of her duties as sovereign led to the rise of an element of republicanism in the land, which was given added impetus by the Prince of Wales's disreputable behaviour towards the much-loved Princess Alexandra. But after three years of excessive mourning and her failure to die 'within the year' after Albert's death, Victoria seems to have taken herself in hand. 'I must try and live on for a while yet,' she wrote recklessly in her Journal. Strangely, the death at last of her beloved Uncle Leopold had an almost galvanising effect on the Queen. She was now the undisputed mother of Europe, or as her daughter Alice put it, 'Now you are head of all the family.'

At the same time two very different men began to fulfil to some degree her need for a male companion in her domestic and professional life. Coincident with her decision to 'bring Brown south', was a growing intimacy with Henry Ponsonby, once one of Albert's equerries, an ex-soldier who combined a light touch with positive opinions which – as with Brown – he was not shy to proclaim. This favourite equerry and 'the Queen's Highland servant' performed wonders for Victoria's spirits and the fulfilment of her duties in old age, including appearing in public. Ponsonby died of a stroke in November 1895. She lost Brown in 1883. A year later, on the first anniversary of Brown's death, she wrote in her Journal, 'I cannot cease lamenting.' She might equally have been referring to Albert, dead now for more than twenty years.

When the Queen died at the age of eighty-one on 22 January 1901 only those over the age of about sixty could recall a time when she was not on the throne. Many of her subjects had been born, married, grown old and died as Victorians. Empires had grown, especially her own, and she had signed herself RI (Regina Imperatrix) since 1875.

The horse was the first means of land travel and transport in 1837; twenty years later even small towns were linked by railway, and at the time of her death a new challenge was making its presence known: the motor car. Within sight of Osborne House, where she died, the men-o'-war, and almost all the big merchantmen in the Solent were steam-driven.

Innumerable inventions, from the camera, telephone and typewriter, to the turbine and electric light, had changed the face of the world during the sixty-four years of Queen Victoria's reign, making the nineteenth century the most productive in history.

What Victoria herself achieved was to change the face of the monarchy in Britain and the empire. In 1837 the reputation of kings and queens was not high, thanks in part to her disreputable and selfish predecessors. By 1901, and for many years before, Queen Victoria's honesty and truthfulness, her simple style of living, her queenly dignity combined with motherly sympathy, engaged the affection of her people, and influenced their own behaviour to a degree unsurpassed by any other monarch.

Prince Albert had been dead for forty years but his influence on the Queen remained powerful to the end of her life. Proper credit must be given to this German-born prince who came to Britain with many reservations and lived long enough to make his mark not only on his wife but on the character and morality of his adopted country.

'Allured to brighter worlds and led the way'

210

Appendix

The lasting popularity of Queen Victoria as a subject for biography has led to a steady flow of books in this century, from Sir Sidney Lee's, published one year after his subject's death, to Giles St Aubyn's biography of ninety years later. During her lifetime there appeared a number of unauthorised and mainly inaccurate biographies, and in this century the apocryphal volumes on every aspect of Queen Victoria's and Prince Albert's lives, and the lives of their children and members of her court have been legion.

Some books have been unashamedly obscene, in particular those on the relationship between the Duchess of Kent and Sir John Conroy, and Queen Victoria and her ghillie, later 'personal servant', John Brown. Contemporary satirical articles, especially from France, in which the Queen was sometimes referred to as Mrs John Brown, formed the basis for much of this ephemeral conjecture.

Almost one hundred years after Queen Victoria's death, there have even been books speculating on the legitimacy of the Queen, citing as 'evidence' that there was no record of haemophilia in the royal family prior to Queen Victoria. But little was known about the bleeding disease 150 years ago. Since then it has been established that the disease can lie dormant for several generations and then unpredictably re-emerge in the male line. At a time when infant mortality was high, males suffering from haemophilia could die in infancy before the disease had been diagnosed. If the sickly Prince

Leopold had died early, as he nearly did, it would never have been known that he was a bleeder.

This biographer has attempted to avoid all such speculative sources, and the works listed in the Condensed Bibliography, from which occasional quotations have been taken, are all sound and authentic.

Prince Albert has, unsurprisingly, not attracted the same number of biographers as the Queen. Perhaps some have been intimidated by the five massive volumes of Martin's official and almost unreadable biography. Those works listed in the Condensed Bibliography are the most informative.

Condensed Bibliography

This is an informal dual biography and references have therefore been kept to a minimum. However, the source of quotations is generally available by referring to the list below.

BENNETT, D, *King without a Crown*, Collins, London, 1977
  Vicky: Princess Royal of England and German Empress,
  Collins, London, 1971
BENSON, A.C. & ESHER, Viscount, (eds.) *The Letters of Queen
  Victoria: a selection*, 3 vols, John Murray, London, 1908
BOLITHO, H, *Victoria & Albert*, Max Parrish, London, 1938
CHARLOT, M, *Victoria, the Young Queen*, Basil Blackwell,
  London, 1991
DUFF, D, *Hessian Tapestry*, Collins, London, 1967
EPTON, N, *Victoria and Her Daughters*, Weidenfeld & Nicolson,
  London, 1971
EYCK, F, *The Prince Consort: a political biography*, Chatto &
  Windus, London, 1959
FULFORD, R, *The Prince Consort*, Macmillan, London, 1949
HIBBERT, C, *Victoria*, Ebury Press, London, 1979
HOUGH, R, *Edward & Alexandra*, Hodder & Stoughton,
  London, 1992
JAGOW, K, (ed.) *Letters of Harriet Countess Granville*, vol i, Smith
  Elder, London, 1894
LONGFORD, E, *Victoria RI*, Weidenfeld & Nicolson, London,
  1964
MARTIN, T, *The Life of HRH The Prince Consort*, V vols, Smith
  Elder, London, 1875–80
NOEL, G, *Princess Alice: Queen Victoria's Forgotten Daughter*,
  Constable, London, 1974

POUND, R, *Albert*, Michael Joseph, London, 1973

The Principal Speeches and Addresses of HRH The Prince Consort, John Murray, 1862

RHODES JAMES, R, *Albert, Prince Consort*, Hamish Hamilton, London, 1983

ST AUBYN, G, *Queen Victoria*, Collins, London, 1991

STRACHEY, L, *Queen Victoria*, Chatto & Windus, London, 1921

WOODHAM-SMITH, C, *Queen Victoria*, Hamish Hamilton, London, 1972

WYNDHAM, Hon Mrs H, (ed.) *The Correspondence of Sarah Spencer, Lady Lyttelton*, Longmans, London, 1912

The author thanks the Hon Gerard Noel and his publishers, Messrs Constable, for permission to quote from *Princess Alice: Queen Victoria's Forgotten Daughter*.

Index

Abercorn, James Hamilton, 2nd Marquis of 108
Aberdeen, George Gordon, 4th Earl of
as Foreign Secretary 82
sells Balmoral to QV 109
1852 government 128
defends Albert against press attacks 137
government falls (1855) 139
Adams, Charles Francis 182
Adelaide, Queen of William IV 22, 33, 68
Adelbert, Prince of Prussia 28
Albemarle, William Charles Keppel, 5th Earl of 42
Albert Hall *see* Royal Albert Hall
Albert, Prince Consort
appearance 9, 11, 13, 30, 56, 177
birth and family background 9–10
character 10
upbringing and education 10–13
early ill-health 11
early rising and sleep needs 11, 71, 123
youthful visit to Berlin 13
first visit to England and meeting with QV 14, 28–31
on QV's learning of succession prospects 22
on QV's accession 35
as prospective suitor for QV 53–4
second visit to QV 53–7
engagement 57–63
honours and titles 57, 67, 76, 148
knowledge of English 62, 71
consciousness of political impartiality 63–4, 74
leaves Germany for England, 64–6
parliamentary allowance 63–4, 149
public attitudes to 64, 66, 76, 110, 135–6
naturalised 66
wedding 67–9
QV excludes from power 70, 73–4
dancing 71–2
dress 71, 76
seeks British-German alliance 71

marriage relations 72–4, 172–5
difficulties with Lehzen 73, 76, 83–6, 172
interest in horses 73
at assassination attempt on QV 75–6
nominated regent 75
organising abilities and reforms 76–7, 124
increasing involvement in QV's monarchical life 77
attends Privy Council meeting 78
children 78–9, 132
and QV's pregnancies and labours 78
and Christmas celebrations 79
skating 79
supports Peel 81
political influence on QV 82
Melbourne praises 83
tours and travels with QV 88–92, 108, 169–70
and father's death 92–3
redesigns and manages Osborne 94–7
closeness to Vicky 99, 103, 106, 161, 173
and Edward's education and upbringing 99–100, 102, 126, 154, 156–7, 163, 166
relations with children 99–101, 103, 105–6, 125, 133, 173
attitude to Edward 100, 102, 105–6, 126, 133, 154–5, 157, 167, 178–9
plays music 103–4
boredom with court 107
at Balmoral 109–10, 127, 168–9, 171
public speaking 110–11
supports public causes 111
plans and organises Great Exhibition (1851) 112–20, 122, 125
hypochondria and poor health 122–4, 157–8, 164, 179–80
sense of duty 124–5, 180
fusses over children 125
political involvement 126
declines to be C-in-C of army 127–8, 138
organises Wellington's funeral 128

Albert, Prince Consort *cont.*
  and redesigning of Balmoral 128–9
  institutes Victoria Cross 129, 153
  elected Chancellor of Cambridge
    University 130–1
  and children's upbringing and education
    133–4, 162
  and Crimean War 135, 137–9, 141
  attacked by press 136–7
  rumoured impeachment for treason 136
  visits Napoleon III in Paris 140
  and German alliance 143–4
  plans Vicky's marriage 143–4
  on Indian Mutiny 147
  made Prince Consort 149
  and Vicky's wedding 150–2
  and Edward's North American visit
    156–7
  concern over possible French invasion
    158
  visits Vicky and Fritz in Germany 158–
    62
  injured in coach accident 160–1
  1860/61 illness 163–4
  and death of QV's mother 165–6
  and Edward's army career 167
  and Edward's sexual initiation in Ireland
    178–9, 201
  health decline 180–92
  visits Edward in Cambridge 180
  on *Trent* affair 182–3
  death 193–6
  posthumous influence on QV 198–200
  causes of death 201–3
  funeral 201
  achievements 209
Albert Memorial, Hyde Park, London 198n
Alexander I, Tsar 6
Alexandra, Princess (*later* Queen of
  Edward VII) 171, 204, 208
Alfred, Prince (*later* Duke of Edinburgh;
  then Duke of Coburg; 'Affie'; QV's
  son)
  birth 98
  qualities 101, 103, 105
  at Balmoral 109, 141
  christening 143
  and Vicky's marriage 151
  naval career 162–3
  absent from Albert's deathbed 192
  later career and marriage 205
Alice, Princess, Countess of Athlone 143
Alice, Princess (QV's daughter)
  birth 98

character and qualities 100–2, 104
  closeness to Bertie 100, 104
  carries haemophilia 143
  and Vicky's marriage 151
  marriage to Louis 168, 204
  in Scotland 168–70
  closeness to Albert 173
  and Albert's decline and death 180, 184–
    5, 188–9, 191–4
  comforts QV after Albert's death 196–7,
    199–200
  death 205
Alma, battle of (1854) 138
Amorbach, Gotha, Germany 12
Anson, George
  and QV-Albert marriage relations 73
  and Captain Childers affair 84
  on QV's hostility to Peel 86
  and Albert's boredom 107
Arthur, Prince (*later* Duke of Connaught;
  QV's son) 132, 192, 206
Augusta, Crown Princess of Prussia 143
Augusta, Dowager Duchess of Coburg
  (QV's maternal grandmother) 2–3, 6,
  10, 66, 74, 97, 122
Augustus Frederick, Duke of Sussex 4–5,
  7, 34, 68, 75
Augustus, Prince of Orange 29–30

Balaclava 138
Balmoral
  QV and Albert acquire and occupy 109–
    10
  life at 127, 133, 168–9, 171
  redesign and construction 128–9, 140
Barry, Sir Charles 114
Bayly, William 164
Beatrice, Princess
  carries haemophilia 143
  birth 148
  childhood 162
  and Albert's death 185, 192, 196
  marriage 206–7
  burns QV's journal 207
  character 207–8
Bedford, Anna Maria, Duchess of 68, 172
Bennett, Daphne 103, 105, 145
Berlin: Albert visits 12–13
Bertie *see* Edward, Prince of Wales
Birch, Henry 102, 126
Blagden, Dr Richard 88
Bloomfield, Harriott, Lady 105
Brighton 41, 91
Brock, Mrs (QV's nurse) 16–18

Brontë, Charlotte 92
Broughton, John Cam Hobhouse, Baron 105
Brown, John 169–71, 207–8, 211
Browning, Elizabeth Barrett 33
Bruce, Lady Augusta (*later* Stanley) 191, 193, 197
Bruce, General Robert 154–6, 166, 193–4
Brunel, Isambard Kingdom 114
Brussels: QV and Albert visit 92
Buchanan, James 156
Buckingham Palace: QV moves to 36–8, 88
Bunsen, Baron Christian 105

Cambridge, Duke of *see* George William, Duke of Cambridge
Cambridge University: Albert elected Chancellor 130–1
Canada: Edward visits (1860) 155–6
Canning, Charles John Canning, Earl ('Clemency') 147
Carlyle, Thomas 177
Carrington, Charles (*later* Marquis of Lincolnshire) 103
Cawnpore, India 147
Charles, Princess of Hesse *see* Elizabeth of Prussia
Charlotte, Queen of George III 79
Charlotte, Princess (Prince Regent's daughter) 6, 8, 12, 75, 77
Chartism 81 & n, 88, 98–9, 127
Childers, Captain 84
Christian, Prince of Schleswig Holstein (Princess Helena's husband) 205
Churchill, Jane, Lady 169–70
Claremont (house) 8, 17, 73
Clarendon, George Villiers, 4th Earl 149, 202
Clark, (Dr) Sir James
    and Lady Flora Hastings affair 46–7, 49
    Albert accuses of mismanaging Vicky 85
    and Lehzen's departure 86
    attends QV for birth of Edward 87
    and Prince Leopold's weakness 142
    warns QV against further children 148
    on Albert's overwork 158, 164
    on death of QV's mother 165
    and Albert's final illness and death 183, 187–8, 190, 193, 195
Clifden, Nellie 167, 178
Cobden, Richard 114
Coburg (state)
    dukedom 8
    QV and Albert visit (1860) 158–62

Cole, Sir Henry 113–14, 116, 120
Combe, George 100
Conroy, Captain Sir John
    accompanies Duchess of Kent to England 2–3, 5
    ambitiousness 15–16, 23, 27
    and QV's upbringing 17, 21
    and Kensington system 20
    QV's hostility to 20, 49
    organises tours for QV 23, 25–6
    supposed relations with QV's mother 24, 211
    excluded from QV's confirmation 26
    conflicts with QV 31, 165
    remains as Duchess of Kent's comptroller 38–9
    aspires to be QV's private secretary 39
    and Lady Flora Hastings 46
Conroy, Victoire (*later* Hanmer; JC's daughter) 20
Conyngham, Francis Conyngham, 2nd Marquis 32–3
Cornwall, Duchy of 76–7
Coronation (1838) 41–5
Couper, Sir George 166
Cranworth, Robert Monsey Rolfe, Baron 136, 148
Crimean War (1854–6) 135, 137–41
Croker, John Wilson 35, 176
Crystal Palace, London
    designed and built 116–18
    relocated in Sydenham 120
    destroyed by fire 121
    see also Great Exhibition
Cubitt, Thomas 94–5, 129
Cumberland, Duke of *see* Ernest Augustus
Cumberland plot 24

Davys, George, Dean of Chester 18, 26
Delane, John Thadeus 137
Delhi 146
Derby, Edward Stanley, 14th Earl of 127–8, 202
Devonshire, William Spencer Cavendish, 6th Duke of 116
Duncannon, John William Ponsonby, Viscount (*later* 4th Earl of Bessborough) 20
Dunfermline, James Abercromby, 1st Baron 20
Durham, John George Lambton, 1st Earl of 20

East India Company 146–7
Edward, Duke of Kent *see* Kent, Edward,
    Duke of
Edward, Prince of Wales (*later* King
    Edward VII; 'Bertie')
  birth 88
  and parental expectations 99–100, 126,
    173
  closeness to Lady Lyttelton 100, 126
  friendship with sister Alice 100, 104
  relations with parents 100, 102, 105–6,
    126, 133, 143–4, 157, 167, 178–9
  as heir to throne 101
  upbringing and education 102–3, 105–6,
    126, 133, 154–5, 163, 166
  enthusiasm for theatre 134
  at Balmoral 141
  and Vicky's marriage 151
  dress 154
  tours Italian art galleries 154–5
  wishes for military career 154–5, 157, 166
  1860 North American tour 155–7
  amiability 155
  Albert seeks bride for 166
  posted to army in Curragh 166–7
  first sexual experience in Ireland 167,
    178–9, 201
  meets Alexandra 171, 204
  Albert visits in Cambridge 180
  with dying Albert 191–4
  and QV after Albert's death 195–6, 198,
    200
  and Albert's funeral 200–1
  QV blames for Albert's death 201–2
  contracts typhoid fever 203
  engagement 204
  as king 207
  ill-treats Alexandra 208
Elizabeth of Prussia (Princess Charles of
    Hesse) 196
Emich Charles, Prince of Leiningen 2
Ernest I, Duke of Coburg (Albert's father)
    8–9, 13, 14, 21, 29
  death 92–3
Ernest II, Duke of Coburg (Albert's
    brother)
  boyhood in Coburg 9–11
  visits to England with Albert 28–30, 54–
    6
  succeeds on death of father 93
  visits Balmoral 110
  flatters QV 150
  QV and Albert visit in Coburg 159–60,
    162

appearance 177
Ernest Augustus, Duke of Cumberland
    (*later* King of Hanover)
  character 15
  and Conroy's supposed relations with
    QVs mother 24
  and QV's accession 34
Ernest, Prince of Leiningen 193–5
Euryalus, HMS 163

Feodora of Leiningen, Princess (*later*
    Hohenlohe; QV's half-sister)
  accompanies mother to England 2
  Lehzen appointed governess to 16
  friendship with QV 18, 20
  and QV's accession 33
  and QV's pregnancy 77
  at Albert's deathbed 193
Ferdinand, Prince of Orange 29–30
Ferdinand, Prince of Portugal 171
Ferguson, Dr Robert 87–8, 184
Fettercairn, Scotland 169–70
Fitzgerald, Hamilton 47–8
Florschütz, Christoph 10–11, 102
France
  QV and Albert visit (1843) 91–2
  in Crimean War 135, 137–8
  Albert fears invasion by 158
  see also Paris
Frederick, Duke of York 16
Frederick, Prince of Prussia 131, 143
Frederick William IV, King of Prussia:
    death 163
Frederick William, Prince of Prussia (*later*
    Emperor of Germany; 'Fritz')
  betrothal to Princess Victoria 143–5
  wedding 149–52
  at VC ceremony 153
  QV and Albert visit in Germany 158–9
  and death of Frederick William IV 164
  ill-treated by son 205
Frogmore 79, 200
Fulford, Roger 9, 105

George III, King 1, 17, 176
George IV, King (*earlier* Prince Regent)
  dislikes brother Duke of Kent 6, 15
  stands godfather to Victoria 6
  character 15
  in line of succession 16
  and QV as child 19
  death and succession 21
  and Buckingham House (Palace) 36–7
  at Brighton 41

INDEX

George William, Duke of Cambridge 167
Gibbs, Frederick 102, 154
Gladstone, William Ewart
  praises Peel 82
  on QV and Albert's love for children 105
  and Great Exhibition 114
Gloucester, Mary, Duchess of 19, 60, 98
Gooch, Daniel 118
Gordon, Sir Robert 109
Grant, Jo 169–70
Great Exhibition (1851)
  Albert proposes and plans 112–16, 122, 125
  exhibits 117–19
  opens 117
  success 119–20
Greville, Charles 34, 46–7
Grey, General Charles 169–70
Gruner, Ludwig 95

haemophilia 142, 206–7, 211
Hardinge, Field Marshal Henry, 1st Viscount 136
Hastings, Francis Rawdon-Hastings, 1st Marquis of 46–8
Hastings, Lady Flora
  replaces Duchess of Northumberland 25
  'pregnancy' scandal 46–7, 50, 60
  death from cancer 47–9
Hawksmoor, Nicholas 4
Helen, Princess of Waldeck-Pyrmont (Prince Leopold's wife) 206
Helena, Princess (QV's daughter; 'Lenchen')
  birth 98
  with dying father 192–4
  marriage and children 205
Henry, Price of Battenberg (Princess Beatrice's husband; 'Liko') 206–7
Hertford, Richard Seymour-Conway, 7th Marquis of 202
Hildyard, Sarah 104, 193
Hill, Sir Rowland 113
Holland, Sir Henry 190
Howley, William, Archbishop of Canterbury 26, 33, 43, 45, 68
Hume, Joseph 1
Hyde Park
  as site for Great Exhibition 114–15
  restored 120

Illustrated London News 115
India
  1857–8 mutiny/rebellion 145–7, 153
  Victoria proclaimed Empress of 148
Inkerman, battle of (1854) 139

Jenner, Dr (Sir) William 180, 183–4, 186, 188, 190, 200

Kensington Palace
  building 3–6
  Kents occupy 16
  QV leaves 37–8
Kensington system 20–1
Kent, Edward, Duke of (QV's father)
  and birth of QV 1–3, 5
  financial difficulties 1–2, 15
  brother Prince Regent dislikes 6, 15
  marriage 8
  character 15
  in line of succession 16
  illness and death 17
Kent, Victoria, Duchess of (QV's mother)
  and birth of QV 1–3, 5
  (second) marriage to Edward 8
  nurses QV 16, 80
  and husband's death 17
  and QV's upbringing 17–18, 21
  and Kensington system 20
  appointed regent 21, 27
  parliamentary allowance increased 22
  accompanies QV on tours 23, 26
  supposed relations with Conroy 24, 211
  and QV's confirmation 25
  QV's deteriorating relations with 25, 49, 53
  and QV's marriage prospects 28
  and Albert's first meeting with QV 31
  and Conroy's disputes with QV 31
  and QV's accession 32–3
  moves to Buckingham Palace 38
  at QV's wedding 67–8
  present during QV's labour 78
  Albert's kindness to 79
  at Balmoral 129
  at Vicky's wedding 152
  death 165–6
Kingsley, Charles 118, 188

Lamb, Lady Caroline (*née* Ponsonby) 37–8
Lansdowne, Henry Petty-Fitzmaurice, 3rd Marquis of 130
Lehzen, Louise, Baroness
  hostility to Conroy 15, 31
  as governess to Princess Feodora 16

Lehzen, Louise, Baroness *cont.*
and QV's upbringing and education 21–2
threatened with dismissal 25
and QV's early tours 26
and QV's marriage prospects 29
at QV's coronation 45
and Lady Flora Hastings scandal 47–8
political attacks on 49
reassures Lady Lyttelton 52
relations with QV 53, 71, 83, 85–6
and Albert's courtship of QV 56
difficulties with Albert 73, 76, 83–6, 172
controls royal household 83
political prejudices 84, 86
retirement and death 85–6, 87, 125
Leopold, King of the Belgians
birth and background 8
marriage to Princess Charlotte 12–13
Stockmar serves 11
plans Albert's marriage 12–13, 28–9, 53–5
and Albert's upbringing 13
allowance to Kents 16–17
and death of QV's father 17
accession to Belgian throne 24
influence on QV 24, 28–9
and QV's accession 32–3, 36
and QV's move to Buckingham Palace 37
visits QV at Windsor 40
and Melbourne's return to power 51
and QV-Albert engagement 58, 62
advises QV and Albert 64
on Albert's departure to marry 65
and QV's pregnancies and children 74–5, 87, 141
QV and Albert visit 92, 159
visits QV in London 93
QV describes Balmoral to 109
QV writes to on Great Exhibition 118
and QV's anxiety over Albert's political involvement 126–7
and QV's complaint of lack of politician friends 128
and Crimean War 138
and QV's 1855 visit to Paris 140
at Vicky's wedding 152
and first VC award ceremony 154
and death of QV's mother 165
concern over QV's shortness 175
and Albert's health decline 185, 187
and QV after Albert's death 198–9
and Edward-Alexandra engagement 204
death 208

Leopold, Prince (*later* Duke of Albany; QV's son)
birth 142
haemophilia 142, 211
character 143
and dying Albert 191–2
marriage and later life 206
Leopold, Prince of Saxe-Coburg-Saalfeld
see Leopold, King of the Belgians
Light Brigade, charge of (1854) 139
Lilly, Mrs (midwife) 78, 87
Lincoln, Abraham 181
Locock, (Dr) Sir Charles 78, 87
Longford, Elizabeth, Countess of 23, 149, 179
Louis Napoleon *see* Napoleon III, Emperor of the French
Louis Philippe, King of France 91, 131–2
Louis, Prince (*later* Grand Duke) of Hesse 168–70, 193, 197, 204
Louise, Duchess of Coburg (Albert's mother) 10
Louise Margaret, Princess of Prussia (*later* Duchess of Connaught) 206
Louise, Princess (*later* Duchess of Argyll; QV's daughter) 443
birth 98, 132
with dying father 192
marriage and later life 205–6
Louise, Queen of the Belgians
visits QV at Windsor 40
congratulates QV and Albert on birth of first child 78
QV and Albert visit 92
visits QV in London 93
and Leopold's illnesses 187
Lyndhurst, John Singleton Copley, Baron 82
Lyttelton, Sarah, Lady (*née* Spencer)
position at court 51
at QV's wedding 68
on QV-Albert marriage relations 72
on Vicky's christening 80
on travelling with QV 90
on building of Osborne 94
on life at Osborne 96
and upbringing of royal children 99, 101–6, 125, 132–4
relations with Bertie 100
on Princess Louise 132

Macintosh, Mrs (wet nurse) 142
Manners-Sutton, Charles, Archbishop of Canterbury 5

INDEX

Marie, Dowager Duchess of Coburg
159
Marie, Grand Duchess of Russia (Prince
Alfred's wife) 205
Marie, Princess of Orleans 45
Marie, Queen of Roumania 9
Martin, Sir Theodore 11, 130–1
Marx, Karl and Engels, Friedrich:
Communist Manifesto 1848
Mary II, Queen 4
Meerut, India 146
Melbourne, William Lamb, 2nd Viscount
on George IV's fondness of children 19
and QV's early tours 26
and William IV's mistrust of Conroy 27
and Albert's first visit to England 28
and QV's accession 33–5
relations with QV 34, 37–9, 53, 61–3,
69–71, 87, 207
marriage to Lady Caroline 37–8
acts as QV's private secretary 39
visits Windsor 40
at QV's coronation 44–5
and Lady Flora Hastings scandal 47–8
1839 government fall and return 50–1
and QV's engagement 57, 61
at QV's wedding 67, 69
and QV-Albert marriage relations 73,
172
and Albert's court reforms 77
and QV's pregnancy and labour 78
gout 80
political decline and resignation 81–2, 87
QV's farewell to 82–3
and QV's Isle of Wight home 93
on Albert's boredom 107
denies royal title for Albert 148
on QV's overeating and appearance 176
Mendelssohn, Felix 104
Millais, John 75n
Millais, Sir John Everett 75n
Morning Advertiser 136
Morning Post 47–8

Napoleon III, Emperor of the French
(Louis Napoleon) 126, 140
Nash, John 36
New York: Edward visits 156
Newcastle, Henry Pelham Clinton, 4th
Duke of 130
Nightingale, Florence 139
Noel, Gerald 101, 104
Normanby, Constantine Henry Phipps, 1st
Marquis of 60

Normanby, Maria, Marchioness of 68
Northumberland, Charlotte Fiorentia,
Duchess of 25

Osborne House, Isle of Wight
QV and Albert acquire and improve 94–
6, 110
life at 96–7, 107, 127, 145
royal children at 132–3
QV and Albert visit 166
QV visits after Albert's death 200–2
Ottawa 156
Oxford, Edward 76

Palmerston, Henry John Temple, 3rd
Viscount
refuses to obstruct Albert and Ernest's
visit to England 13
relations with QV 72
and QV's pregnancy and labour 78
loses office (1841) 82
controversy with Albert 126
1851 resignation 135
seeks office in Crimean War 138
1855 government 139
approves royal title for Albert 148
arranges marriage dowry for Princess
Victoria 149
and Edward's proposed Canadian tour
155
on Albert's overwork 158
1861 new year message to QV and Albert
163
Albert recommends breech-loading army
rifles to 168
and *Trent* affair 182
and Albert's health decline 183–4, 186,
189–90, 193
and Albert's death 196
and QV's blaming Edward for Albert's
death 202
Panmure, Fox Maule, Baron (*later* 11th Earl
of Dalhousie) 137
Paris
1849 *Exposition* 112–13
QV and Albert visit (1855) 140
see also France
Paxton, Sir Joseph 115–16, 120
Pedro, King of Portugal 155, 171, 190
Peel, Sir Robert
and QV's accession 35
and 'bedchamber crisis' 50, 81
QV dislikes 63, 86
Albert supports 81–2

Peel, Sir Robert *cont.*
  1841 government 82
  advises against QV travelling by road 89
  recommends Isle of Wight for royal
    home 92–3
Phipps, Sir Charles 186, 189–90, 193–6
Ponsonby, Colonel (*later* General Sir)
  Henry 161, 208
Powis, Edward Herbert, 2nd Earl of 130–
  1
Prussia: proposed alliance with Britain 144
Public Health Act (1866) 203
Punch (magazine) 115–16, 137

Raglan, Lord Fitzroy James Henry
  Somerset, Baron 136, 139
railways: development 64, 88, 112
Ramsay, Admiral Sir Alexander 206
Ramsay, Victoria Patricia, Lady 206
Ross, Sir William Charles 145
Royal Albert Hall, London 120
Royal Society of Arts 113
Russell, Lord John 60, 114, 119, 138, 182
Russell, William Howard 139, 147
Russia: in Crimean War 135, 137, 139

Salisbury, Robert Arthur Talbot
  Gascoyne-Cecil, 3rd Marquis of 205
Saxe-Coburg, Francis, Duke of 8
Scotland
  QV and Albert travel in 88–9, 108, 169–
    70
  see also Balmoral
Scott, Sir Walter 108
Scourge, HMS 155
Scutari 139
Sebastopol 135, 139–41
Shaftesbury, Anthony Ashley Cooper, 7th
  Earl of 111
Sibthorpe, Col. Charles de Laet Waldo 63
Siebold, Marianne 2
Simpson, General Sir James 140
Smith, William 128–9
Society for the Abolition of Slavery 111
Society for Improving the Conditions of the
  Working Classes 111
Somerset, Edward Adolphus Seymour,
  12th Duke of 182
Spectator, The (magazine) 136–7
Stanhope, Lady (QV's bridesmaid) 68
Stanley, Lady Augusta *see* Bruce, Lady
  Augusta
Stanley, Eleanor 97, 105
Stockmar, Baron Christian Frederick

on Albert's character 9, 12
plans Albert's marriage to QV 12–13
and death of QV's father 17
and QV's upbringing 17, 20
at QV's accession 33
learns of QV-Albert engagement 58, 62
as royal adviser 64
and QV-Albert marriage relations 73
and nomination of Albert as regent 75
on birth of Princess Victoria 79
Albert complains of Lehzen to 84–5
and death of Albert's father 93
and Edward's upbringing 102
and Princess Victoria 103
and Great Exhibition (1851) 116
on Albert's hypochondria 123–4, 158
and Albert's domestic reforms 124
and Albert's nomination to Cambridge
  Chancellorship 130
and press attacks on Albert 136
and birth of Prince Leopold 142
QV and Albert meet in Germany 159
and Albert's 21st wedding anniversary
  168
informs Albert of Edward's sexual
  initiation 178
and Albert's final illness 190
Strachey, Lytton 184
Sumner, John Bird, Archbishop of
  Canterbury 152
Sussex, Duke of *see* Augustus Frederick,
  Duke of Sussex
Sutherland, Elizabeth, Duchess of 37, 42,
  52, 99

Tavistock, Anna Maria, Marchioness of
  47
Tennyson, Alfred, Lord
  ode on death of Wellington 128
  on charge of Light Brigade 139
  and QV's praise of John Brown 207
Thackeray, William Makepeace: 'May Day
  Ode' 117
Times, The
  on QV's marriage prospects 27
  opposes Hyde Park as site for Great
    Exhibition 114, 116
  criticises press attacks on Albert 137
  reports Crimean War 139
  on Albert's illness and death 195
Torrington, George Byng, 7th Viscount
  178
Toward, Mr (land steward) 95
Trent (ship) 181–3

Turkey (Ottoman Empire): and Crimean War 135

United States of America
Edward visits 156
Civil War 181
and *Trent* affair 181–3
Uxbridge, Henry Paget, Earl of (*later* 2nd Marquis of Anglesey) 84

Victoria, Queen
birth 1, 5
christening 6–7, 15
early childhood memories 7–8
marriage prospects 14, 27–9, 53–4
babyhood 16–17
in line of succession 16, 22, 27
upbringing and education 17–21, 107, 168
appearance 19, 34–5, 40–1, 150, 175–6
wariness of Conroy 20
dolls 21
promises to be good 22
early tours of England 23, 25–6
name used for public places 23
confirmation 25
relations with mother 25, 49, 53, 165
first meets Albert 29–31, 53
fondness for dancing 30–1, 71–2, 123
accession (1837) 31–6
parliamentary allowance 31
relations with Melbourne 34, 37–8, 53, 61–2, 70–1, 82, 87
voice 34, 52
moves to Buckingham Palace 36–8
court dissensions 38–9
conduct of official duties 39–41, 51–2, 60
early popularity 39–40, 45
enjoys games and riding 40–1
coronation (1838) 41–4
attacked over Lady Flora Hastings affair 47–9
Whig sympathies 48, 62–4, 74
isolation from contemporaries 53
temper 54, 61, 174
meets Albert on second visit 55–7
proposal to Albert and engagement 57–60, 63
travels by rail 64, 88
and Albert's arrival for wedding 65–6
wedding 67–9
preserves power from Albert 70, 73–4
speaks German 71

marriage relations 72–3, 172–5
pregnancies and children 74–5, 77–82, 87, 98, 131–2, 141–2, 148, 173
assassination attempts on 75–6, 88
and Albert-Lehzen difficulties 84–6
tours with Albert 88–92, 108, 169–70
at Osborne House 94–7, 132
sea-bathing 96
relations with Vicky 99, 173
and education and upbringing of children 101, 133–4, 163
relations with children 106, 125, 133, 173, 204–5
proficiency in languages 107
acquires Balmoral 109
at Balmoral 109–10, 127, 168–9, 171
and planning of Great Exhibition 114
admires Crystal Palace 116
opens Great Exhibition 117
and Albert's hypochondria 123–4, 158
fusses over children 125
and Albert's political involvement 126
life at Balmoral 127
and Wellington's death and funeral 127–8
lays foundation stone for new Balmoral 129
on Crimean War 138, 141
visits Napoleon III in Paris 140
takes chloroform during childbirth 141–2, 148
and haemophilia 143
and Vicky's betrothal 143–5
on Indian Mutiny 147
makes Albert Prince Consort 148–9
proclaimed Empress of India 148
and Vicky's marriage 149–52
awards first VC's 153–4
and Edward's visit to North America 154–6
relations with Edward 157
visits Vicky and Fritz in Germany 158–62
and Albert's coach accident 161
and mother's death 165–6
and Edward's army career 167
fears blindness 176
and Edward's sexual initiation 179
and Albert's health decline 181, 183–93
and Albert's memo on *Trent* affair 183
and Albert's death 192, 194–6
grief and mourning for Albert 197–200, 203
Victoria, Queen *cont.*

blames Edward for Albert's death 201–
2
withdrawal from public life 203–4, 208
and children's marriages 204–7
death 208
jubilees 208
achievements of reign 209
Victoria, Princess Royal ('Pussy'; 'Vicky';
QV's eldest child)
birth and babyhood 78–80
christening 80–1
upbringing 85, 99, 102–4
health anxieties 87
closeness to Albert 99, 103, 106, 161,
173
relations with QV 99, 173
character and qualities 100–1, 103–4
betrothal 143–5
as haemophilia carrier 143
parliamentary marriage dowry 149
wedding 149–52
parents visit in Germany 158–60
and father's coach accident 161
and death of Frederick William IV 164
attends grandmother's funeral 165
attempts to find bride for Edward 166,
171
introduces Edward and Alexandra 171,
204
and parents' marriage relations 173–5
and Albert's health decline 180, 188
comforts QV after death of Albert 197
and QV's blaming Edward for Albert's
death 201
and Alice's wedding 204
life in Germany 204, 207
accident, cancer and death 205
and son's treatment of Fritz 205
Victoria and Albert (royal yacht) 108–9,
152, 162
Victoria Cross
instituted 139
first award ceremony 153–4

Walmer Castle: QV and Albert visit 90–1
Watson, Dr (Sir) Thomas 190–1
Wellesley, Gerald, Dean of Windsor 193–
4
Wellington, Arthur Wellesley, 1st Duke of
at QV's birth 5
and Cumberland plot 24
on Waterloo 31

and QV's accession 35
and Lady Flora Hastings scandal 47
declines to form 1839 government 50
not invited to QV's wedding 69
at Princess Victoria's christening 80
in Peel's 1841 Cabinet 82
QV visits at Walmer Castle 90
suggests sparrowhawks for Crystal
Palace 116
at opening of Great Exhibition 118
death and funeral 127–8
successor as C-in-C 136
Wetherall, General Sir Frederick Augustus
5
Wharncliffe, Elizabeth Caroline Mary,
Lady 175
Wheeler, General Sir Hugh 147
Whewell, William 130
Wight, Isle of 25, 92–3
see also Osborne House
Wilhelm II, Kaiser (earlier Prince Wilhelm
of Prussia; Vicky's son) 159, 204–5
William I, King of Prussia (Fritz's father)
164
William III (of Orange), King 4
William IV, King (earlier Duke of Clarence)
succession to 12–14, 22, 27
objects to visit by Albert and brother 14,
28, 30
and QV's marriage prospects 14, 28–9
in line of succession 16
accession 21
and QV's tours 23, 25–6
and QV's confirmation 25
mistrusts Conroy 27, 31
decline 28
death 31–3
William, Prince Regent of Prussia 159
Windsor
QV resides at 40–1
Great Park military review 41
Albert revisits QV at 55–6
QV-Albert honeymoon at 69–70
QV-Albert's home in 88
unhygienic state 123, 203
life at 133
1853 fire 174
Winterhalter, Franz 145
Woodham-Smith, Cecil 21, 105
Wren, Sir Christopher 4

York, Duke of see Frederick, Duke of York